SALT 11

In the Mix:
International Regionalism & Hypermodernism 1

Editor
John Kinsella

Fremantle Arts Centre Press / Folio (Salt)

First published 1999 by
FREMANTLE ARTS CENTRE PRESS / FOLIO (SALT)
PO Box 320, South Fremantle
Western Australia 6162.

Fremantle Arts Centre Press   http://www.facp.iinet.net.au
John Kinsella   http://www.geocities.com/SoHo/Square/8574/

Opinions expressed in this journal are those of the contributors
and not necessarily those of the editor.

This publication has no connection, nor intends to bear resemblance, to the
Australian Army Education Service magazine *SALT* (September 1941-April 1946).

Publication Editor Tracy Ryan
Designer John Douglass
Production Manager Cate Sutherland

Typeset by Fremantle Arts Centre Press
and printed by Sands Print Group, Bassendean.

ISBN 1 86368 229 5
ISSN 1324-7131

The State of Western Australia has made an investment in this project
through ArtsWA in association with the Lotteries Commission.

Cover image by Richard Woldendorp.

CONTENTS

Peter Porter

SLEEPING WITH THE LIGHT ON

It makes good sense to organise your sun.
You switch it on and wait to be a star
Asleep, content with such a sweet eclipse
Arrived at naturally: light equips
Your birthright's quark, your memory's pulsar.
An inside moon would be a dreamer's pun.

And we are for the dark. The dark is for
The race re-run in Helios's car.
A light bulb's still on sentry duty, one
More squaddy of the all-enlisting sun.
The darkness fails to tell us who we are.
A rare lake only seeks to map its shore.

The sun, the Aten of what is, may seem
The Devil's emissary. Monks awake
Are only drones, but dreams point every way.
We're playing *Simon Says*: hear Simon say
Turn out the light for credulousness' sake
And leave it on that Lucifer may dream.

LE JUGEMENT DES URNES

Where does she sit, casting her vote,
His ordinary and spectacular mother,
Seeing everything in Heaven, afloat
On love of her son, supreme survivor
Of death and disfiguration? Remote
From responsibility, will she wrap
Him in happiness, her many-coloured coat?

And across a divide of fear from her,
His other guardian, still dressed in pain,
Dawn-gazing ever — is she thinking of how
She can help him, or is she dreaming again
Of never existing? And should she try,
A forsaken Ariadne, to explain
Forgiveness to him, because he weeps for her?

His two angels have not yet spoken
And did he but know it are his accusers
As well as his intercessors. Woken
From their dreams of blaming, they must listen
To his plea of extenuation: a broken
Trust in one and in the other a broken heart,
And from each one's hand the casting token.

Ass Insight

The righteous Balaam set out on a journey,
His purpose certain; he was God's attorney;
His ass reared up and would not take him where
It saw what God saw; what he saw was air.

Buridan's ass stalled at its timely hay,
So many bundles, pointing every way.
But we, intending herbivores, will carve
And bloody-minded see we do not starve.

James Tate

SAME AS YOU

I put my pants on one day at a time.
Then I hop around in circles hobbledehoy.
A projectile of some sort pokes me
in the eye — I think it's a bird
or a flying pyramid that resembles a bird.
Well it sure hurts and I'm swelling
even in areas where it's inappropriate
such as my cupola, also my cup of tea.
Flapdoodle is my middle name so I know
two specks about what's coming next:
the leopard's spots and their humorous sayings.
There are those who would suggest that
I am hog-tied and frequently late to work.
To which I reply: Indeed I am.
As a former ranchero and postmodern
farmerette I think we can speak freely
of the current crisis — the soil is creeping
out from under us and the haycocks
appear lubberly. If it's true
that you can judge a man's character
by the shape of his sandcastle,
then I say you are a squint-eyed stormy petrel,
and I a piebald crabstick,
which is like a dream come true.
We're practically carved out of the same carrot.
I for one can barely tell where I trail off
and you begin, since human beings are reported
to be ninety-eight percent duct tape
and feathers anyway. It's hard
to pull the pants on over all of this debris,
and once the greensward has been wrenched
into shape the going is so smooth
it's almost like not going at all.
Where have I been, where have I been?
Thus I was led into paths I had not known.

James Tate

REVENGE OF THE JAGGED AMBUSH BUG

Please don't taunt the scrivener
unless he's plopping around in a useless plot,
then you may lampoon him at will.
Don't butter the monkeys, just don't.
And no *études* on the ball field after eight.
Permits are required for flagellation,
keep your messianic woes to yourself.
Breathing on the bumblebees is strictly forbidden.
No muffins permitted in the aviary.
Talking dogs must keep it to a whisper.
Neither should you pee on the piglet.
You may boogie on the bridge but only lightly.
Try not to spend the summer in a state of torpor.
If you must eructate at the funeral
do so behind a bush, and make it sound
as if a rhinoceros is charging.
Do not write on the gazebo.
Do not sleep during the ranting.
Do not rant during the sleeping.
This is just a fragment of what I remember
of my childhood, and a roller coaster
I never dared ride, and some daisies,
and ghouls, thousands of ghouls
dancing on our graves. I mean rules,
thousands of rules digging our graves.
That's much better, that's approaching
the gazebo and deliberately, fiercely
writing on it, words that will cauterize
the delicate, the wan and sickly passerby:
Marcus Aurelius is a horse's ass.
There, now I can die with my boots on.

Fleur Adcock

Easter 1997

On the curved staircase he embraced me.
'You've got a ladybird in your hair.
Without hurting it, come closer',
one of us said, in a daze of dream.

But I thought we were in Jerusalem?
— That is indeed the name of this city.
It would be difficult to wind down further
below the ground than to this cave of birth.

All the best dreams have a baby in them.
Year after year I give birth to my son.
Clutch him in his blanket, close in your arms;
the chill from the walls burns colder than marble.

30 March 1997

Peter Boyle

GARDENER

'You practise the silent art,' she said
looking into the narrow garden where a bird
passed rapidly. 'You move in isolation
from recognition or audience.
And what you place on the page
is mostly read by no one and
what you value in the way the words fall
or run together,
pointing outwards to the world
and inwards to a private reticence,
is something not explicable to others.
Your silent unwanted art draws me.
I have been dead long enough to hear
the cadences you hum under your breath at midnight.

'The garden is small — the fence hedges it round.
One dawn of extraordinary lightness I first entered here:
with the being of a small grey bird
I quizzed the stone, followed the long crack
in the concrete that led to a garden bed,
the peach tree with its hard green kernels,
the herbs, the blue and pink flowers.
There is always water here —
dripping quietly from a tap
or the end of a hose,
water languid and dark in bowls below the potplants —
and that small fullness of presence
the mouth grows round with.
From the other side of earth
from the underside of the night stars
I came back to wait by this small desk
in a kitchen that looks out
on my garden with its roses and carnations,
its apricot and peach trees.

'All night the bird of darkness that shelters on your roof
cracks and taps his debris,
sweeping stones and the bones of fruit
crashing into oblivion.
I don't know his purposes
or if the brush of his wings is truly demonic
while the garden lies lost in such deep darkness.
Flowers and death —
it is always so late in the world.
For you too it must seem so late and lost,
shaping what never really comes to birth.
I wanted to weave around you
a little of that patience the wind knows
as it ceaselessly gathers leaves and flowers
hurrying them down the endless cycles
between life and death.
Thinbk of musicians unearthing buried sound,
the first man to construct a transverse flute
or the girl who found herself one day
on the edge of a new sonority.
(And for how many
those unresolved new continents died with them.)
Or to wake one day
and discover in your hands
the open shell for a feeling that has left the earth
like the holder of abandoned instruments,
caressing the silver stops that still hold sounds
people have forgotten how to make —
bird-clappers left behind in a land where the birds have vanished,
tree-felling songs transported to Iceland.
Your small suburban garden is open to the sky.
You glance out, your eyes half closed.
All through the cold you sit here
trying to write.
My skin is like the wall —
an intricate face you see reappearing
beyond each coat of paint:
the circled turning of the cosmos
mirrored on a garden wall.
What outlives me are trees I once lived under,

the earth I moulded and returned to,
a daily usage of things.

'Just as the sun moves around the garden
so when I come back your chair is in a different place,
your neck tilted differently,
the scattered papers express
a different state of disrepair.
Yet I understand your words
when I peek over your shoulder at midnight
or at first dawn when you move your chair out under the trees
to catch the stillness of the garden.
Through you I relive
a serene witness to uselessness.
My eye reduced to zero dimensions
on the backyard's concrete floor,
I stand at the pure angle of shadowless being
while you live in and out of shadows,
cut by light.

'The tree invents the tree.
The river invents the river.

'A line of pink and white flowers
that summon birds.
The line of hesitant words
summoning these solicitous
glances from the dead.

'And work
and dejection
and the line
that trails down.
Slashing and pruning.
Feeding that they may blossom
in nowhere.

'Don't think that because I only ever cultivated
the living art of the perishable
I can't see in you the methodical joys
of a gardener.'

Dorothy Hewett

The Safe House

I will sit under the peach tree
reading in the drone of summer
the peaches will drop bump in the grass
and the ants will swarm for their sweetness

in the bright light from the kitchen window
my grandmother sews her thimble flashes
her little feet crossed as she bites off the thread

my grandfather potters and rakes out in the garden
rolling his Havelock Ready Rubbed through his fingers
his moustache ends tickle my cheeks
he will love me forever.

I will lie in bed stretching my toes
for the warm brick covered in flannel
listening to the blind bumping
in the wind off the river
smell the old people in their iron bedstead
at the far end of the sleepout.

I will run out into the moonlit garden
shivering in my chaste white nightgown
to metamorphose into a silver wattle
I will sprout leaves and branches
the wind will blow through me
I will be forever as virginal as this.

Dorothy Hewett

THE RUNNER

I never ran as fast as I do now
down the white tracks through the scrub
dazzled with cabbage moths
on the way to the sea.

I never ran as fast as I do now
down the long wet beaches
where the tide hardens the sand.

I can run as fast
as a runaway horse
dodging the low branches
the foam from its jaws
splashing its rough breast.

All this running I do
in my bed under the window
while a chained dog howls
on the other side of the cutting.

Am I running to some destination
or just for the memory of it?

I think of my son at 42
(believing he has the body of a 20 year old)
he runs 15 miles down the straight chalk roads
of the island springs a muscle
and lies on the verge for hours.

We are all puzzled by age
how quickly it comes on
until moonstruck under a window
with swollen knees we are running away.

Simon Armitage

THE GIRAFFE

A gift, with its camel's face and leopard's spots,
the only place for its height was the hall, its feet
biting into the lino floor, and its head half-asleep
with one eye open, like a dog, outside the bedroom door.

Of no practical use at all, we found room for the thing;
followed its neck downstairs like a bannister rail, tugged
every once in a while, in passing, and meaning no harm,
at the bell-rope, light-pull, toilet-chain length of its tail.

THE WATER SNAKE

We sat on the green bank at the side of the road,
passing the time with the girl who wanted to top herself
but somehow managed to stop herself
from driving her mother's car into the stream below.

The cops were called on a mobile phone, and came,
but not before the village fire brigade, eight men
with cartoon bodies and animal heads, hell bent
on doing something useless with the hose, the hose

which had, as they say, a mind of its own. Alive,
and way too strong for the one with the donkey's face to hold,
it stood up straight, spun round, and spat at the girl,
the girl who wanted to die but was too wet now and too cold.

Simon Armitage

SCORPIUS

The weapons we used for tearing each other in two
were dipped to the hilt in secret potion, an oil
for the stemming of blood and the cleansing of wounds.
This solution, applied to ourselves, was a poison.

THE LIZARD

Today, being Monday, I think of the lizard, at prayer
for years of his life in the one position, who forks out
double meanings with his tongue, or nothing at all,
and faces the sun, without blinking, through a stone wall.

HYDRA

At the jungle research station in Manaus, they keep
a brown electric eel in a dishwater-coloured goyt
that looked to me, when it was pointed out, more like
a dead palm leaf, or, side-on, a length of gutter pipe.

But as I said to the man who was showing us round,
dingy or not, you have to take your hat off to a beast
that keeps itself to itself for the most part, but when touched
transforms a single thought into several hundred volts.

Wendy Jenkins

WHITE DREAMS

1.
Classical Perspective
(a romance)

Classical perspective's
a thing of the past
(naturally)

providing only
a seeming
order

but I want
to lie
down with you
on a white sheet
at the point where all lines
converge

and be captured
by an old master
sure
            of his measure

and be held there

resonant

enthralled

as your flesh tones
deepen and convince
    (can I say just once that
            they become you?)

until smiling
like the Mona Lisa
you slide
   across the sheet
                    to me

raise
a roseate arm
   (plump, perfect)

and pull
the horizon   down

2.
Metaphor Murder
(a thriller)

Something is at large
and very sexy it draws you
to it like a diction   running
a line on itself it slides
through language
                    slips
into your throat like
a tongue
 a knife
   that first last drink

something keen
  something cold
    something you have
to have

Your tongue is suddenly a blade
that cuts all ways

the shapes it makes seem true
to you

and just the case
        perfect   so good   oh *yes*

(who is speaking?)

from far away
you realise

        marks on the clean white sheets

you have committed metaphor murder

CAESURA

Every now &
then
a break
in traffic

respite
& the shadowing
urge

to surf
the pause
or even

jump it

    nerve pulse
        synaptic gap

poets high
on caesurae
give one pause

on/off
they step
from bridges

rest a
                beat
on the frozen
air

DOLPHIN SIGHTINGS

1. First time

The first time
we saw them together
was at Deep Water Point

whether they were
four or five
we couldn't tell

the rhythm
of their surfacing
being more akin to music
than mathematics

anticipation
riding the gaps
like shadow notes.

2. You were talking

The second time
they were right in by the shore
at East Fremantle

traversing and doubling
the same stretch of water

and you were talking
about the space
where arrival and departure are
the same thing

about trying to hold
that moment
as vision and tone

about how sweet
and sad it feels

unspeakable
unspeakable
you know?

3. Flatlining

At the still point
of the argument

(my silence
now equal
   to yours)

I saw them break
the surface
at the opposite bank

two of them in unison
and a third
tracking
in a kind of
counterpoint

the man in the kayak
stopped his paddle
at once (ecstatic)

and slid smoothly soundlessly backwards
on the tide

flatline   still trace
about which
dolphins blipped and jumped
like a fibrillating heart.

Bert Almon

A Voyage through the Three Kingdoms of the Cosmos

— Montreal World Trade Centre

Zeus

An atrium covers a multitude of scenes.
It is an outside inside, overhead to underfoot,
leaving me in a space neither within nor without,
on a street between two long brick slabs, one red, one grey,
with eleven façades of old buildings embedded in them.
A detached bit of the Berlin Wall is on display.
The sky is over me and I am under glass.
The atrium holds it all but not together.

Wife of Poseidon

The long black fountain doesn't gush or jet.
A slab of granite bearing yellow images
of the yellow lamps that ring it,
it brims over, a slight increment
of water seeping into the basin beneath.
The coins lying in the water made me see
how shallow it is. Facing it is a dry fountain
with a statue of Amphitrite, daughter of Ocean
wife of Poseidon, recumbent on a plinth,
one hand holding a jar from which no water flows.
She came here from northern France,
where Dieudonné-Barthélemy Guibal
carved her in the 18th century. The goddess
had her marriage brokered by a dolphin,
and it was rewarded by translation into stars.
Power Corporation funded her journey here.
The statue, pure calcium carbonate,
is a motionless fountain of white.
Her reflection floats in the black lozenge,

but she is not inclined to look into it.
There are more things in heaven and earth
than can be joined by an atrium.

Hades

I thought the black fountain was deathly,
then as I follow the downward arrow
into the Métro I become a shadow
circulating in a system of signs, shuttling
from the Green line to the Orange. A wind
steady and warm stirs on the platforms,
blowing from nowhere to nowhere.
The compass has no points down here
where live rails promise forgetfulness,
and the train is a pure vector.
I surrender my small red ticket to enter
this kingdom, trusting the escalator to carry me up,
transformed to flesh as I stand blinking in the sun.

Edwin Morgan

MARGINALIZATION

'We have increasingly become phantoms.'
You can almost see our starving atoms.
We flit from Areopagus to Patmos

to Jupiter to Hell and any place
where we might find the remnants of the race
we're severed from, but there is no trace.

We pass through bastions, dungeons, pyramids.
Nothing stirs in the stone. Our heavy lids
drowse on the grilles and tills and screens and bids

of an unclassic time. Everything stirs
but falls again like dust, a soot of futures.
Dismay and deprivation hug the stairs.

Phantoms pushing nothing across counters,
phantoms in malls, a maze of non-encounters,
phantoms clocked by cameras and bouncers —

a blur, a shadow, something grey, half seen,
things to think back to, never really been,
an unclicked turnstile — the undead, the unclean!

Who has not felt this, as Gramsci once,
hammered by forces hard as distant suns,
made thirsty for a spring that dries, not runs?

Within the walls he writes most steadily,
encourages his friends, freely, readily,
heads letters with hope, and not wrong-headedly.

Edwin Morgan

In a Bar

Bona homie, bona partso, hey?
Don't wind him up though, or he'll never play.
Leather gods can be a leery lay.

Did I ever tell you — oh, it's not fair,
see the polisman's helmet, no underwear,
keeps shifting leg to leg, look, don't *stare*! —

I never told you about my leatherman,
turned out to be a rubberman, oh *man*,
got out a huge rubber bag, I almost *ran*,

put me in it and brought me off, drew me
a hot bubble-bath, stepped in and blew me
through a slit in his rubber suit, threw me

a vast scented mother of all towels,
said 'that was all right' with his rubbery vowels,
delved on pointy rubber feet like trowels

into the kitchen debris, found an egg,
poured coffee like a diver at a keg,
my merman, and he'd neither brag nor beg,

just *was*, the life he led, I thought it weird
but then I thought it not so weird, geared
to a generous camaraderie, not feared

after the first frisson, and at least no part
of exchange floor, wine-bar, Porsche, the art
of greed — he didn't even have to start

a cahootchy factory, a Soho shop would do! —
it must seem unbelievable to you,
a suit, a nice one but, that I went through

that perfectly normal — to some! — hoop,
trolling about in a bag, looping the loop —
it's true though — God there's a whole troop

come to loll at the bar now, chaps in chaps,
all caps and studs and bulges and tight straps —
let's get closer, hear them creak, perhaps.

A ROOF OF FIREFLIES

I am not sure that I believe in the old adage that 'the unexamined life is not worth having', the sources of whatever power one has are not too fond of being poked and prodded to see how they are doing, and may withdraw their cooperation. A few years ago I visited the Waitomo underground caves in New Zealand, where you descend by a series of roughly cut staircases to a large underground lake and are taken in boats over the dark still waters, gliding in silence so that no conversation or other noise will disturb the thousands of fireflies shining in the roof of the cavern. It is a remarkable and beautiful sight, and like any other visitor I found it thrilling, but somehow it was more than thrilling, it was moving, it was saying things that only things can say, and my mind kept recurring to it for days and months afterwards, and I can feel a tingling even while I write about it now. But if what it said could be put in a letter, I was not going to open the envelope. I have not written a poem about it, though it might well come into a poem if it could do so unawares, with no tedious moralizing or clumsy piling of analogies (Charon's ferry or Auden's limestone or whatever). The subterraneanness, both physical and mental, enfolds its value, as a geode its flash, and that is where this visitor at least is going to leave it.

With that proviso, I have to say that I felt I must ask myself, and did ask myself, why I was not writing poetry about the Second World War at the time when I was engaged in it, as a private soldier in the Royal Army Medical Corps in various parts of the Middle East. If Owen and Rosenberg, whom I much admired, could do it in the first war, why could I not do it in the second? I knew the situations were different, both because the apocalyptic surprise and horror of trench warfare in France, with its intense emotional involvement, could not be matched in the African desert campaign of the

1940s, and also because I belonged to a hospital unit which by its nature had to be some distance behind the front line. For all that, I felt guilty, and angry with myself, at least during the times when I had leisure to reflect. Did something tell me, or was something trying to tell me, that it didn't matter? That there is no pattern in the poetic life which decrees one must write about the immediacy of forceful or strident events? I didn't even keep a journal, which doesn't mean I didn't think the things that were happening around me and to me weren't important, but that possibly my instinct about subterranean workings preferred to leave them in the limbo of memory. A risky pool to leave prized things swimming in! Would I live long enough for the right moment to come for fishing them out? It turned out in fact that the images and incidents of that time and place remained fresh and vigorous thirty years later, when I cast my mind back and wrote my hundred-poem sequence *The New Divan*, embedding long-belated war poems in a geographically horizontal and historically vertical panorama of the Middle East where Hafiz and Sindbad and Scheherazade could watch as tutelary spirits over 'the thud of land-mines'. (It is my hidden poem, which no one ever writes about!). While it is tempting to say therefore that nothing is lost, I would have to admit to myself that that sequence would not have been instigated if the Middle East had not been again so much in the news in the 1970s, driving my mind through memorial labyrinths that were almost labyrinths of witness. — To which I add a sudden lateral thought: what sort of inevitability was it that sent me to the Middle East in the first place, since at school I had been strongly attracted by Egypt and Mesopotamia and not at all by the classical world of Greece and Rome?

Relating art to life may be dodgy at the best of times, but I would have almost too many, certainly not too few, reasons why I found the 1960s such a productive period that it seemed to have lifted me totally out of the slough of self-doubt I was in some danger of creeping about in during the aftermath of the war. I daresay some backlash against that remarkable decade was bound to come, but I would never find myself subscribing to the downgrading it has received in would-be virtuous quarters. The unexamined life in me — let us bring it back — does not know whether the decade was waiting for me or I was waiting for the decade. Do I want to know? I don't think so! I was in love, and that casts a light and a glow that transform everything else. But without that I would still have thrilled to the new music, to the exploration of space, to the exploratory international poetries, beat, concrete, aural, oral, to the political and sexual radicalisms that were at last putting their heads above the parapet. I was at the same time, and without any sense of strain or strangeness, writing love poems, space poems, verbally experimental poems, and poems about social conditions in a Glasgow poised between grimness and potential renewal. Looking back, I would find it hard to scrub any of these interests, or to say that whatever it was I had to do in poetry was harmed by the diversity. I knew that it was not my job to 'find my own voice', as reviewers are always encouraging young writers to do. That is one kind of poetry, which is not mine. Good luck to Seamus Heaney, but I pushed out, and continue to push out, a different boat. What about a boat that is itself a shapeshifter: the nuclear-powered icebreaker is now a light white felucca triangle fading in the heat-haze and then a bathyscaphe goggling at black smokers and it emerges as an oily junk on the contraband run and before you know it it is a ship of space out there up there riding the solar wind.

Poets of many voices — Dunbar, Blake, Khlebnikov, Voznesensky, Weöres, Prigov — have therefore always exerted an appeal that I am aware of and acknowledge. I liked to see exploration, divergence, risk-taking. I liked the idea of an avant-garde, and the common assumption that *The Iliad*, to say nothing of the much older *Gilgamesh*, had not been 'beaten' by anything later and greater did not seem to me to validate an anti-evolutionary view of art. Biodiversity, whether vegetal, animal, human, geophysical, or astrophysical, is surely the key. The range of poetries has grown enormously and continues to grow. Unknown territories beckon. Alien territories beckon. I recall the military origin of the term avant-garde, the band of scouts who went ahead of the main troop, not out of bravado or to gain kudos but in order to facilitate or encourage a general advance. In this sense, both Whitman and Hopkins were a true avant-garde of their times. The extreme dislocations of the twentieth century have naturally manipulated the use of the term, sharpening or roughening it according to one's point of view, but certainly allowing it to problematize the idea of trailblazing. Dmitry Prigov (b.1940), arch-perestroikist and deconstructor of Soviet social realities, has used an enormous variety of forms to roll back what he saw as the timorous traditionalism and incipient sentimentalism of Russian lyric poetry, and he has made a large impact. I sense a kinship with his work, and yet I also realize that his task cannot be the same as mine. He has said: 'I don't deal with human emotions directly, neither am I able to identify myself with any individual feeling or idea.' I, on the contrary, don't find in myself the either-or of the personal and the impersonal, the direct or the deconstructional. I have poems in invented languages; poems with compressed or dislocated syntax; permutational poems; simulated computer poems; poems in code; poems of one word, and even of one letter. But the pleasure of writing such poems, of making something meaningful out of something very new, the pleasure in language itself, its malleability, its untapped potential, is not enough. I need, with another part of me, the very things Prigov is suspicious of: a direct poetry of human relationships, friends, lovers, family, a poetry of vulnerabilities, desires, losses, encounters missed and encounters won. This being so, who would not be impatient of categories?

An English astronomer was interviewed recently about the severe problems being undergone by the Russian space station Mir, including problems that might involve the actual survival of the astronauts. He scarcely disguised his belief that the whole operation was little better than a waste of valuable resources and time. Why risk men's lives when machines could do everything we wanted? Space telescopes, space probes, as automated as technology can provide, that was the cleancut way to do things, no crewmen fumbling and bumbling about among the — oops — cables. Cut to his American counterpart at NASA: no sir, we have to go up there; we have already learned good lessons from the troubles in Mir; everything we do is a step forward, not a setback; even disasters don't stop what is a matter of destiny. Needless to say, I rejoiced in the positiveness of the second interview after being depressed (though it was a familiar pattern) by the first. Poetry, just like Mir and the greater space stations which are planned as launchpads for planetary exploration, seems to me to want to take its human load wherever it is possible for that human load to go. When Gagarin first saw the blue glow round the globe of the earth, he commented on its beauty in a way no machine would be able to do. What good is beauty? We don't know. But if we sense it, we ought to record it. Words go with everything human. Poetry is a brilliant vibrating interface between the human and the non-human. A gutter in Calcutta or a rille on the moon, we're there, and if we're not there, push us, drive us! And don't try to tell us that the gutters of Calcutta will run with milk and honey if we dismantle the space programme; they won't, the world is not like that. *Médecins sans frontières* — oui, assurément! *Astronautes sans frontières* — naturellement! *Poètes sans frontières* — pourquoi pas?

As I write this, Scotland has voted to have its own parliament, with lawmaking and tax-varying powers and a fair measure of autonomy, though still within the United Kingdom. As a member of the universe, Scotland does seem to be twinkling, however faintly. It is my place, and I shall continue to write about it as occasion arises. Its fate, as an entity, haunts me, and will not haunt me the less if I stand on a hill in Glasgow and look up on a clear night at a dash of stars.

Susan M Schultz

PLURALISMS OF ONE

The Peace Bridge goes either
to Canada or to the next century;
can't remember which. Fire trucks

savage a high school band's one
lost tune, as Tweedledum serenades
email partners with loud rounds

of thumb-sucking. Eggs, like virtue,
sacrificed to higher clauses, poems
rinsed by an ulterior rain, regimented

weather interrupted by school bell
harassment policies. Whose pluralism
shall I conceive or mention, I whose

favorite ism is somewhere between
here and another border crossing, or
is it a dead end built into the system

as bland tolerance, where power
tolerates weakness but not counter-
strength, or lunch, as Aussies say?

Chrome fenders distinguish one class
from the other, which drives dented
past islands of urban commerce, all

men (Donne) cogged into abandoned
warehouses, bards shot by counter-
bards whose words have real value.

Oral exchange, multiply printed,
postulates an air of difference
intolerant of same. Who defines such

sameness, either, since the 'different
same' is a national ideal, or at least
a deal for anthologists of brain candy,

the game kids punching buzzers like
links untruthfully reached by prior
counsel of none's peers. The state

abandons them as welfare cheats, nay
queens (hardly cross-dressers) set up
in LBJ housing to be soothed by free-

way whine and rain, toting up ill-gotten
gain like the poet carbuncular adjusting
columns to fit the ethereal era of be-

lated capital. Cultural studies are a wash,
she says, wish lists for liberal command-
ments, words bleached clear of meaning's

meat. I remember Hubert like it was later
yesterday, who lost 'by the margin of our
despair' (Jackson), legacy exhumed at

reunions of '68 vets listening to old
musics and misremembering bloody sticks
that mark our history as one of idealists

repeatedly ruined by passion, remnant
worshipers of a father's sentiments; old
age has taken so many away from us,

line breaks of a begotten syntax eloping
just now with the furtive essence of a
strategic transparency that translates.

Susan M Schultz

ADDENDA

Erstwhile argonaut of the word.
The lightning strike flared, was
then fantasized as a place
to stand, bus shelter where
exchange makes no concession
to value in being historical
speech: the bench bears names
Anonymous might covet, were
he not so aloof, like a country
philosopher bent on making
an academy of his principles,
those numbered one through
three. Not number but incident
or access to accident as potential
rubric for our nostrums whose
grace is in our ability to turn
away and still gather in
that flex of the verb or agency
created to aggravate intention
into something we can trust.

Plain sculpture, thicker than
a Shaker desk, ordinary log
planed to give the heel
of the grain its due; peace
is in the modest light that
unveils its angle or niche
where, seated, we remainder
experience in order to forget
passage for a while.
This bark does not float
but waits and weights on air.

Explain process or form.
Explain the form of your process,

that form at which you arrive, breathing
hard, at some reconcilement of need
and place, the place our need takes,
seated like a family at the outer gate.

Reluctance. That is mine
to know either as acceptance or
as hesitation before onset, least predicated
of my vows to this going toward, or away from,
the scheduled arrival of my sentences and their
correspondences, those that float and those that stop.

Prepare awareness, like a weed.
Go inside this cluster, this cloistered
message scrawled on paper or on screen:
her glasses never fit to read those most portable
of phrases, flickering, inept, reminders
of spiritís desire to move off
the shelf and into armchairs, seasons once
again predictable according to where the leaves are.
Disgrace is no option, though degradation
in love is ordinary enough, state she fled
when mind trampolined off skull
or circumstance. Was there windfall
from that spareness, or did those
separated leaves blacken, block what risk
there was to be taken, or indeed given?

Hammock potential, the potentate
of this age of infinite reduceability,
reproduced in plates or pixels
to stretch the web past each site,
space where nothing is, is only
projected onto or from, as if
the slide projector stood down
a ravine and blew out blues
and greens, commingled with
colorless substance, whether
of air or nebulous rock spray.
The falls cast doubt on fact,
like stone, and yet are continuous

even when, as rumor tells it,
they're shut off for the night,
not frozen but stalled as are
our projects, stretching hours
into word auras, if not exactly
well defined. The snow is not
general, but scattered, like museums,
within the trophied white, green patches
formed like mange that falls prey to its own
backward promise. Secret operations
(oh redundancy!) sell missions short
with greed of getting in exchange
for words and pictures a settled view,
the suburbs' easy annihilation of content
for form, the grid of streets and stops
imposed to be invisible to eyes
but not to one's sense of self as itemized,
growing on a dish, nothing but off-shoots.

Our beams high, though none falls
from them except the proverbial dust
that colors air, governs its essence
by marking its place inside our sight.
Those who believe do so quietly,
inhabit righteousness like a tent
about to fold at a circus, before
the authorities grab their chance
to collect taxes, or runaways, sting
operations filmed for later, barren,
inspection: Always the motel room,
gray mirror and gray men, dealing out
their desires like cards to be read
as clairvoyance, the past's clear view
and precedent, having learned to get
out before complications earn us
the title of truth seekers. Pagans
go home from the beach to candles
and prayers half-consumed by surf's
fuzzy logics which we can't
accommodate and so worship
if only things other than motion

are tethered to this shore, this sea,
this tangle of metaphysics and plain noise.

Solipsism's home, having run
her errands, performed a self
that's freshness dated for today—
no need for redesign until
the morrow welcomes her with
its solitary equivalent of open
arms. That hug a day collapsed
with widowhood or other loss,
onto the flat affect of an empty
wind with its cargo of spray
or snow, embracing nothing
that is not absolute and so un-
changing as the one who only
fears loss, not frames it.

Priceless one-of-a-kinds
taken as baggage in Chicago
from citizens returning to Belgrade:
redundant loss unprincipled
accident whose worth returns
to nil on opening.

The hoped for sequence narrative,
shrugged principle shagged near home
by the armed catcher whose bullet
throw to second saves a run
and tidies the action so we can
tell relatives where we were when
it happened, not Pearl Harbor, but
its sequel, the sadness that is
incidental to any telling, its tolling
as final evidence of unrepeatability,
video stuck in the machine as paradox,
as palm.

The word, like lettuce, crisps
under the humid eye of copy editors
and clowns. Disenfranchise my part

of speech and the plurality wins
its long commute to the polls
favoring a candidate who splits
infinitives like Lincoln wood.
Itís the inner theater, now,
that operates as chancel house
or special prosecutor, sworn
to uphold his past and parcel
of a story long suspected, yet
not flushed out, plumbed.
For this is our evidence
and this our indictment,
misdemeanors demons
treated before a judge
at the last resort, gavel
clogged with sand and gravel,
no earthly reason to
stay behind bars, as islands
are the perfect breeding
ground for insider trading
that goes nowhere on
the Dow, abrupt platonic
excuse for a dividend that
costs only as much as
the contents of your mouth,
half-open, as if you were
asleep.

Hypothetical resonance, resident
manager of the Hyperion, the romanticsí
hotel fronting Mt. Blanc and other
sublime getaways, your salad days
showing up later in every generation,
as if anklets were to link todayís teens
to flappers, and so to ancient Rome,
chains marking a slowdown of affect,
hysterical weepers crying anon
as their bread is baked by slaves,
for whom expense is itself a luxury,
hence are dry-eyed, counting
their hours to release when at least
theyíll be graced with the term 'barbarian.'

Counselors contend, repeatedly,
that anxious governance insures
mutability. The cantos were just
drafts, so whereís the final product?
I put my money down already
& advertised my abilities
as scribe & weather forecaster
(better to specialize in more
than one art, lest
the economy shut
my one window
of opportunity,
and the white-
haired senator
again condemn
the draft as he
had before).

Debacle of the latter days,
this straining toward cash flow,
this health care scam that is not
a plan, these gypsies paid to teach
but not to live as we tenured do,
walled away from the bitter touch
of economy, act foretold with brevity
by your nearest broker. If it ainít
brokered, donít fix it.

Evidence of. Arch rival to.
Story pre-packaged to your
immediate pleasure. Tin foil
cover art, the price of foiling
another plot in your plot.
iI have a plot!î she said,
for whom the stutter is
the plot. No platitudes
here, just earnest addenda,
which is all thatís left
to add when prefaces
are sold out, forever
promising but never
delivering. Buy two

conclusions for the price
of one argument; that
way you donít have
to follow the evidence
through its peaks
and valleys (brochures
now available) or
flooded lots where
your cottage, too, can
sink and so become
the province of eager
archeologists with
their toothbrushes
poised to scour
your dentures,
explain why late
20th-century culture
was so beholden
to laxatives, why
no catalogue
properly places
us: Sioux Falls,
Dubuque, Kahului,
all the mythical
outposts there on
the old maps that
warp a continent
(and its blips)
to fit the scheme
of the Dirt Lucky
Gold Mine she
bought shares in
and couldnít
redeem for the
cost of a high
glass of cold water.

What is added on is meaning,
reminder the outlying areas
can stun central suburbs with
nonchalance, ease that is

another mode of control:
only from here does
democracy make senseó
or from the place of
almost dying, the astronomer
said, for whom point
of view was only
the start: a star
and then another
star, and then
a region where
location is instinct,
pool of dark
communicating
absent light
to those who
look up, even
when seeing
is past the point.
Telescope
or panopticon
launches from
inside out, even
when the lens
needs a transplant
or graft, its correction
the nebulous
warrant for arrest
of certainty,
as when
the brief-
case closed
& you hadnít
seen the
toothbrush
or shot
glass, only
flashlight
& tiny mega-
phone, sans
voix. Test

passed, the tube
becomes a way
to be there at
the start
or midstream,
like a skater
whose cilia
embrace surface
water or is it
air, error timed
to coincide with
discoveries never
made, arrived
at, or fostered. I'm
never home, said
Zeno, so don't
wait for me,
my alarm's stuck
and I can't get
out of my door
anymore; I
witness events
like the way
light falls on
leaves that is
everywhere
the same so
I can't discount
it, though I
grow rooted
to amazement
and its bargains;
I'll take two
autumn remnants
for a tropic
holiday
and then give
them back
to see bougainvillea
climb the stones,

                      violet flash

> against a late
> last
> setting.

And distress fled to the outlying regions. She was left with a band of content-
ment over her brow, the one that had throbbed violently in the past, and
couldnít know why sheíd been chosen to lose herself in ongoingness: the pre-
sent belongs only to those who relinquish desire as a good against absence or
the threat it leaves like a homeless manís mattress at the door; he doesnít
threaten you, but his circumstance does, so you retreat into the sanctity of
your castle, sacred if only because it stops the drafts from disrobing your secu-
rity zone. So contentment is always at the mercy of the next plunge in stocks
(at best) or thermometers (at most contingent). The invitation obviously false,
you arrive late to find the company banded, like endangered birds (not those
of prey but other more delicate ones, those whose beaks canít reach into most
flowers for their rudimentary nectars), conceived in discourse and bounded
by it, as I am bounded by these narrower than usual margins. The culture
shock eased, white people seeming more or less inevitable in every circum-
stance, and so did the reflex anger that greeted my first public exposures to
the old rules. Yet the purpose is to conjoin elements, allow them their clash,
than recuperate whateverís left as sediment for the newer dispensation, the
one that promises to arrive like the express mail, a day or two later than
promised. The local is real, as my students remind me, white woman shuttling
unpredictably in and out of her symbolic value, the duck/rabbit example
hardly an instance of autobiographical excess. Fluttering like a lid or nervous
astronaut in front of a zoom lens, space between him and more space, you
recoup your losses as evidence there was a gain, again, embarrassed knowl-
edge taken like a fortress, or the egoís precarious pylon on the far cliff, ropes
in arrears as usual. Guilt greets you less as fact than as necessary outback to
operate through, though your ancestors did not, and etc. Intellect is molasses
compared to historical necessity arbitrated by oppressionís stern rehearsals
historyís over for you guys, but not for us. The phone rang and you neglect-
ed it, hoping instead for more direct speech, the blood knowledge that the
wanderer set his chips on. Plantations run by such as you, ìdiscoveryî made
by such as you, evidence that agency sells disaster and an outsider referring
to 'the rape of the land' is a fool even for noticing it. Metaphor as defense, or
irony, and I love them both, donít do it when communication occurs on the
head of a pin and there's no time for prettiness (considered with or without its
'r'). Old judges told tales predicated on outside value; the newer ones start
from a siege and then take the shelter of their sufficient arguments for enclo-

sure, which later bites them as instance of bourgeois power realignments. The gap is there to slip through, so take up your pen and write (if not here, oh crucial 'f') a measured dialogue with other selves, even where the landscape falls away and all you see is ruin around the billboard advertising your front yard as paradise, lest you prick the bubble to which you signed a loyalty oath. I wouldn't cheer for that, if I were you.

Sometimes I get lonely, but it's nice to be alone.
—Tatjana Patitz

Arena packed for the last game.
In a bid for audience, the lyric poet
with her 'if not here's' in tow,
promised to run the borough according
to sound business principles. Unacknowledged
legislator, she 'didn't just spend all day writing poems,'
preferring to display her culinary talents to the first
floor world that kept calling, like Publisherís Clearing
House in a childís imagination. Vegas has eaten New York,
installed skyscrapers on the strip; whoís to say itís not
worth the risk of ownership for a stroll over the pint-sized
Brooklyn Bridge? Or stashing oneís chips on Wall Street,
shaded by a Liberty who welcomes no immigrants
but those with easy money to ìgrow the economy.î
One poet invited another to tell the class that white
men have nothing to add but irony, who trust the adage
about double negatives. Tell that to ironyís cheering
section, pompoms dipped in paint, kinetic fields
of color strewn over the stands where simple rhetorics
soon acquire the shade of someone else's volition.
I cannot speak for anyone but myself (Thoreau is
right on a few things), yet risk cancellation of my
subscription to Metaphors of the Month Club, fore-
most among them the 'melting pot', the 'soup'
and the 'salad.' At least some figures of speech
are healthy, antidotes prescribed to cure too much
presumed clarity.

How I do things with words
is by letting them forage on their training
leash, sometimes pulling them in, telling them how
proud Susan is of their performance, marking out
territory, barking up a storm or tree, eliding hope
and hostility in single stark acts of fertilizing the earth
of this page, or other.

I've looked in the mirror for 20 years.
It's the same face.
                        —Claudia Schiffer

What I saw was my own face
brought to the cracking point, identity
framed no longer by wood but by context:
if I look the part, I am in and of it, playing
my role with accelerated attentiveness to my culture's
Fed Ex package, the one that moves with frightening
alacrity into new areas, then takes notes and offers
lectures on 'the religious practices of early Hawaiians',
with footnotes to relics discovered beside the new highway
that tears an island in two. Speed is always part of it,
the acculturated tide that refuses to stall or stay
like farmers in a single patch of taro
who wait until the earth draws its own conclusions.

Sobriety checkpoint.
Checkpoint Charley.
The guards are in
tonight so lower
your high beams,
weíre coming
to take the wheel
and turn it like
roulette by clients
whose poetsí
eyes widen at
visions of higher

imagination or
lower fancy,
piles of chips
to rival pyramids
as their kids
play Nintendo
in the cellar,
practicing
compulsions
necessary to
adult practice.
Trace your
genealogy here,
not by blood
but by type,
driving wedges
in personal
growth, driving
down the cost
of contrition,
not mass culture
but trickle down
soulistics introduced
on Oprah so
how can they
not be authentic,
if only in a fraudulent
way, the good fraud
that keeps us hoping
for a second coming,
rising once more
like the sun on
a supermodel's
self-worth.

Add ons. Adjuncts of the real:
extra notes infiltrate the line,
torching ambiguity with actual
delirium, word that contains
the verb 'to read' beyond pale

equilibria these suburbs promise
if never quite deliver, even though quiet
desperation doesnít exactly describe
it either. Let 'sleeping dogmatists
lie', in both senses of the word,
walking around their nucleus like
a kitchen philosopher taking recipes
from the book of Terezinís dead.

You canít think too much or it doesn't work.
                    —Paulina Porizkova

Meditative practice accrues
by diminishment: its extra, [remainder,
annex, wing] takes those notes
and improvises their disappearance
until still music trims itself
like a wick defeated by its flame.
Simplicity locks in the rifle sight,
eye focused on what must be undone.
The bird bath frozen, only squirrels
stay in the yard, looking for what birds left behind.

Compression is usually the way,
word warped into other words
and then unpacked as cause or
effect, if not in order, non-narrative
narrated to make approximate
sense of nominal chaos. This is not
that way, is slower, like a caravan
stalled between watering holes, camels
trading dialogues on the origin of humps,
meditation on process that tries to step
outside like an ambassador freed from
the consulate; is not terror but considers
its existence possible. As spur or head-
land, panic conceals only its own
procedure, adrenal rush ending at pitch

of thoughtlessness, having climbed
the stations of fret and skid, fallen
through ice to numbness. A fast
talker meets a slow talker and loves
her hesitancy, her inclination to listen;
Slow Talker marvels at Fast Talkerís
pace, her evident relish in thinking out
of sound, rubato beaten against strings,
stringing out assertions within the quaver
of her voice. Between them the history
of western philosophy lurks on the list,
for a ìlistenerî tabulates the score until
someone announces that disciplines are dead.
In the meantime, Slow Talker walks
home to feed her deaf dalmatian.

Loss of momentum is to be feared and then accepted
as in all losses that shape us and are gone.
Red cross knights leaving the mall parking lot lay
siege on consumption, their breastplates polished,
if a bit use (in the French locution). He who pricketh
· on the plain pays no taxes in this state, nor sets
aside income to fill potholes and ease congestion
that is more than metaphor, less than fact.
The presidents are missing, and we regret their
passing like gamblers in an era when risk is taken
off the table, negotiations halted for lack
of a mother tongue to enumerate demands,
process like that of carving a perfect sphere,
peeling the onion to trade scent for substance,
marking boundaries only when there's nothing
left to get teary over in cafÈs devoted to grief.
The block has closed, try us again in two years.

Pressure behind the eyes pushes
sense forward like a mirror whose
objects appear closer than they are
or books whose characters
bear no relation to us, romans

a clef in name only, racial
violence always possible,
especially in the schools.
Another non-communicant
would feel fewer responsibilities,
especially since committees are
seen as a womanís province.
As lines grow, so does my sense
that outerwear is heavier this
time of year, even for Darwinís
Camp Galapagos' kids, for
whom wise investments
created an inheritance of
lizards, surviving well if not
gracefully. Leave my words
out of this, that know how
to forsake their god, eyes
open like pearls against
eveningís hamstrung sun

Everyone should have enough money to get plastic surgery.
          —Beverly Johnson

A homeless man stands in front of the Sheraton,
his story scrawled on a piece of cardboard.
Steam rises from a heating vent, embraces
the sleeping bag, man inside.
Man in a wheelchair begs for change.
A city is pastoral only in the sense that its landscape moralizes.
Occupied fronts: images walled in to keep the children away.
Most encounters are more appropriating than not.
What do we make of them in striped pajamas
building cardboard cities beside the boxcars?

Coal dark shoes, the brushes and hair clips,
small and large jackets, photo gallery of 15,000
pounds of human hair baled at Auschwitz. A boy writes:
'do not let time happen again', meaning history

that is ours not to re-member as body but as
fragment, these three smiling faces posing
in a meadow, circa 1910, and we know
their story ended. Scale of horror: dead bodies
less gruesome than the dwarf who was given
to science before he died, his tender eyes looking out
at us from the well set behind a protective wall.

The work of forgiveness is not kind.
Forgiveness is not yellow paint on a white tile
like sunflowers or a childís accident.

Self-opinions vary within the frame
that holds us to the garden whose flowers
pay homage to a season's pretext,
certainty of blossoms weighed
against the uncertain context within
which they appear as lost faces,
what foreknowledge allows us
only at moments clouds open
like curtains and we see the storm
approaching, unable to cross this
pressure system that makes us hope
for order within the classical sense
of chaos, no fractals to burden us
with spontaneous generations of
unmarketable patterns outside
the lexicon, homeless words
telling no story but still disturbing
our belief the telling's necessary
to fend off socratic questions
since you have no legal precedent
for reply unless you sue yourself
for differences irreconcilable
if easily predicted, predicated
on an itinerary of moving
forward into weather (the colloquial
sense of it) or back to standpoints
as yet unimagined in philosophy.

A man bleeds inside the chalk
marks that register his death
into a murder mystery whose
pleasure is ours to tell and tell
again, cameras roiling away
from incident into history,
domestic servant to stories
that encompass incident as
delirium, hum of prelinguistic
matter filling rooms like bug
bombs: leave to return when
the house is pure as a policy
statement gone bad: what
impresses most is efficiency,
governance holding hostage
more messy ideals, the hybrid
confluence of less abrupt
foreclosures: I leave here wanting
to lose myself in a child's coloring
book, no matter yellow's a weak
color, since it describes escape's
wish so well as to bathe us,
like Serranoís Christ, in
the beauty that voids self
of excrescence, sacrifice
in a dance of daffodils.

　　　　Once I got past my anger toward my mother, I began
　　　　to excel in volleyball and modeling.
　　　　　　　　　　　　　　　—Gabrielle Reece

Last year the snow made the street a sheet of unrumpled linen.
Cold additive, it marked out presence in earth's absence,
lurking as on an email list beneath the conversation.
Desired escape accomplished, we circled Illinois
an hour in the fog as if going around were going somewhere.
We canít see jet streams except those displaced on other
travels. The misery index rises, though this January's warmth
prepares a lesser deviation between partial lives; transition's

an art that demands constant attention; it takes its prisoners
and locks them up as souvenirs, in the French sense, not that
of Niagara Falls fake china, ashtray of broken water marking
a visit to the urban sublime and wreck not of Hesperus
but of manufacture. The line between
economies is as clear as the tightrope
over the falls and you need a permit to risk
your life, awares, awash in a ruffled fog like
a twin engine over Hatteras. A private war
as deadly as the public, marchers gather
on the 50th day to protest nondisclosures,
votes returned to dusty boxes in provincial
stations. Have I cleared too great a space
in which to think these thoughts that lead
either forward or aft, daft as this sentence is,
led from the scruff of its syntax into unregistered
meaning (requiring a 7 day waiting period)
on which tax is levied or the dam breaks
thatís like a garde-fou, raft over the roiling
water a drug to instill in us the speed we require
to change our track, resettle in the silt of
another riverís salt? Or can this trance
accommodate a truce's end, onset of insult
meant to cover losses with accusatory rushes
of adrenaline and reaching out not as welcome
but as avoidance. The central fact is there to hold
to like a glove or instep arch, ribbons of rain
making bows, the intensest color of this space,
mediations as anchors against stasis; no thought
can rightly halt, even at escalators (you called
them elevators once) though the turn can negate
what sense you arrive at through the coin-op
binoculars that offer sight at a discount, erasing
the far hotels for nearer rebounds water inscribes
in air like words once the video spigot's closed
and the PC goes down for the night, conflation
of virtue with virtual links, mysticism computed
to make a milky way from these information
showers along way-stations between sites,
and I wonder why the jazz home page has
links to an asthma drug unless the fact of breath

belongs with castles melody elides to make
an elsewhere incorporated to mortgage air
for time, the only medium that tells us everything
we need to know about our futures, pork or
cattle or enigmas therein. Bungie cords make hay
out of our inability to fly, bonanza for the fun
industry combining danger with later tranquil
recollection, a romantic truism taken
to its final channel as you surf the blue note
for another Monk whose hands are real.
The notes are never ours to claim unless
new chord progressions can be funded
when mistakes are made, improvisation
the art of inadvertent landfall, motion toward
nowhere but where the chord breaks,
parachutist warned the hazardís there,
ride a short reach through
the all-encompassed air:
a final half note, and then you're here.

Anthony Mellors

TOY OF THOUGHT: PRYNNE AND THE DIALECTICS OF READING
N H Reeve and Richard Kerridge, *Nearly Too Much: The Poetry of J H Prynne*. Liverpool University Press, 1995.

I have not yet seen a review of *Nearly Too Much* in the academic press. Having spent years working on their study of Prynne N H Reeve and Richard Kerridge may now find that their efforts are ignored or at best treated to a display of pugilistic ignorance of the kind usually reserved for higher profile bogeymen like Jacques Derrida. For Prynne represents everything that is alien to the pretend consensus on post-war British writing: he is a modernist of the Poundian stripe, detached, mandarin, esoteric; there is no trace in his poetry of tidily manufactured populist gestures, which Robert Crawford and Simon Armitage call 'the democratic voice'; his ethic appears to be one of strict self-denial and intellectual resistance to aesthetic ease; if his inaccessible writing at least looks accessibly fixed to a critique of commodity culture, its politics nevertheless remain maddeningly unclear; and there is nothing about the poet or his work which could be endorsed by identity politics. To quote Andrew Ross on Celan, there is nothing here 'which we are going to be able to find socially useful.' ('The Oxygen of Publicity' in *Poetics Journal*, No. 6, 65) Prynne occupies a privileged space for poetry reviewers in the supplements, a zone of unredeemable obscurity or 'gobbledygook', as Robert Potts puts it in a *TLS* review of the Picador anthology *Conductors of Chaos*, where 'the lines continue to resist interpretation; nor do their linguistic shifts and confusions allow for any other pleasure.' This is a poetic of utter abjection, offering none of the popular joys of reading: no identity represented by the verse itself, and no comforting recourse to an identity behind them.

Reeve and Kerridge are keen to present a critique of the cultural assumptions on which this negative reception of Prynne's poetry is based, and they argue for a poetic that responds to its material dialectically. 'Dialectical' here means to question the positioning of concepts and registers of experience as unassailable entities tied to explicit or implied empirical identities. Ideally, Prynne's writing requires an act of attention from its readers which keeps interpretation as open as possible to the construction, dissolution, and reconstruction of cultural meanings. The poem exists as an unstable conjunction of the reader's fleet-footedness and wrong-footedness; it is primarily a nomadic form, not ruling out the possibility of a resting place but insisting that identity is never at home to itself, never more than a contingent point from which we must move on, being 'this we must leave in some quite / specific place if we are not to carry it / everywhere with us.' ('Thoughts on the Esterhazy Court Uniform') The aim is to create the heuristic conditions for a reading subject who would be fully alert to the paradox of the *Unheimliche* in the way Heidegger describes as *Dasein*, 'primordial, thrown Being-in-the-world as the "not-at-home" — the bare "that it is" in the "nothing of the world" … it is something like an *alien* voice.' (*Being and Time*, § 277.) One of the strengths of *Nearly Too Much* is its authors' ability to see that a dialectical reading must be reflexive enough to question its very positing of dialectic, and that — I can and cannot say it — this is the *essence* of Prynne's poetic: even in a collection as early as *The White Stones* it is too easy to identify the figure of the nomad and extrapolate a neat Heideggerian formulation from it, because as a utopia of 'complete migration' the nomadic model is itself open to question, and the refusal of home comforts may be an evasion based on the romantic allure of a non-Western otherness that merely supports a fantasy of alienated nobility:

> To become the 'complete stranger' would be too extreme a solution; it would be to 'live in a sovereign point', a self-sufficient state around which the world could only revolve indiscriminately. Since nothing outside could effectively impinge on it, the condition of total estrangement would thus increasingly appear to be merely the obverse of the one in which the tie to 'home' was never broken or even stretched. (63)

Throughout *The White Stones*, identificatory positions are offered but suspended. When Prynne writes that 'home is easily our / idea of it' ('Thoughts') he doesn't make it 'easy' to decide whether this ease should be rejected or affirmed. The plea for 'worked self-transcendence' in 'Questions for the Time Being' is not necessarily incompatible with being 'warm and tired / without some impossible flame in the heart.' ('The Common Gain, Reverted') The desire for some form of transcendence, whether pastoral, political, or spiritual, is a necessary condition for moving forward, but it is also prone to misrecognition as a hope for imaginary plenitude, the filling of lack promised by the commodity form, nationalism, the family, etc., which, being impossible, inevitably results in splenetic, passive acceptance of the damaged lifeworld. The sanguine 'recognition' of this 'deep, blunting damage of hope' ('In the Long Run, to be Stranded') checks the longing which both inspires progress and stifles it: 'The consequence of this / pastoral desire is prolonged / as our condition, but / I know there is more than the mere wish to / wander at large, since the wish itself diffuses / beyond this and will never end' ('Moon Poem'). If the poet goes on to assert that 'the wish is gift to the / spirit, is where we may dwell' (a dwelling that is Sisyphean, accepting the beyond of mere wish as more wish), his songs and/or psalms shine in the night, a night of 'negligence and still passion' ('Moon Poem'). In these poems, assertions of spiritual illumination vie with stoical reserve. The moment of epiphany is also the moment of error; vigilance or watchfulness is everything: 'There is a tradition, derived from Christ's unassisted watch in the garden, of regarding sleep as a weakness on a pilgrim's part, a slackening-off from the clear march to the trusted home' (*NTM*, 82). '[W]e carry ourselves by ritual / observance, even sleeping in the library'('First Notes on Daylight'); 'But sleep may also be a necessary nourishment from which good may emerge, if identity is reconstituted on waking' (*NTM*, 82), and Prynne does defer to what he calls 'that extremity of false vigilance' ('Questions for the Time Being'), with which he checks even the stoic response.

Whether you want to call this dialectic or mere equivocation depends on how you are disposed towards the rigours of Prynne's poetic. In this dark light, 'Questions for the Time Being' should perhaps be taken literally as an indication of Prynne's intent. The text is a blatant contradiction: more prose manifesto than poem, it is a splenetic diatribe against splenetic tendencies in late sixties political mores, a 'defence' of stoicism which infringes the decorum of its own ethics. The indignant opening line, 'All right then *no* stoic composure' says as much, declaring the thetic speaker's decline into the very rhetoric he would prefer to avoid. The outburst which follows takes a Nietzschean view on the relation of grammar to will, insisting on caution regarding problems of mastery and transgression. The current 'masters' of language may be 'self-styled', but they do 'own and / control the means of production', a fact which has escaped those who assume a revolutionary stance without any understanding of realpolitik:

> so much talk
> about the underground is silly when it would re-
> quire a constant effort to keep below the surface,
> when almost everything is exactly that, the
> mirror of a would-be alien who won't see how
> much he is at home.

Modish talk of an underground by (presumably) bourgeois bohemians et al. masks the lack of action on the part of what Prynne describes sceptically as 'any discrete / class with an envisaged part in the social process'. The idea of revolution is thus no more than fashion, the 'idea of change is briskly seasonal' and 'scout-camp' militants are so bound by their (and our) separate desires that any possibly genuine action is interminably delayed, being 'not part of any mode or con- / dition except language & there they rest on / the false mantelpiece, like ornaments of style.' The 'historic shift' is in actuality subject to forces outside telic fantasies ('hope', once again, here reviled as 'Micawberish') and any response to a 'really crucial moment' must be able to reject the blind world of wish: 'the wheel is permanently / red-hot, no one on a new course sits back and / switches on the automatic pilot.' Prynne remains stoical because he resists the sleep of desire (qua misrecognition) while ultimately seeing no escape from it. Nevertheless, he makes a claim for overcoming the self and its narcotic fantasy politics: 'What goes on in a / language is the corporate & prolonged action / of worked self-transcendence'. Whatever this means — the dodgy authority of its abstraction should not blind us to its lack of qualification, for if it is a case of 'language speaks, not man', where is the ground for agency? — it stands opposed to the culture of teeming *ressentiment* in which even this text is enmeshed: 'No one has any right / to mere idle discontent, even in conditions of most / extreme privation, since such a state of arrested / insight is actively counter-productive'. Nor does it follow that the alternative is a state of Epicurean disregard: 'Contentment or sceptical calm will produce instant death …' But the poet is on the ropes, and he knows it; the whole diatribe is just, well, *too personal*. As a last despondent snipe suggests that 'luminous take-off' is merely another pose, the poem sinks into nihilistic pathos: 'in a given con- / dition such as now not even elegance will come / of the contemporary nothing in which life goes on.'

In *The White Stones*, then, Prynne appears to be struggling to overcome his allegiance to the Olsonian ethic of *Kitchen Poems*, for which the 'politics … is for one man' ('The Numbers'), but he is stuck oscillating wildly between sceptical spleen and cosmic ideal ('Where we go is a loved side of the temple', etc.). Civic virtue is a desirable but impossible aim, and the turmoil produced in trying to achieve it is contrasted with projections of *ataraxia* in the 'thereness' of 'love' and 'the world', an oxymoronic concreteness in abstraction. In a sharply critical essay drawing attention to what he calls Prynne's 'neo-Stoical, Senecan *consolatio* of argument', D S Marriott has described this as '[t]he world as sacred object subjectively intuited in the sound of the sentient as immutable and timeless as contrasted to the privacy of individual time as a form of knowing within terrestrial process.' ('Contemporary British Poetry and Resistance: Reading J H Prynne' in *Parataxis* 8/9 (1996), 170.)

Reeve and Kerridge are acutely aware of the modernist oppositions of activity and passivity, subjectivity and objectivity in Prynne's work, arguing that the poems resist the cartesian stranglehold. But at times their dialectical approach gives way to Empsonian decision-making. Eliding the problem that Prynne's use of the definite article may simply reify dualist abstractions, they plump for a pastoral ethic derived from Heidegger to explain what they see as Prynne's 'Wordsworthian' answer to despondency:

> The desire here is for 'the world' to keep up the kind of unrelenting pressure on its inhabitants that would prevent their egos from disengaging themselves from it and bringing it under command. (*NTM*, 53)

Without wanting to labour the point, it strikes me that *the* world here is too Wordsworthian to be of much use to Reeve and Kerridge's larger argument for Prynne as the poet of radically shifting perspectives, of 'questions of scale' and positional contingency. Admittedly, this comes in a discussion of Olson's influence on *The White Stones*, and Reeve and Kerridge note that the poems often feature 'a rather vapid inclusiveness where large emotive terms are not able to carry the burdens placed on them.' (*NTM*, 50) Yet they also want to claim an avoidance of 'power worship' for Prynne's poetic as whole, for which 'Wordsworthian wise passiveness, or emotional reserve' would be too conventional (*NTM*, 32). The desire to avoid Donald Davie's reading of Prynne as 'lowering the sights, settling for limited objectives' (*Thomas Hardy and British Poetry*, 113) is understandable, but if the poet does propose an alternative, as Reeve and Kerridge seem to suggest, they can't put their finger on it. Prynne may never have subscribed to the right-wing cult of strength in modernism, but in a writer whose early rhetoric mimics the tirades of Wyndham Lewis, the possibility should at least be entertained that his poetic supports the distinction between subject and object à la *Time and Western Man*.

In general, Reeve and Kerridge are so keen to prove that Prynne's poetry is 'potentially democratic' (*NTM*, 2) that they ignore any aspects of the work which might counter this already hesitant proposition. Moreover, they struggle to clear away any taint of interpretation which might make the work appear conservative rather than progressively 'postmodern'. For example, even though we have already seen nomadism considered as a prime figure, and Wordsworth and Heidegger have been invoked as showing conceptual links, and there is a reading of 'Rates of Return' from *Bands Around the Throat* as a text involving 'Ecological concern [as] one of the pressures necessitating some sense of shared "horizon" and collective responsibility for the relations that constitute public environments' (*NTM*, 143), the authors argue flatly against the presence of pastoral in Prynne's poetry as if it were too risky to talk about modern British poetry's continuing preoccupation with the pastoral mode. More than any other poet, Prynne has radically changed the form and force of English pastoral writing, dismantling its Georgian nostalgia and shifting attention away from dreams of otium towards the prospect of care extended from the uncanny dialectic of 'home' and otherness. But in *Nearly Too Much*, the term 'pastoral' remains shorthand for a golden landscape of nymphs and shepherds and is treated throughout as a signifier of reaction: 'Prynne's reader is not invited to find consolation in nostalgic ideologies, in pastoral, or in any sense of wholeness gained through distance ...' (*NTM*, 134) The statement is simply too general, leaving questions begging about the direction taken by Prynne since *Kitchen Poems*, where at one level the reader is 'invited' to indulge in just the sort of ironic mourning for commodified nature described by Andrew Lawson in 'On Modern Pastoral' (*fragmente* 3 (Spring 1991), 35-41): 'the water of life / is all in bottles & ready for invoice.' ('Die A Millionaire'). Crucially, the naive rejection of pastoral threatens to contradict remarks made elsewhere in *Nearly Too Much*. *The Oval Window*, for example, is described as reviving the prospect poem, where 'the journeys that occur are contemplated from a *distance*' (my italics) and the poem

> touches on various Romantic negotiations towards a place for the self, a place of at least provisional stability amid the boundless organicism of the world, when we come across what appears to be a rough shepherd's hut ... It would offer some rudimentary shelter, and a prospect on the surrounding landscape, like a Wordsworthian occasion for reflection and insight (It is hard not to think of the ruined cottage in *The Excursion*, or the heap of stones in *Michael*). (*NTM*, 171-2.)

It is not that Reeve and Kerridge are wrong to reject the pastoral tag in order to avoid collapsing Prynne's poetry into the parochial tradition espoused by Davie and criticized by Lawson. Indeed, they work hard to disentangle Prynne's historical concern for landscape from 'vague and sentimental ego-mysticism', which they admit to be a 'risk' in the early poems (*NTM*, 42). The problem is that their own position offers a critique of pastoral while remaining unresolved: 'Ecology means the emergence of a new process of negotiation between different narratives and systems of cultural meaning.' (143.) In other words, care and vigilance; but the reader is left guessing how this is distinguished from pastoral. And no account is taken of Prynne's important text 'A Pedantic Note', featured in *The English Intelligencer* (1967), which charts the philological extent of the runic wynn into 'bliss' by way of 'meadow' and 'pasture'. In this essay the connection made between pastoral and spiritual travel concludes with a Blakean affirmation of the 'cultivation' of intellect.

By the early seventies, Prynne's poetry has begun to work itself free from its dependence on the personal voice struggling for impersonality, intensifying the most valuable aspects of *The White Stones*: ' ... small pieces of language can suggest the presence of competing interests and attitudes, from "objectivity" to outright emotionalism, without resolving them into a hierarchy of value' (*NTM*, 46) and 'By opening the moment of intense feeling to implicit comparative analysis, technical language ... can perform a similar function to the lyric strategies elsewhere, which undermine the claim of subjective experience to uniqueness and self-sufficiency.' (64) This suspension of hierarchical value belongs to the heuristic imperative of modernism, opposed to 'realist' forms of narrative order and completion. From *Brass* onwards, Prynne's poems display a textual profusion which is 'hermetic' to the extent that it appears to offer access to a buried signified; but the more the reader accepts this lure of meaning and strives for interpretative closure the further the text retreats into ungrounded specificity. A poem becomes 'self-reflexive', not in the now hackneyed manner of referring to its own procedures, but by reflecting the reading subject's anxiety about the act of interpretation. As Reeve and Kerridge conclude, echoing the title of their study, '[t]he effort required — moral, intellectual and imaginative — to sustain such alertness, in the midst of all that would close over and smother it, may be nearly too much to make.' (*NTM*, 189)

The rigorous attention required here would appear to identify Prynne as a high modernist, with all the élitist connotations so despised by the supplements and the Academy. However, in keeping with their aim to 'introduce Prynne's poetry to a larger audience' (dust-jacket blurb), Reeve and Kerridge make a brave case for the poetry as being capable of empowering readers rather than marginalizing them. If 'the reader remains intimidated and marginalized … the poet in turn will merely occupy the heroic position of isolated visionary' (*NTM*, 2): the threat of romantic élitism remains worryingly persistent throughout this book, and the authors can only counter it with the problematic notion of a compact between poet and reader based on the acknowledgement of 'risk'. Prynne 'faces' the risk that his poetry will be regarded by '[u]nconvinced readers' as 'an extreme of self-isolating élitism' (2), just as we have seen that he 'risks handing the poem over to the most vague and sentimental eco-mysticism' (42). In 'Aristeas' there is 'always a risk' that the treatment of the cultural otherness of shamanic flight 'could be reclaimed and converted into Western terms' (68), and because Prynne's text imperils the subject's sense of self-identity, preventing readerly absorption, it 'threatens the reader with absorption into larger discursive processes and time-scales. In other words, the dissolution of the speaker in Prynne's work threatens the reader with dissolution also.' (123.)

All these risks and threats may be necessary to a poetic which ruthlessly brackets thesis and identity in order to relocate the subject as both effect and agent of reflection, but they are a far cry from the contemporary discourse of marginality, which is concerned with specific social relations of mastery and dispossession (real or imagined) and for which the conceptual rigours of intransigent modernist writing already implies a bourgeois subject with the education and freedom to choose to question self-identity. Reeve and Kerridge do not face this risk in their own appraisal of modernism, which in Prynne's case they try unconvincingly to render as 'post-modern'. Accounts of this nebulous concept tend either to locate it as an essence of works of art (even to the extent of positing the work of art as non-essence), in which case it becomes indistinguishable from various modernist projects, or as the *condition* of late capitalism, in which case all 'works of art' are postmodern in that they are appropriated as objects of symbolic capital. In both tendencies, postmodernism is seen as being informed by a crisis of legitimation, the absence of a universal ground of knowledge, in the face of which 'art' collapses into the after-life of the avant-garde, the spectre of art as the theoretical impossibility of its own being. Postmodernists either mourn this loss of 'metanarrative' (Habermas) or celebrate it (Lyotard). In their chapter on 'Theories', Reeve and Kerridge represent both these positions, and they try to show that Prynne's poetry is consonant with the most positive aspects of each. Prynne's poetry, therefore, might be said to follow Lyotard in calling into question all grand narratives as contingent constructions of identity; but it also takes account of Habermas's critique of the 'privatization of the self' in Lyotard's notion of subjective mobility, reviving the need for an intersubjectively shared lifeworld. This looks like quite a neat dovetailing of two apparently opposed positions, but the reading remains dependent on the assumption that

> [w]hen Prynne confronts a reader with alien, specialist discourses, he is challenging that reader to resist being pushed to the side; to enter, instead, intersubjective relations with a world most of which will always be external. The reader is not only asked to examine the conditions of his or her own marginalization in relation to powerful instrumental discourses, but also drawn from the margins into a kind of public space, for an encounter with these discourses. (*NTM*, 134-5)

This passage moves from the tentative 'a reader.' to the universal 'the reader', but it cannot escape the hesitancy of 'a *kind* of public space'. While it is fair to say that Prynne's poetry insists on negotiating forms of discourse not normally associated with the poetic, which focus attention on what poetry consists of, and what the reader's role might be in relation to it, it is questionable whether 'marginalization' is being anything other than reinforced. Is it possible to have 'intersubjective relations' with an always external 'world'? Reeve and Kerridge try to play two language games at once, one phenomenological, for which apprehension is highly partial and contingent, and one sociological, which requires firm identifications of social space. Although of course hardly incompatible, the two jostle uneasily here in an unresolved relationship which suggests that the demand to make Prynne 'relevant' to postmodern identity politics is at loggerheads with a more discreet poetic inquiry.

Two other 'theories' are at issue. The first is Bakhtin's idea of the dialogic text, an odd choice because it leads Reeve and Kerridge to describe Prynne's work as predominantly prose-based. This is somewhat awkward as it threatens to shore up Davie's criticism that it 'makes for good impatient prose, if not for anything that we can usefully call verse.' (*NTM*, 108) Fortunately, Reeve and Kerridge knock this on the head by challenging Jakobson's equation of poetry as fundamentally metaphoric and prose as metonymic, and later, in a fine exposition of Prynne's interest in Chinese poetry they show that he disturbs this romantic opposition. The poems in Anne Birrell's *Jade Terrace* anthology tend to be read through a Western convention of poetic metaphor as vaguely evocative sets of images, divorced from the context in which they were written. In fact, Prynne argues, their technique has more in common with what we call metonymy, having been composed in a courtly tradition of emotional displacement for which recurring patterns of imagery become 'points of entry to a sophisticated network of meanings, which is called into play whenever its components are mentioned. The tradition of encodings allows for the entire cultural world of the subject to be registered in the nuances and hints of its detail' (*NTM*, 182). Prynne's own poetry shares something of this 'conventionalism', an 'awareness of the large, sometimes overpowering consequences that can be brought on by the slightest changes, whether they be the least displacement of an oolith crystal or the skipping of a letter in a [computer] programme …' (183.) This is not a poetic of self-enclosed metaphor (which in much modern verse resolves into simile, forging clear hierarchical distinctions between literal and figurative significance), but a text in which internally organised condensations and displacements are themselves synecdochal, always open to contextual possibilities which can inform but not exhaust the space of the poem.

Reeve and Kerridge also show that Bakhtin's distinction between monologic and dialogic discourse becomes problematic, because although it is useful to see Prynne's *bricolage* of utterances as a form of dialogism, many of his poems include a 'sardonic', 'satirical', and sometimes 'contemptuous' voice (*NTM*, 114) which 'spits out its reader' (116), confirming the Bakhtinian argument that lyric poetry tends toward the monologic. They are sharp on what they call the 'pattern of contraction and expansion' in Prynne's rhetoric, questioning their own earlier point about his dissent from the modernist flirtation with authoritarianism. But rather than leaving the argument at this impasse, they seek explanation in a second influential theory, Kristeva's extension of Bakhtin into psychoanalysis. Kristeva might be said to go some way in accounting for Prynne's aggressive tone when she writes about 'avant-garde practice in terms of rupture and reformation, sometimes in quite violent terms' (120).

For Kristeva, avant-garde writing is characterised by its dialectical response to the two orders of being which motivate the subject, the pre-Oedipal state of somatic drives (the semiotic), and the entry into language, which grounds the self qua Subject of the law of the Father and society (the symbolic). The maternal *chora* of the semiotic is a zone of discontinuous sensations, rhythms, bodily feedoms and constraints which gradually becomes displaced, repressed, and ordered by the development of self-identity, which is a misrecognition of the identification of the self by family and state. Although Kristeva insists that the two conditions are inseparable — this is not a nostalgic plea for return to primal selfhood, as no such essence exists — she marks out fundamental tensions between them: the semiotic is associated with the Mother's Yes, the symbolic with the Father's No; the semiotic with 'intuition', the symbolic with 'rationality'; the semiotic with fluidity, the symbolic with stasis, and so on. There are political consequences: bluntly, the more authoritarian the pressure exerted by family and state on the subject, the greater the imbalance between semiotic and symbolic realms, resulting in the need for revolution. Avant-garde writing disrupts the symbolic's dominant hold on the semiotic by pushing communicative language beyond the bounds of sense, creating in its radical disjunctions of syntax and its stress on rhythm, word-play, etc., a space in which the semiotic is allowed to resurface. This process, which Kristeva calls *significance*, should be distinguished from mere fragmentation; it is, as Reeve and Kerridge put it, 'continuous formation, rupture, and reformation', which 'seems applicable to Prynne, particularly in its emphasis on the movement of a poem, the requirement that the reader should move on before sense has been stabilized, gathered and sorted.' (*NTM*, 119.) It is the triumph of the 'dialogical and polyphonic over the monologic.' (121.)

The immediate theoretical problem here is that the description of such binary oppositions (and perhaps the notion of binarism as such) comes from the symbolic realm, which always *represents* the semiotic. If this is so, how can one propose to know the difference between the two states? The infant (*in fans* 'non speaking') has observable desires and responses, but whether they translate into the basis for the oppositions posited remains questionable. Kristeva may be proposing a dialectical relationship that simply does not exist, especially if its epistemological basis in the 'mirror-stage' is anything to go by (see *NTM*, 120). This early formulation by Lacan has no clinical credentials, and is phenomenologically bogus. So far as the child is concerned, there is no mirror-stage prior to symbolic access, the deixis informing the gaze. Kristeva is aware that in the process of individuation the child's apprehension of its objects are configured in the symbolic (the 'thetic' stages), but she cannot adequately account for the origin of the process. That said, the violence and negativity of much avant-garde writing is accounted for as a release of the expulsive drives which give pleasure to the pre-Oedipal child but, because they must later be repressed, become a source of trauma in the symbolic. Therefore, by giving voice to this withheld desire for play, the experimental texts of the avant-garde put the subject both in process and on trial, allowing for the break up and re-formation of symbolic energy.

A related concept is 'abjection'. Abjection is the emergence of self-disgust arising in the symbolic as a failure to come to terms with the pre-symbolic rejection of the mother, who is identified with that which is expelled from the body, and which occurs in the first thetic moments of individuation. The subject exists as a crisis in the state of being 'individual': the sense of self-identity as self-sufficiency is gained by rejecting that which the infant absolutely depended on to satisfy needs. The refusal of the mother, therefore, marks the shift to a phallic phantasy of the self as independent, without lack. However, because in the symbolic the I is already positioned by the desire of the other, is already the other's desire, it can never fulfil the desire of the self to be inviolable, a 'body without holes'. I think as an individual, but I am always already divided from myself by the spectre of dependence. Obsessively, I seek to expel all traces of the other, but only succeed in spitting out myself, wasting what I love (which becomes inseparable from what I hate). As Catullus famously puts it,

> Odi et amo. quare id faciam, fortasse requiris?
> nescio, sed fieri sentio et excrucior.

Paradoxically, abjection, 'like rejection, is connected to the death drive, the drive towards dissolution of subjectivity.' (*NTM*, 123.)

Reeve and Kerridge make a good case for applying this theory to Prynne's thematic of loss, which extends non-thematically to the experience of the reading subject who struggles to identify meaning only to have each interpretative position confounded by the proliferating text. Prynne's poems are abject gaps or holes which cannot be filled by the subject's representations, and therefore stage the subject as mediated, dependent on an ungraspable knowledge in and of the 'other': 'the dissolution of the speaker in Prynne's poems threatens the reader with dissolution also.' (*NTM*, 123.) The crucial point is made at the beginning of the book, in a preparatory mention of Kristeva. Prynne's obsession with questions of loss, waste, and rubbish exemplifies his concern with the residue of meaning which is

> a rebuke and challenge to instrumental systems, and to subject-positions, because rubbish is what is left when the operation of the system is complete and nothing should be left. When the rubbish is language, the

words which lie around conspicuously on various surfaces, rather than disappearing once they have been used, contain all sorts of secondary, multiple meanings not required by the user. These meanings articulate and fill the poem, in an unmanageable excess of meaning which reveals the repressed and concealed relations between discourses. (10.)

I am not about to disagree with this analysis, as it seems to me to be central to approaching Prynne's work. It also shows why our fulminating *TLS* reviewer is so right and yet so wrong in calling this poetry 'meaningless'. Prynne puts meaning on the line; if his work is abject it is because it does not flinch from the fact of abjection pervading the most sentimental and most violent actions and representations in Western culture. The pleasure of the text is the creation of a space in which inner contradiction — of the text and of the reading subject — may be negotiated and accepted, the joy of going beyond the self that is the basis of play and intellection.

Where I have trouble with Reeve and Kerridge's account is firstly, as I have already said, that it ropes Prynne's work into an inappropriate discourse of margins, and, secondly, that there is a mismatch between theoretical statements and critical practice, which Reeve and Kerridge then try to make good by disclaimers or conceptual turnarounds. The discussion of Kristeva ends with an important reservation from Leslie Hill: Kristeva's 'attempts to plot the path of the semiotic always end up making the semiotic reinforce the symbolic or thematic.' (*NTM*, 132.) This point would have benefitted from a comparison with Derrida's deconstruction of thematic analysis, but Reeve and Kerridge evade the problem by proposing it as 'a new light in which to see the "unreadability" of Prynne's work' and by making nonsense of what they have claimed earlier: 'Prynne's work is unusual in not polarizing the semiotic and symbolic as separate vocabularies. At the level of vocabulary there is indeed only the symbolic: all the language in Prynne's poems is public.' (132.) But this is not the point. Hill is asking, to what extent do the presuppositions of psychoanalytic theory lead to a method of interpretation for which all the semantic cards are marked in advance by what amounts to a typological formalism? And this is precisely what happens with Reeve and Kerridge's treatment of Prynne's more tendentious poems. Throughout the book, they find themselves in the subjunctive mood; in an exegesis of 'Royal Fern', for example, 'beads could, distantly, be the fern's', '[t]he "wing" may, by remote etymologies, be the fern', 'to stare something blind may be to look so hard at it as to be unable to see it', 'there may be a suggestion of snow-blindness', '[t]he key "takes cover", as if huddling under the blankets a little longer', etc. (*NTM*, 88-91) The marks of contingency here do nothing to alter the fact that the reading is constructed as a projected unity of discreetly related units, when in fact the text offers no such resolution. Similarly, Reeve and Kerridge choose to illustrate their discussion of Kristeva with just this kind of thematic reading of 'Rich in Vitamin C' and 'Cool as a Mountain Stream', where supposed contiguities of the 'this suggests that' variety are forced into impressionistic unity and made to fit the theory.

This is not to say that Prynne's poems outlaw such appropriation; indeed, it is a constituent of their dialectical 'lure' to offer the promise of unity. But Reeve and Kerridge tend to fall back on New Critical method as if they have forgotten the necessity to reflect their own investment as reading subjects in process / on trial: 'we will take exegesis as far as we can, and then acknowledge the residue or bulk of poem remaining, as a surrounding context of otherness which ensures that our position is always partial, always inside rather than outside.' (*NTM*, 4) A laudable ambition, but it does not answer the question as to why 'exegesis' should proceed as an assemblage of positive, if hesitant, references in the first place. Nor does it prevent them from describing 'Landing Area' as 'formidable in its unity ... full to capacity, but not overcrowded or stretched' (19) (how on earth do they know?), or *The Oval Window* as a 'moving', ironic sequence which culminates in 'increasingly rare moments of affirmative celebration' (188), as if it were too risky to end the study on a downer. Moreover, the authors are urged to conclude thetically that '[f]or the moment, anyway, in the opening lines of this last stanza, the subject is stable, standing amidst the "crossing flow", as discourses pass through and around it ... it is upright, confident in what it knows, asserting the authority of the senses ...' (189) *It's alright then*, phallic poise has been reasserted, in the irony of nocturnal laughter. This last 'toy hard to bear' strikes me as an inept return to the stoical Prynnean persona, which is surely what Reeve and Kerridge have been arguing against. Prynne steps in through the back door as 'a deeply concealed ironist, secretly laughing at those who insist on reading his words literally'. This is Allan Megill, writing about Heidegger (*Prophets of Extremity*, 148); but it would be more in keeping with the aims of this study to see Prynne's poetry as a version of what Gillian Rose describes as the Hegelian divine comedy: 'No human being possesses *sureness of self*: this can only mean being bounded and unbounded, selved and unselved, "sure" only of this untiring exercise. Then, this sureness of self, which is ready to be unsure, makes the laughter at the mismatch between aim and achievement comic, not cynical; holy, not demonic.' (*Love's Work*, 125)

A final note on scholarship: although this study is packed with well-researched explications of literary borrowings and technical references in Prynne's poems (e.g., *The Oval Window*'s fragmentation of Lavatch's speech from *All's Well That Ends Well*, and the brilliant exposition of the line 'a haploid cyclone of insect lust' from *Wound Response*), for the most part few sources are given, especially where scientific language is concerned. Clearly, this is due to the publisher's constraints on space, but detailed referencing would have been interesting and useful. Also, the authors are astonishingly remiss concerning their awareness of what is now a substantial body of Prynne criticism. This publication is not, as the jacket blurb claims, 'the first book-length study' of Prynne, there is no mention of Prynne's reception in Europe and the US (Bernard Dubourg, for instance, does not get a look in), and Reeve and Kerridge only acknowledge a handful of articles written by ex-students of Prynne at Cambridge. D S Marriott's work, which seriously challenges many of the book's assumptions, has not been considered, and nor has my own work, even though it deals extensively with the questions of psychoanalytic reading taken up in *Nearly Too Much*. Even Prynne's own essays and letters receive scanty attention. In a study which makes so much of the importance of context, the overall impression is of a curiously contextless encounter with the subject.

Drew Milne

BELLIGERENT LACONICISM
review of Rod Mengham, *Unsung: New & Selected Poems* **(Folio / Salt, 1996),
pp. 108.**

Unsung is an elegantly produced book which in one volume collects almost all
of the poems Rod Mengham has published in the last twenty years. Mengham
has featured in anthologies such as Iain Sinclair's *Conductors of Chaos* (1996),
and he is well known as the editor and publisher of the exceptional Equipage
pamphlets. Critical discussion of his poetry, however, has been relatively
scarce. Despite the engaging and illuminating manner of readings he has
given, the work has a somewhat enigmatic reputation for measured obscuri-
ty. Moreover, his critical writings provide only oblique illuminations of his
poems. This collection, then, provides an opportunity to assess the develop-
ment of his poetic work thus far, and to suggest why the quality of his poetry
should not remain unsung.

Unsung's opening poem in prose, 'Local History', reads as an almost pro-
grammatic allegory of the book's art of the local. 'Local History' combines
reflection on historical events with reflections on the impact of such events on
a more immediate person, a person it is difficult not to presume is closely
related to the poet. In Mengham's poems, however, the prose remains tem-
pered and lyrically impersonal, as if abashed by too much sentiment, but
determined not to go private. 'Local History' describes a father in terms which
prefigure the book's mood: 'He was crippled by defiance. Grief had nothing
to do with it.' (p. 7) The poems ask that the silent interlocutions between sen-
tences be recognised, but it is the tone of the narrator which is the central lyric
drama of the book.

These poems, then, are always close to the rhythms of prose statements and
the narrative voices associated with prose. In some of the earlier poems this
can give an impression of detached remarks, remarks which lack the momen-
tum or desire either to hang together or to hang out. Superficially this sug-
gests affinities with the detached listing of L=A=N=G=U=G=E sentences. But
Mengham has elsewhere suggested scepticism regarding the claims of
Language poetry, and his distinctively restrained muse comes into sharper
focus if it is contrasted with Tom Raworth's poetry. Whereas much of
Raworth's work strains to break the power of the sentence into a music of
phrasing, Mengham's poetic line is more enclosed and contained, with a more
decisive use of the full stop.

In the earlier poems this poetic line often involves a drama of she, I and we. 'Beds & Scrapings' offers metaphors of bodies embedded in resistance to the sentimentality of sexuality. This might be called a phenomenology of pillow talk. For example, the line 'Ice sing with passion' (p. 17) turns the 'I sing' of love poetry into a contrast between ice and passion. This might be compared with W R Bion's discussion of how, as an analyst, he became aware of the phrase 'I scream' as the condensed content of an analysand's use of the expression 'ice-cream'. The lines can seem painfully explicit: 'He wrenched off like a mussel in two parts in petrol.' (p. 26). But if these poems are careful not to overplay the angst of sexuality, they also have to fend off a tendency to imply a Lawrencian language of animality. On occasion, this is perhaps a risk too far: 'An elephant came to rest / and blew a jet of steam into her eye.' (p. 20). If this, so to speak, doesn't quite come off, the sequence does dramatise the conflict between desire and language. The danger is that all language appears over-determined as an expression of condensed and displaced sexuality.

Many of Mengham's lines resist this in imperatives and enigmatic aphorisms which separate the teller from what is told. This is most explicit where a pun transforms a cliché into a double edged knife. In 'Polyalbum', for example, 'All the rage is red herring.' (p. 37) folds clichés in on each other, leaving the reader to decide who is responsible for the associations. Where internal combustion reaches for neologism, for example 'logo-/ motive' (p. 42), the effect can be strained. But where the familiar is brought up against itself and left gawping, the effect is more enlivening: 'I open sesame' (p. 43). The apparent overlap of the Arabian Nights and sesame seeds was always already part of the expression.

Puns are often dismissed as cheap effects, perhaps because if understood speculatively, or indeed poetically, all words are puns. The question as to how to escape the expensive cheapness of puns is perhaps posed most directly by the final lines of *Unsung*: 'inlaid box, crying what news what news / not a sausage' (p. 108). Rumour has it that Out to Lunch, no mean punster himself, has threatened to throw a string of sausages at the poet when next he reads these lines out. We may wonder at the reader who would jump off the precipice of puns into the abyss of literalism, but the important question is the fragility of tone in such moments, and the relation between the energy of wit and the perils of irony. 'Glossy Matter' is the finest of these early poems, perhaps because its interrupted moments are carried over across phrasal prose patterns into the more metrical urgings of a continuous line.

Out of the early poems, Mengham has developed two characteristic modes. The first and more representative mode in this collection consists of sentences which unfurl over lines marked out predominantly in couplets and single lines. These poems resist becoming seamless, but weave together a range of social, political and aesthetic references through a texture of imperatives and injunctions. 'Neutrinos', for example, cross hatches neutrinal structures — a 'neutrino' is an uncharged particle with zero mass — and experiences of Eastern Europe, including, according to an aside at one of Mengham's readings, the experience of watching Tarkofsky's *Solaris* in Russian with Polish subtitles.

Experiences of Eastern Europe figure in many of the poems, and the poems register local responses to the evolution of a Europe which is both modern and yet haunted by its past. 'Unsung', the poem from which the book takes its title, traverses references to the myths of unsung heroes. From Adam, 'the man whose wife the apple / gets more sick' (p. 69); to 'the crazy flight of Icarus' (p. 69); 'a rag-picking native like / Tantalus' (p. 70) and 'the pump-action of Goya' the poem describes a world recognisably ancient and modern, searching out of blind roots for 'remigration where it belongs.' (p. 71). The movement of migration from a colony back to where 'it' belongs suggests the international homelessness of these poems, a homelessness quite different from the transcendental homelessness described by Lukacs.

The most important theme of these poems, then, is the critique of the desire to return to worlds secure from the babel of language:

> Transcaucasia like a burning wheel, 27 languages
> On the verge of saying 'cosa nostra'
>
> How can·you tell, the shadow of home rule
> has a toothed edge in the wounds of capital   (p. 75)

In poems such as 'Dogs on Sticks' and '31/12/92' a transnational world of language relates more identifiably British characters — Kenneth Baker and Norman Lamont — to the world of Havel and actually existing European economic markets. In these poems, Mengham attempts to track the implosion of the local within the international experience of capital, in what might be called a phenomenology of anti-spirit.

If there is a problem with this exploration of the difficulty of the local it is that the tension between fact and value is not always sustained. There is a preponderance of definite articles and verbs in the indicative, such that description installs its unlocated poetic authority within authoritarian prose steps. This perhaps explains the preponderance of imperatives which appear to be ironic while unable to wish away the voice that gives the marching orders. 'Take a Bite' exemplifies this by assembling a series of violent but imploding imperatives: 'Kill the messenger, burn your hand, know the names / you are inside ... / find out who among them recommend weeping / or desire instruction with the closed fist ...' (p. 95). The sequence tempers the violence of these resonant commands, but one is left wondering if the sequence offers only an 'Achilles fang', a bite at the weak heels of power. 'The Boeotarchs Shall Hear of This' begins with a counter-imperative against the perils of sustaining such explorations: 'Never put a razor inside your thoughts / even for a joke.' (p. 101) The poem reflects on Les Murray's essay 'On Sitting Back and Thinking about Porter's Boeotia', in *The Paperback Tree* (1992). Murray attempts to imagine an alternative tradition of poetry stemming from Hesiod out of rural Boeotia. The opposition between this tradition and that of the Athens praised by Pindar, also a Boeotian, is resisted by Mengham. His poem moves towards 'another redoubt / killing two birds with one song' (p. 102). The redoubled doubt of the violent metropolitan song will be heard by the Boeotarchs, and may be better than embracing the rural idiocy of Boeotia's 'snowed-in / capital of stoics' (p. 101). Mengham, then, challenges the urge to celebrate a supposedly non-metropolitan local history, preferring the awkward struggle to reconcile the feuds of modernity.

Mengham's second and more distinctive mode consists of prose poems more accurately described as poems in prose. 'Down in the Mouth' takes up the enigmatic aphorisms so common in Mengham's poems to combine reflection on the formal resources deployed within a more sustained argument: 'Too much mildewed freight was left in pallets on the docks of ancient Europe, and the history of being in beds has many more things to answer for than sheer afflation at the roots of the burning crops.' (p. 80) This poem provides a more explicitly articulated framework for resisting the 'xenophobic relays of idiot vetch' (p. 80) which the other poems explore. The force of its paragraphing makes it clearer that we cannot afford to remain intimate with the unspeakable apparent in the more fragmented poems. 'The Dog Star' is more programmatic, offering reflections on the contributions which might still be made by old empires now rethinking the legacy of Columbus, and working to develop a refluxive script out of the 'rubbish-compacting dens of the avant-garde' (p. 93).

If a larger collection of these poems in prose is forthcoming it promises to be Mengham's most distinctive and original contribution to contemporary poetics. This contribution suggests a new prose poetics of modernity which knows the cost of the freedoms it expresses. This collection reveals a developing oeuvre which deepens and strengthens as it progresses. With an unusually clear ear for the formal relation between prose and poetry, the poetry extends its forms into social and political explorations of the discontents of prose. The poems bear witness to local histories of experience without collapsing the locality of modernity into sentiment. Walter Benjamin once described how Proust 'brings to the most feeble perceptions a beautiful, belligerent laconicism'. This surprising description of Proust's more prolix oeuvre might serve as a description of Mengham's emerging achievement.

Fiona Templeton

RECOGNITION
A POETIC PLAY — TEXT ONLY VERSION

in memory of Michael Ratomski

(The play is set in a courtroom. 12 of the audience are jury. Michael is on videotape, and is also played by Fiona. There is no judge. The dreams are by the light of video blue, in which the prosecution and defense tables become beds.)

First Dream

Fiona: Why am I asking a question?

I'm giving you a memory to will have had to will have known the answer I'll tell you.

Why am I asking a question? Because words are a honey to why.

How can you not have known? Must I spill in his language, backwards, kneeling, in act without action, naming, act out of action, jobless, cannibal, be him? You knew till I asked you, and telling, blow free in its ignorant giving. But I have a freedom and giving and ignorance you copy in ignorance of knowing that's equal to bearing. I've given all of my place. And I've given the ignorance.

Why am I asking a question?

***

ACT I — i

(In the courtroom, answering that question as witness.)

(eyes open)   There is death in my language, a grimace, jawless. (In yours a ma–a–ad bleating, that in hers cuts fucking.) Cut.

· 73

(eyes closed) Bind. In the words of going to you, going to you. In the speech of influence. I feel you all through me. What are you doing? I'm feeling you. What are you looking for? You through me. You are not on the carpet because I am dressed.

(eyes open) Cut. Protected by specific daylight, allowed by a specific weight on the body, here because a place here, its weight gives me weight, I'm here. So ok the mind.

(eyes closed) 'To' was to have inside. Held inside, how inside is. Contain him how a part of means gone from. Him is how what's inside is, how out. He said gone from, he said inside his. I heard. Inside his is each thing he hears with me.

(eyes open) Splice the cadenza. Star which schizo? Nobody speaks through me, and my mouth opens and closes, healing to a familiar indifference. Life never was like action replay, real tears for false eyes. Good thing I wasn't overidentifying, tripping into someone else's room like a bad snapshot, me to a T, incomplete and free.

(eyes closed) Risk things away, leading tearing torn. No, you don't get used to it. And now no tearing? For two.

(eyes open) My accident and I, well, the body's mutual. In this state, what story could I give? The plot thins. Pawn for pawn, trying to lapse, to be true, to witness, to seed.

(eyes closed) A motorbike pulls up like a match. Flared is a new and active silence, his. His, this name of him, holds. Holds his body holds. Held himself out of the discussion, in one stroke, instead of it. The likeness is unmistakable. I, too, imitate him into life, into my mouth. The fooling is his. Here. Hey. Have your, hisself.

(eyes open) We hit a neck, sweet ko'd me. What's this struggle? Of course I want him to be real. When I want him to be. You didn't even notice I was gone, missed the real show while memorizing deja vus to hold against us. Your irises flick their catalogue, can't lick his body, how pass back to what's his, here, hey, have. Today he ... born, into his. We hit efface.

(eyes closed) To free him inside,

(eyes open) he.

(She becomes a man.)

Limited. Already. Token. Help. Relentless. Indifferent, satisfied. Open secret. Live here. See me. Change, that is, on, productive, treading till, I don't know why, it's been a long time. Wrong. I'm new. She is speaking through me, unfairly, a cold and steady breath in the corridor, absorbing attitude, straining us. I am not unconscious. Where is my motorbike? Behind the empty walls she exits far away and returns immediately, the life–deed done in the time for me to see the empty walls. I'm lost but I'm speaking. Build a house, polish a beat, the sea through the cleft through the window. What do they say, in profile, in windows, in parentheses, in bodies, in stories, in clefts? Noooooothiiiiingg. On the other hand, tattoos. I extend this masculine, amnesiac breach into your possibility. Born whole as silence, what have I begun?

***

ACT I — ii

(As the same man.)

Michael: For the one, the other dies; for the other, death is the other. I will fold you into each other, man and man.

Deaf as a postmortem, well into the matter in hand. We may say 'it is warm', but we don't bother to say 'there's weather'. There's no weather without change. Why should being be any different?

It thundered in him, so far ahead of diagnosis, of being stuck in a place by time. Hands in the guts of the machine, I announce a beginning, a slap in the face of eternity. Not him, back at design central, but being got in the end; nor he, claustrophobic in the barren belly of brightness forever. Briefly, I need not be all of you, aahhh; all you want to know is what kills me. Of course, that's your job.

But I'm the apparition of code. I crack myself, from all of you, into signal 61, a fight, or 88, an assault, into now. In homicide, it's just you and your partner and the action's over. By the time there's the here you're the subject of, you're not now, now not. You go in, make your notes, write your narrative, make your case. Leaving is beginning. Blue visor, blue lettering: 'Our day begins when yours vanishes.' You wear that to scenes of limit, neither variable nor permanent, just you at the crime?

(Lies down.)

I see. Sight spills below you. For you, incognito is my real name. Has it happened or do I still bear you? (Rising:) You are borne.

(Lights down.)

***

Second Dream

(Fiona sings, to the tune of The Farmer Wants A Wife)

> The dog wants a bone
> The dog wants a bone
> Hey ho my daddy o the dog wants a bone
>
> The bone won't break
> The bone won't break
> Hey ho my daddy o the bone won't break
>
> Hammer on the bone
> Hammer on the bone
> Hey ho my daddy o hammer on the bone
>
> The bone wants the dog
> The bone wants the dog
> Hey ho my daddy o the bone wants the dog
>
> The dog buries the bone
> The dog buries the bone
> The bike without a rider comes chasing you down
>
> The dinner's on the table
> The man is in the chair
> Who would you have for dinner if the table wasn't there?

The boot is on the foot
The man is in the chair
What would you do on the table with your mouth made of air?

The shit is on the boot
The pie is in the sky
If all the sea were paper this song might wipe my eyes

The bird is in the hand
But the beat will not be held
Its breath is on the glass and I have swallowed the world

The breath will not be held
Though the sky is in the bed
What do you call a girl with a boot on her head?

The dog wants a nurse
The nurse wants a child
The child wants a wife and the wife wants a farmer

***

ACT II

(Court again.

References to glasses or other props should be accompanied by making a move with the piece and/or preceded by downing the contents.

The dialogue is mostly two monologues, especially Michael's.)

Michael:	Fiona:
	What do they *say*, fella?
He is lying in the bread. He gets up, rearranges it, lies down.	
	What's in doesn't look out.
He gets up, she puts a cup of water in the arrangement. Another puts an apple. Another puts a price on the bread. The first eats the apple.	

The third steals the bread.

Your only motive's to follow the hinge, but you find yourself next door.

If the universe is a place in your schoolboy address, habitation of the pluriverse is not amnesiac. Like a gaggle of geese, a creepy–crawly of realities.

It was the body that asked me the question, where did he go?

It's the body for whom bread is moral.

Keeping your freedom dialectic keeps your killers pure.

Between yourself and you, a death is as good as a change.

They knock; the door opens; and a new set of guards takes charge on the other side. The walls close.

Or the walls open. I may be the walls, or I may pop out, me, mine, ma.

You had to be there.

I seed myself. Painfully, visibly, don't let up.

Let me in, prisoner.

Opening falls silent, clangs to.

You gotta secret?

Tests offer the refuge of possibility, but my retreat accompanies me.

They don't need me.

They don't need me at all.

They know what to do without me.

Ain't no nuthin'.

None of them are ever going to leave
here, and the worst is there might
be worse.

I finished my cake and he led me to
what did not come from me.

Single stood alone, rearranging a
styrofoam cup, a tube of toothpaste
and a bottle of mouthwash,

stepping back and looking at what
he's done even when brimming with …
at least his own nature.

It is not a thing and can't be had.

They are piled.

It is never a present.

It all made sense,
but it was all a
deception.

It is not suffering.

Observe me observing my held fast.

This drunk or sober game for life is
played on a table, a bed, a nighttable,
a nightcourt or nightmare.

What had he heard to make him
deaf forever?

Its breath is on the glass and I
have swallowed the world.

Hermits need outs, too.

Dross of the day is not-the-full
decks still compel playing.

And art a ruse a sleight of mind to
fleece the poor in spirit?

So it's clear that on a biting night
twice shy of slammed teeth,
preferring the window to the
corridor to powerlessness, that all
you have to do is rename your
universe, not so much Mama opening
the wall as one woman's motorbike is
another mother's glass,
see?

Is this a room for miscalculation?

He is too delicate to speak his
kill, sob his secret from himself,
from his audience.

You are not in two places at once.

Starting from scratch match is only
a trick

Not a reality. Come back.

to deny particular absences any
active value.

In my dream, I mean lines, it's he
who says, we are unable to be able.
They lie in the place, an event
arrives, that is, she was there, but
the writer wrote his coming. He
devised an alphabet. Most others
are assimilated through joy. He had
another name. Death multiplies, and
sings it just before. How should
being be any different? The women
take it out of your hands. I don't
need one. They even the score, not
apart but parted, impossible to say.
We can't live together, I spit
myself clean, and we can't live at
distance, toes clenched to the earth
and to you. The pain is perfumed by
an elsewhere of violins.

Just that I'm a violin doesn't mean
I'm passive.

Everyone was talking

I'm not free, therefore I mean?

had the drone,

You worry that this has nothing to
do with truth, yet your radio's on
all day, sausage.

is no I,

Contact me at my one-armed address-
book,

not even weather

but weatherness.

my register of little births,
gasping.

An offer of Puffed What might make
the adult well, too, blanketed dark
between peaked windows, stilled into
my world.

Upon arrival at the scene

Here begins the ineffable tenderness
of his later mispronunciation,
strapped from and inside the hot
world's gag steaming into
reiterations;

this writer was advised by Mrs.
S-H-E-L-L-S

a mist of blue-black wets our
unspecified and separate faces,
match to the page.

that the above–listed victim L-Y-N-N
would say loudly,
'Please don't hit me no more.'

'Please don't hit me no more.'

She lay down in the bread.

'This speaker is spoken and evilled
and endless and you're a man and
afraid and in France. I who have
always rained and shined, now leave
from somewhere, you.'

This speaker is spoken and evilled
and endless and you're a man and
afraid and in France. I who have
always rained and shined, now leave
from somewhere, you.'

When the noise stopped, after some
time,

To have not changed, ah, finally.

Mrs Shells stated she could hear
A-C-E saying,

'Lynn, please wake up.'

At this time, this writer was
advised that there was freedom in
the fact of the subject, and
loneliness in its single beginning.

The punch line had spread out
newspapers so as not to make a mess
of the matter in hand,

the weight of itself as weather now,

neither after the joke nor before
the blow spreads from the center of
its above–listed

heavy self.

For every mark there was a maker;
but not me. For every advised there
was an adviser. Every body was a
negative that could be processed to
reveal a subject, a weight of a
having, so a thing. But I speak
from my body. You have taken away
my gold standard ring, which you
claim is to protect it. I don't
protect my speech. The cup of your
ear tinkles with the wave of my
silence. If you're free because you
have, take yourself; and in that
tragedy, divide. So link the chain
to your image. So see your edge and
end as privilege, poor thing. So
write your terminal case.

***

ACT III – i

(At home, across a large pool of water, Michael is preparing medication and directing Fiona to write him. Fiona is in court.)

Michael: You don't know me, but I take the long cut, and I give the lie to
the lie. Interrupt me, your breath into my laughter, my body
into your …

82

Fiona: What are little boys made of?

Michael: I love presents, but I take myself away.

Fiona: You give yourself away.

Michael: A liquid secret's hard to jail.

Fiona: Disguise says take me off, even when you've seen the lights go out for the birthday candles. Who made the cake?

Michael: Oh, I did. When I came out of that coma I just didn't know what to do with myself.

Fiona: A hawk stops to see, and we see silence. Report, shatter.

Michael: I was never part of you, but I made what you made.

Fiona: You studied how to change my wits.

Michael: Take your witness out of mine.

Fiona: You are borne.

Michael: If this is the changing room, where's the habit at?

Fiona: Oof. By the end of the answer, it's older.

Michael: I understand you were present when the body was found.

Fiona: Into its pockets seeped doubt of its kind, from the corners of its mouth a letting hard for them to figure.

Michael: Change places with me.

Fiona: Again? Don't quote me.

Michael: It was a foreign body, remember?

Fiona: Aren't we all?

Michael: Bound to answer? Bound for treatment?

Fiona: And now it isn't, so … missense, deletion, termination.

Michael: But not the same the next time.

Fiona: But a fine figure of a door.

Michael: With my hat raised, the difference between not being there and no birthday.

Fiona: If I can't see you, I've no excuse. This is the last avoidance before toll.

Michael: The only invitation's to between. Eating, for example, or folding a bedsheet together, and wanting to find always another in the basket.

Fiona: Before the blind sheet of the unreal billows black back, and need, and no hawk, and silence anyway.

Michael: The affinity's different, not the avidity, in and out in the power of the sitter over the chair he conforms to.

Fiona: Where are you going? I hear you but my hips asked as I turned, my foot asked as at an unexpected ditch.

Michael: Yeah, with costumes, gestures, handshakes, works spoken to you but that can also reach the ear of an innocent bystander.

Fiona: To lurk in that gossip's forensic bowl? Till swallowed?

Michael: At close quarters we assume understanding from the beat back. And know the now to tell.

Fiona: Let's be introduced again. To tell with one hand, knowing the now to question. The telling of the weaker closes in, dancing.

Michael: Deeper into routine is the story. What do you do?

Fiona: Act at short range. Your turf, my song. Grew there. Fruits on you.

Michael: Sweet aim.

Fiona:	Sweet wandering.
Michael:	The lie, I said, to the lie. Do you recognise anything yet?
Fiona:	What, exhausted from change?
Michael:	What, be him?
Fiona:	The angel of plot? Or river of telling?
Michael:	My solo submerged by my own chatter. Or the one that denies me?
Fiona:	The sodden wings are the lie of the man. And you? Who denies whose question?
Michael:	Give place, time. Details. Preference.
Fiona:	Build shelter on the precipice?
Michael:	Yes, ladder to the foam.
Fiona:	What?
Michael:	Do you hear something?
Fiona:	No, I don't think so.
Michael:	The effect can't be acted. Tell it with the lips of each blood beat bubble. Are you sure you didn't hear something?
Fiona:	Should I?
Michael:	I don't know. You looked like you heard something.
Fiona:	No.
Michael:	And on the outside, a picture.
Fiona:	The picture of what was inside now it's not? Or the picture of the third in the bed of the warp and the woof? Who's going anywhere?

Michael: Here we are again, hand to hand.

Fiona: Close quarters feel different after all your skins.

Michael: No secret or no jail?

Fiona: No thing. Sweat your way through.

Michael: To? Help comes.

Fiona: Comes is will come, takes no space, gives it. Lying tells too.

Michael: Let me look for you. *(Leaves. Closed door on video pause.)*

***

ACT III – ii

Fiona: That touch became its own body. Taken away is again, again, own pulsing gash in gravity. Discloses how to lose longer, hear something. Now is new so never learnt.

Michael: *(Offstage.)* Can you dance?

Fiona: I am dancing. Just not for anyone. Walking endows time's silken binding, not to tell here for there.

Michael: Where do you live?

Fiona: Hello, well well. Hello, well well. Play it by touch. Her spider space measures the user's resistance.

Michael: Are you available?

Fiona: Specifically.

Michael: Is it true? Is it certain? Is it allowed?

Fiona: Do you have to? Can I? Are we here?

Michael: Skip the sheets. Draw in the rain. No, skipping defends against specific pain, even in a specific home.

Fiona: *(Scrubbing draws the floor's violent corps.)* I've stopped dreaming, can't speak.

Michael: Specific. Fine. Whose was the body?

Fiona: The third in the bed belonged to the body. How she swims can't be woken to there. Prompt me with witness.

Michael: How she swims didn't ask its spell onto you.

Fiona: Her haunts and woods signal the material. Sheets dry.

Michael: Are you acting?

Fiona: Haunting, close quarters, no family, and back.

Michael: Get to an edge. Good, go in.

Fiona: But it's my edge. I'm in.

Michael: And then?

Fiona: What do they say? None of this has happened to me.

Michael: There, there's a door. You take the next one. The meeting place encodes the help within.

Fiona: *(Looking at 2 doors.)* Sitting. Or standing.

Michael: What do you need to know?

Fiona: Keeling. What do <u>they</u> need to know?

Michael: How old are you?

Fiona: Timely. The birds in the field fly up in a mad whirl and the sky seems dark and noisy. We turn back. The cows are running around, breaking things and anxious.

Michael: Waits.

Fiona: Waits.

Michael: Waits.

Fiona: Binds!

Michael: Waits.

Fiona: Interiorizes.

Michael: Waits.

Fiona: Processes (but protects).

Michael: Waits and hopes.

Fiona: Re–exposes!

Michael: Binds! Is stimulated! Stimulates!

Fiona: Secretes! Produces! Is simulated! Proliferates!

Michael: He placed man's countenance on top of his body, and bade him look at the sky.

Fiona: J reminds us that Mr. B. maintains a dungheap on a piece of land of which he is supposed to be joint owner with his brother A. If you want my guess, the sky starts here, like the photo of any fool pressed in your wallet.

Michael: Precedent's act waits months, years for you, in walls, doors.

Fiona: The foundations survive the fire, but are mocked by the thought of life on their new antiquity. Shells, not hearts.

Michael: Condemn me then, gutted and unfrequented.

Fiona: Oh no, dear, it doesn't go away. Night and day the house lies open, for she has given it a thousand apertures, with never a door to barricade their thresholds. The whole structure is of echoing brass, repeating words and giving back the sounds it hears. There is no quiet within, and yet there is no loud din, but only murmured whisperings. Some of them pour their stories into idle ears.

Michael:	Dead actors direct the judge. The accused degenerates under the chain's specific link. the ear. Yes, you, yes, the law is a line and tellings are spills.
Fiona:	The three are poised on the bridge away. Catching but never caught.
Michael:	A classic competitive inhibition in a double reciprocal plot.
Fiona:	So call me names and give me a map, and where they meet, I'll draw my body.
Michael:	<u>A</u> body, in your dark.
Fiona:	Help! Cross the line, please!
Michael:	The edge?
Fiona:	Between the lines. Bleeding. My heart pounding back to my ears.
Michael:	Take a good look at this woman.
Fiona:	That's enough! It's your story I'm betraying!
Michael:	*(Paused door opens. M as Madonna.)* You're right.
	(Slow vogue interlude in.)
	You can't vogue. You can't do the accent. And take your goddam edge with you.
Fiona:	How hard it is to make up stories. But I will let the two of them off with a good night's sleep.

***

Third Dream

(Fiona tells what Michael would have told in testimony (from Ovid's Metamorphoses Book III 300–340 approx.):

'I'm Tiresias. I'm an out–of–work blind prophet. I used to move around in some pretty lofty circles. I would hang out at Olympus with, like, Jupiter and Juno. What happened? Well it happened that Jupiter decided to have a night off from all his weighty responsibilities, and he was lying around bantering with Juno, and they were drinking. A lot. And Jupiter got really mellowed out on that nectar, and he's a bit macho, so he says, 'You know, Juno, of course, you women get far more pleasure out of love than men do.' well, illa negat. I mean she had never noticed this. So they started to get a little out of hand. And that's when they called me in to settle the argument, because I had lived life both as a man and as a woman. How come? Oh boy, you're really digging into my past. Well …

'One day, I was walking in the woods, in the deep green woods, when I came across these two huge green slimy serpents inter-twining and winding, and I was so disgusted that I took my staff that I used to walk and I hit them, bam. And wham bam thank you ma'am, I'm a woman. Well, this was not an easy thing, I mean, seven years of psychotherapy and I still hadn't really dealt with it. So in the eighth year my therapist suggested that I go back and confront the scene of the trauma. So I go back to the woods, to the deep green woods, and there I see these same two slimy snakes slithering and writhing around each other, and I say I'm going to get them this time and I hit them and I hit them, and … Guess what's back.

So that's when they called me in to adjudicate in this argument between Jupiter and Juno. And, I had to say, I'm afraid, ma'am, it's true, women get far more pleasure out of love than men do. Oh, rage, PMS, don't know what it was, she flew off the handle, and she condemned me to eternal blindness. Well, all the other gods thought she had really overdone this, I mean, it wasn't my fault she hadn't gotten it. But there was nothing they could do about it. Because if one god does something another god can't undo it. They have, like, autonomous powers. So the omnipotent father gave me, as the booby prize, the power to see the future.'

***

90

ACT IV

(Michael receives a letter in hospital. Fiona asks a member of the jury to read it. Michael and Fiona change channels.

They are not in the same place, but the underlined words in this scene belong also to the other performer.)

Michael: (Reads.) Dear Michael ... It's from you.

Fiona: I don't recognize myself.

Michael/Jury:

In water or on land, I've housed drift. A bridge seen as a drawbridge swallowing voices into the illegal or illegible, to construct the unreal in the presence of <u>the real wound</u>? No, I build leaks for you where your voices can burst as the mountain buckles the father's legs, <u>wounds within wounds</u>. Speaking wasn't a place to be true or false in, but the openings on your body are answering me back, Michael, <u>the wound in the world</u>.

The actor affirms, not the transience of life, but the permanence of the moment ...

But toll counts the moments, tells on the body, clipes in betrayal, and naming, and law.

The body was placed in a supine position, a term in the contract ... <u>Heart</u>: without murmur, rub or gallop ... The rub of the hand on the page of the chest is excited to witness ... <u>Was cut.</u> Correlation with the history is recommended.

Fiona: I schal send ow my–self seint Mihel myn Angel ...

Michael: Obtaining the reaffirmating second signal from the B cell's further activation has required a transformation of the offered first sign.

Fiona: He holds the secret of the mighty 'word' by which God created heaven and earth. <u>It can bind.</u> So much the fear of thunder and the sword of Michael still wrought in them.

Michael:	The killer T cells need to recognize a foreign (nonself) antigen in the context of a particular histocompatibility protein, usually the same one carried by the T cell <u>itself</u>,
Fiona:	<u>ow</u> my–self seint Mihel myn Angel …
Michael:	<u>Appear</u> in disguises, after revelation.

But your nakedness is always visible beneath the parasitic host or tool.

The presence of the corpse is the fiction. The stories go back to the moment of change, again, again, to lead us back forwards to a present changed by the uncovered past.

'Yeah, your disbelief is compassionate.'

But swim to your surfaces, sing your small adventures of welcome in declared disguise. Take on, Michael. It's you give who the shirt off your back to the naked performer with a door. <u>(takes off his shirt.)</u> This is one role.

'… The skin stuck to me. It stuck to me all over. It's not an analogue. It's not simultaneous. It doesn't have to match.

Saint Roch, traditionally invoked by plague victims, is sometimes represented as a pilgrim, but is most often recognized by a sore on his thigh. <u>(takes off his pants.)</u>

'Okay. Come over here and stand with your back to me.

Wait for me.

Fool me …'

Fiona:	Liquid threatens its box. Would the witness please stick to the question?

In witness, in tongues, the answer(s) that drown(s) the question that could never have asked for it, as many as you want, as far as you want. Between the lines, between the legal/legible/ lethal/lexical. Michael, your aria.

Michael:	*()*
Fiona:	Now sign. To bind.
Michael:	Love, Fiona.

***

ACT V

Fiona: *(To self, to jury, to TV, to audience. Crashes the court tables together into the hospital bed, forces the video to drink:)*

Love skulks home the worst for waste, its telling between its legs. Let's not breathe revenge of the being.

See hand–held smile, fits the slot, or would, the soul of witness. Wrist–held at close halves, don't be in it, do it. Later for in it, on earth, in me.

But as we suspect our own secrets, we must listen to their secrets' secrets, out of the mouth and into the future.

Moving like strangers through the house of language, our bodies speak to understand. Your attention's our material, though we spoke before attention's answering bruise. But you read that blue story. Once upon a voice, we bed in blue chambers. Hearsay was placed in the mouth and denied standing room.

Dreams are obeyed, names denied the weather for fear of treading a mortal boundary.

But to have and to head–hold, too, buffets air home with another cheek. Searches the mouth for the word the heart held. And we attend to this of each other.

The lure of her other is imagining that the other can imagine what she can not. A let–me–bring–you–to–your–senses, without introductions, spoken in intakes, unsutured, of breath. You know, eking the tongue, ow, till blue in the face. Not law's habit or must's maze, how can the sky–blushed throat of air be for saying no?

If you're an actor, where's the infinite? the camera?

(So softly I knocked on the window–pane: o love, are you with-in?)

Wings of an impossible mirror, partialities suspend each other. He is not to be discovered behind this blank that holds motion-less.

Show, shout, the last closet of all. Be not captured, be in mouths, be impossible to resist.

(The cadenza is spliced to say, this was written before.)

Write the actor off?

He will slip out by the door of immobility. Taking place takes the time you're in.

Our death is our own as dreams are.

***

Fourth Dream

And after? Death is an utter change in meaning.

(Michael turns on by himself, laughing.)

***

Dara Wier

THE LONG STORY

Sometime later he said
I want to rot in your arms.

The mind/body question
resolved itself finally.

I could no longer name
the subspecies of American cars.

He said I love your flowers.
Great numbers of precious species

went extinct. He said I still will
love you forever deeply.

Summers raced to sunnier lands.
He said he loved me dearly.

Who knows sincerely about sincerity?
He said he loved me, clearly.

He said he loved me madly.
A few leaves had peaked.

Susan Wheeler

TESTIFY

This is a great and august time.
The saddle sky shot with red.
The diamond in the nostril, passing by.
Refrigerator dough. The helispont.

A smallish flange redeems the bowl.
In halls the poems come and go.
I could not brave. The pugilist.
Barking other on the leash going by.

Bosco, benwit, johnson brown.
Seven hung and strung out clouds.
Blowfish from Asian waters, packing.
This is a great and august time.

Louis Armand

Autobus Urbano 45 (Madrid)

in its rainslashed headlights
i am a crouched hyena
who has here awaited the revelations
of hieronymus bosch
on the avenida of thousands murdered
forgotten unforgotten

with treacherous claws i give
to franco what is franco's
the driver sightless
slips my five coins into their coffins

La Parodie Terrestre

in the darkened amphitheatre
a pair
of human lungs

(neither voice nor
oxygen) ...

in more remote places
some believe:
silence is golden

draws the zealots
like flies to a corpse

Peter Minter

FROM EMPTY TEXAS 1967-97

1967 Linguige

Content is a slippery glimpse, or so the light
of three bodies, authenticated grace stretched blue under laying out the notes
the Pacific Highway riddles into Sunne, moves northward as light tauter

takes it or leaving it
She lifts the terraform and
and lays out escarpments of opposition, *tubes of frozen magma*, to have across
again plains beneath the turquoise, the blue hills, the gum emigration

Épouvantail, espanta pájaros

even birdshit creates an open figure, composition by field marking out
what one might, essentially, know, the syllable
counting every movement.

1968 Odalisk

The lovely stuff, you know, is *livelier*
tongue erasing frantic hammer &
suspended by the right ankle, the Musician, too far deliberately

              the dozen happy love poems written every day,
the extermination of the crossed.

In fact, you already define it
as derivative, abstraction disguised as particularity, the boundaries

Boogie Woog the approach, descend or subtracting the low hill
old sun, curious millennial half light

              and *The Blue Macaw* wanting the jet's arc to follow, say
Believe You Me, or so she heard this

to eat here, answers pile up as
lite imitation and

considering selection and appetite
                                        spoonbills
                actually trace between reeds.

1971 Scenic

The winter it came here, he looked up. Leaves pixillate
to invisibility
because we know this is it, the sky

ice forms on the fingernail, the periphery falling

& We say the bird falls, visibility falls
False Harbour runs
out over coral, detritus flaring up neon as
                The Next Ibis
                stands on the same point, your legs'
red orange tubular discharge
branching into water, some sort of odd performance from the Great
Copper Pipe
and the common act compulsion is to watch!

She says she
she fears the flag, salt torn ligament evaporating cooch
& From upstream — save it for the dream of production,
a mirror of cities mistaken as petals
arched lines
knots into water (dark
chronic pattern with one primary
stress — another
Body of Air.

Simon Perril

THROUGH THE OPEN PORES INDEFINITELY SEEPS THE OPEN PAUSE IN DEFINITELY

tethered ends endeavour to greet
effete polar regions
the heart a-smoke in its holster

now there's a thought
curling languidly at the edges
the way laid

crazily paving
like minds
we have

to somehow cope with
the extraneous circumstances
of a night on earth

and a day blanched
in prospect
still flinching

the bay a
gelatinous bowl
add sun to set

and serve
on architectonic platter
annexed best thing

Simon Perril

NEWLY TENDERED

1

the sea's curled lip
Elvis style synchs innumerable chinks
in amour to be

flagrantly fragrant and newly tendered
for the offering
putting yourself on the line pre-

-cariously cursory and curiously tertiary i
split ends in the mirror that re
-flexes me a thousand folds

my flesh is air to nothing, hereto
fore nothing else than your
convenience stored in data

based on ergo some ego another
fine mess you gotten me into
now so

close o
figure me
reluctantly to be known or noun

2

walking sheer into nonsense
your re-nouned for it
a new thing at some remove

cardinal points skewed
and shot full of glances
exquisite fractures

sewn passing over simple objects
music is the muscle
taut across them

x-rays that graphic displays don't equalise
into a higher resolution
the great lengths I never made it to wave

in the corrugated heat between us
sickening for something to be said
against a noisy background

join the dots
close-mic the intervals
integral to you to

amplify star-burst
cerebral mistrale cor
textual noise in the head of the prince

micro-tonal erotics of location
the spine's bass-line throbs
a wired stem-stammer

3

sleep's edges blunt through
overuse until they bevel
oblique below sea-level

tide lines across the forehead
some violent transport
a liminal sub cruises the straits

taking the temperature of our distance
with a wish
two notes breathe more easily

into a third resulting stress
3 accidents in a soundscape
we are

a hum on selective frequencies
clung to the sides and sites
the centre of attention

a mobile disloyalty taken
as read by light fingers
of emotional braille

4

the wear and tear of eyelids
elope with good sense
only to strike a balance

full in the face, blooms in
carnations ready pressed
not to breathe a word only

have it rest
in febrile fabrics
the grey mat

sat on the cat
causing distress for all concerned
not to mention

the moon's acned prospect
unworthy of telescope
heresay

or over here say
as i write this i a
mend in the bend of space-time

colloquially yours
for the bidding
fresh as mint's legal garnish

Steve McCaffery

EVENTUAL RESEARCH

'Summers suckings Williams Whiteheads of explosions.'

Tried breaking down into eighteen parts 'but didnt.'

in a concise but amusing road to spiral proclivities
one has entered or entertained here the root system of aortas
destination: nutrition
approximation: goosequill

about the same time it takes to peel an apple

'smaller?
'continuous?
'outward?
'criss-cross?

(entering or entertaining
a lung mélange blancmange
mixture ridden modern cuticle)

'fibrillose ?
'reddish-brown ?
'or cap it ?

as we on a sunny morning connect conatives
to black twine-like strands
in a rhizomorphic space

a fetid wood called Marquette

September to November

the economy expands to
'guillemot ?
'tungsten ?
'Hopalong Caffery ?

the small (Eustachian) meningeal (valve)

sometimes derives from the preceeding

to drug-store
by inner side
without jaw

a double current fossilized
inside a cunnilingual Brecht

(Tuesday Alan) (Morning Sue)
same temporal esperanto

'Trees identified as elms accompanied by nerves give off
a few twigs which are lost in

the cancellous tissue by the turnstile.'

My half-sister Claire for instance is a set of operations transforming
tellings into showings.

'apparently wheels ?
'suggestion of a spore analysis ?'
'performance in a seedy part of town ?

hailstone equals referent

a town bell called Seattle
the sense in which it defines
the shape of the previous forest

one is heard ascending an infra-orbital canal
into denser traffic
as a single repetition
Outposts = Ottawa = upwards

Cairo numinous between the cuspid teeth
But through the trace called form
a purer specimen obtains
Coventry passed more

inward through the nose and shatters
teat-time tick-tock

patina   abyss in this distance

(a smile described)

'Washington ?
'Belgrade ?
'Helsinki ?

the contents of a palatine canal

or Lilith network complication
glassine figurex surroundelles

the myth of protection remains small
its habitat
ground leaves
among debris

'hardly that sense of donor will emergent'

in hemlock
colophon adapts to cedar swamps

a theme of the unreal

'Sunscape and shade here is a gratitude to thank before the eye.'

spent Christmas in Hertfordshire
'the four bones'

(synovial (membraned (conifers

central North Michigan stem with a cavity
on decaying leaves

the Soviet tropes in Proust

'infrequent amino amigo ?
'concurrent glabrosity ?
'faint spillage imminent ?

This pause in prosody delays our proper names.

Obtuse at ends means smooth to the boy-scout mutant apex.

Sights arrive and even this is a listening.

No one explains the tessellated Edsel where replication expands.

one is entering the abdomen at the umbilicus
half-pulmonary decent
transverse fissure division
larger joints at the the portal vein

Blocks out the world in oral tales.

Clove pinks become an item stitched on Sarah's crowded tawny edge.

One is entering a narrative about thinking with a small semantic scar
to show
the cause.

cylindrical ?
gregarious infrequency ?
peculiarly light-red stains ?

(Each gulley notched but in the way a path contracts the mass
of space to navigate a narrative
between the concept of syzygy and elsewhere)

covered routes now coincide with observation
(hardly a barge at best or else)

(sea)

(lake)

(pond)

(narrow creek)

the function returning as my head grows corners

entering the lobe as Pittsburgh

'cup-shape   ?
'hemispherically depressed sort of thing   ?
'no compresssion squeezing through each stanza   ?

Nine is the cotyloid capital of Washington

can you name it

all parts superior to its border's power

Jim's being the truer pelvis
separated by the intervals of sound

'is it gray-brown   ?
'is it an intervening viscid stench   ?
'do the spores cover the gills as they did in the Leningrad-effect   ?

tries this for sizes

if roof means power or else an inner will
and France is the face of a man transmitting it

handling a lake with left wrists brings

in a secondary sense of ripple

eventually all cats return to bourgeois dogs

'yet it all depends on vocal bonds'
a thin
and fragile
flesh with
snazzy metallic
lustre when
dry walled

'a striated agony epigone   ?
'a goofy fusiformality   ?
'a white cheddar rice cake cacophony   ?

(placed) (examined) (taxonomised within)

the mythic intermission

five four three two none

known as Kant.

ETYMOLOGY OF DISPLEASURE

I was asked: tell us what happened. Nothing. I said. Nothing clear nothing really to talk about. 'You were its reader once but you survived a wooden bullet.' The present I in a present past. Come on they said. Nowhere to go. Something they asked. Nothing I said.

'The mountains are an uncommon blue this time of year.' 'But the turnips remain the same.' The *nunc* or nowness of this felicity stays the same in the same way 'turnips' stay the same. Nothing they asked. Yet someone said it. There is a gap said in the mountain range where a mountain disappears. We look at a condition here we haven't reached.

Does each word mark this step. Sometimes it said. Sometimes it stays and remains in 'to breathe' as-if-truly-present-in exhaustion. So the word 'edge' is more profound. Edge of productivity, edge of obeyed. Inside a happy farm beyond the edge of beauty in manure. 'Stood chance' in necessary white that's all. Nothing they asked. At all some said.

'Standing in front of Mrs. Stacey's frozen turnips this morning I realized that the entire reductionist abuse of empirical data was quite unfrozen.' One of the wolves is dead as well. *Methodenstreit*. One of the sharper teeth at the front could still be understood as lacking. 'But deconstruction too has its own place in a tradition of skepticism going back in history to at least David Hume.'

'Come off it it asked.' A camel flies at night whose wings open suddenly to stress the singularities that make the game impossible as social signs. Encyclopedias then of an obvious irritation. 'Just an old man speaking inwards Mary.'

'Detective fiction they asked.' 'The body was eventually transferred to Eli Carter's pasture' 'to be placed in a' 'totality.' 'The man from the Social Institute turned up as well and built himself a high tower' '(not Babel again)' 'one asked' 'and placed himself on it in order to shoot crows.' 'A world thus negotiated can never be described in a clear and adequate picture.' 'Yet abandoning agency is hardly sufficient.' '(Therefore).' He pulled the trigger at the slightest quivette from a nuthatch.

Through each context of consciousness the self stays older than the ego. 'There is a factor 'colour' in this series.' As in this tree was green. Which the love of bubbles spilled. But are the turnips still possessed of meaning. No one asks. To treat turnips as an absolute analogue to mathematics would still reduce them to a series of tautologies without meaning. On Mrs Stacey's farm at least. No one says that. When water is exhibited in small quantitites it wants the agitation of a torrent. What follows is a break for thirst and toast. Aid aims support at more reflections.

('Meanwhile') the meaning 'he insisted' 'being turnip' must constitute a collective drive towards a state of absolute rationality. Appearance on the outside gives a nearer view and as we enter it we see a distant country equally enriched. Contracting forms assume an empty pause and in the fullness of its channels the river itself becomes a winding surface of description. 'Let us enter its cascades.' 'Through the beautiful category of the shelving.' 'At last.' 'My heat is latent to you.' 'If the truth were known which I don't know.' 'I would reject all claims to absolute demonstration.' If it is a book these ways remember stories. That way I'm reading it. But there's a garden somewhere in the way at the threshold of a window called inert.

Is it about myth 'they asked.' She insisted. It all depends on who wrote the volume, no one answered, on which writer wrote it, someone claims, and which reader read. 'I fold this on a sheet then pressed for time push passed it.' It's discussed because it stirs. David devotes 'a whole chapter to this.' A turnip in a clause consists of two nominal groupings. Noun of oak. 'Nobody asked.' A curb extends this spoken phrase into some agitated bid for ornament. 'But the bell is perhaps a distant oxymoron for the boat itself.' 'But we think of wholes as trips beyond exchange.'

A tongue avoids a bar a supper good for three within a mile. 'So the story begins again and again.' 'Particles spin off from an expert grammar.' 'That's all that comes back about written language.' A game for all players.

Starting a novel with the sentence 'We don't know what happened after that.' (The words too are frequent; they are formal copses quintessential amid white spots bursting everywhere from chalky soil. A valley on an edge. Some other easy mode for otherwise. 'Going back to page nine.' No one asking. 'Moving from the last line up to line eight but not before moving across to the fourth word then down four lines to the middle of the third.'

Why describe this denial. No one says so. Doesn't metal begin in it. Pond evasion barely sight in treatment. Ink syrinx a gallery two pipes connect disintegrates. The dust a Dutch mud dahlia. All the words describing pick-axe, single blast sledge wallet punctual habits knocking train departures. Mosaic Yahoo triumphs catalogue catastrophes these kittens purr. Name of beehive: glacier.

Sensation of a pond gone hungry. 'Macro-afternoon reshedding world twelve councils triplicate spice from the major stress of those crucifix days.' Advancing to 'property' you take a third and willfull sequestration of a fact. 'It's just to hear you say hello inside a telephone gone wrong.' Rain is entering a tiny hole in the floor. This limits copyright. 'Some hills' 'open inwards.' A finger on language as the invoice curls. 'Confirmation of a caveat.' In fact a reciprocal obligation invades. 'And Titian painted her.' Nobody said so.

'The stitching glows in the anonymous house of the Person.' Fresh air brought as 'nose.' It's noise. A culprit's 'inner' cigarettes. This is just to know you. Someone would say. Get a feel of what it's like to squeeze the square night slackening. Every different way is gradually. No one thought it. More rain enters through a tiny hole.

'The formidable dialogue which followed this passage is reported to have induced a panic in the Chamberlain's office that was unparalleled in peturbation.'

'Nobody said so.'

'Tell me what happened.'

'Nothing they said.' Nothing clear, nothing to really talk about. The present we in the present past.

'Come on I said.' There's nowhere to go.

(A man finds a mine.)

'The hull is blue.'

'They can't be the same.' I asked.

Nothing. 'They said.'

Pam Brown

THE ING THING

Transgressing
        a brilliant surface,
little slanted forays
      lead to bonding
over
      trivia-quiz nights

way off
      in the lucre wilderness —
an exponential increase
     in indistinct bundles
      huddling in
   to buildings,
adapting to circumstance

quoting
  'The Portable Financier'
the minister for something or other
    berates
        co-operation —
the nation's mind's
      a blank

      ***

scrolling through
    your best concerns,
having an admiration
    for institution, for
   committee, for quislings,
you must address
    the technicians —

     touch a balloon
  to talk to one

of our people.
touch a question
to hear a reply.

***

        next, you're
outperforming
        those spacy
            year planners!

    lead us to your
    Writers' Centres!
    dot dot dot

***

dismantling
    web sites
    brings you sorrow,
eating
        disorders,
    attention deficit syndromes,
                virii

    this *is* the same
    project isn't it?
    you just get
    older on the job.

***

staying
    out late   you're
        a public nuisance,
then staying awake
    for the infomercials —
morning's nothing
    floats along
like an unrecovered
    flight recorder

114

***

tilting
   into
       image suck-out.
   talk is cheap
   but
   money talks
'Today,'
   declares
      the art critic
'money doesn't
   only talk,
it may criticise
       & curate.'
   an especially
   schizoid blah
   de blah —
   &
   I feel guilty
   all the time!

***

serving up
   delicious gizzards
      with two-tone pilled
         dessert

   'whose hair
   is in the jam?'

say something, supermodel!

   'an echo in the handset
   every time I pick it up

   no dial tone here
   something wrong'

   'Hi Anon!'

115

***

                    this
shambling
     contingency,
          (writing a poem) —

work's,
   for me, a sanctuary
          from building sites
from something else
   from evil duco-scratching
                    truants
   if-not-already, soon-to-be
excluded
          from its realm —
                    work's

***

               so, now
who's driving?

reversing freighters'
soothing sound
          just a brick away
stuffed into
     the narrowest lane

               whole days
drifting away
 this way

***

taking so long
     to write the book —
only to be
 remaindered.

Ian Pople

DERKER

Cows' new shit steams
to early fog that sunlight
will release and pigs snuffle.
Beyond the barn door a goat
stands between the farm's first
mechanical drill, the harrow
and the clam shell tractor seat.
A golf course on the farm now
brings buggies to the land
hooves' soft clefts relied on.
Cows' eyes bulge to shine,
tongues lick, the smeary tails'
brown flick compasses dawns
of stout veins opened for puddings.

Peter Larkin

From 'Throwley Plantation' (Section 2 of Parallels Plantations Apart)

Pungent in pine, snared candid across the remainder's uncovered hillside, a wood outside any majority.

Squatter with no furniture of the mobile, plant your hug diminished off salient, no huger unchange constantly thins thus.

The stubby roost in mantle, where a slighted unnew pilots return, upon a hillside's recent luckless accordance.

This provinced central creep, secular steep, sacral speed come direct upon correct reduct, trees tipt to known zone for their crouchable: a mechanic of radiance spits local imposit.

Arid-mutant, but bought off attested barrier, as the better of small-change branch in tree-defiled area.

A satellite abroad from the inner famish, to where it furnishes ungovernable shade of the thinned-out: this the human clue launches up the hillside, towards a nakedness of stakes.

Perduration all swarthy espalier. What had detained an open from its parish-infinity will still presume on sapling, a subject scaled down to the seal of the world. Slits together at confinity.

That clear unripe face of remove never to grip beyond the moor's empty ridge. The varnished slope smooths deep under wind, the naked hill flush with this new static, where folded tree-table is tied to vertical twist.

A poll of the woods set opinionate, pine-lenten. Uncharging as winter leaf, a light too sessioned to spurn a sky able to invite safe season windowed into, pennanted from below: as blocked beneath, there dis-taunted.

A stubborn filter sets launched upon its standing toward the nails of place, fixity surviving as only half the shelter, though through edges fought over for an intimacy of outsitting: palpable instrument to crouch and retract horizon by the half of absorbable light which flies it by. The same half of shelter which flies and fixes to keep it half.

Tenuous pressing together. In a photo-herence slender returns on the openness of light: but unfelled radiance from this tender loss of result.

Only the trees admitted back to squares of kernel no longer rob us of horizon, reduced now to their swabs of replenishment.

Bony parapet at an untorrential hedge of themselves, takes refuge upon the usual unsurrounding of light.

Throbbing impediment turned alcove, a rota moulded on the pandered shelves of tree-level.

Then small forts, squarely, merely, browse on their danger, encombing a light of the hunches of defence. With hazy rotation, it scrutinises the needle deferences.

Insinuate selvage, cadaverous but with filter set selfish green. Some unemergent regularities, composure conning common proposal. Green hostility seduced to a perpetual clot in the wood, peck chain from holistic braid.

As though shelter can be done in team, unruined in ream: frequent brush with impassible love acquainted with the lowering that honours salvation. Brushwood not naturalised to the passings of light, perfervid at its panel.

Squat tower of the green-grey trudge of regulars, bearing on the ridge, a proneness unburied but unwieldy nearing its marriage: links of shelter immoveably unfallen, for a stasis can rear no heavier impermanence. Gives root shelter to what is identical-uninvented of a differently suffixed earth.

Insufficiency must be stasis freed to be no less patient than its own continuance up the planted hill: overtakes advance as its cladding does an unopenable readiness in the seed.

Production rushes a spectre of world to sector, the human order lacking spathe, slight-spiked shelter to speak redress in type, here ties itself to an agenda of the slots of resonance, aprovident set-aside. All the woods of it one plantation incarnate: stake the step between itself and plentifiable horizon, our solitary provided set-before.

In this placard of wood, fractionally granting thorn its tremble. A green sharpness of the never uncovered. The copse has ebbed into valid attrition, ragged dimness to a setting of defence.

Anchored to poke the gust toward sighable impasse, scatter glades from the pick, an axe-band of site. Petal-verdure in its mean of distributed order, one pine decipherable for a tranche of unfilled time along the spokes.

Infestant grapple, a cluster engreens succeeding to a latter rake-out of earth in tree habit, a distinction 'bright horizon' which can't be cut out of battening on woods: in aura of this scopious, over-sewn dimension, untorpidly knit and shaven.

A wire-like stretch of stimulant glade, the clamps fetch all that won't forsake a real of trees by plantation. These green racks are the fault which roots me to conjunction, squirms the shelves of since well over the top of any joint in previous rock: the stone stands to first call, its repeat begs shelter's smarting knock.

Oppressive uncovering thrown to the pounce of reparation, the leap of the construct onto its awning: with cropped shins of harmony's arisen memory, the ounce of completion. Unicited green, the curing myriad uncitied.

A waning bower with no sense of end other than the plantation's stark contrary assart across ample, empty, sufficient hill. A slide of belonging planted; streamlined, to a standstill. That a dwarf share of thickest orchard will linger at the shade's stump. Green neon of a forest's aversion, was the city precursor so much ironed out as porch to the woods?

The row is content with brushwood with which to scour an earth alone with itself, the satellite of loss raised to invasive heights, requital upon boggy loft now observing green forebearance. These trees will be harvested without flush, detectable still in their interlude.

meika von samorzewski

A large moving twist
of bark leaves the trunk
but hangs around,
down,
to rattle the winds and
snare an ear by turn,
here,
where a seed unfurled
once the fire passed,
and fell into growth
to meet the rain,
never still amongst
waves of visitors
and light;

... thirty years since we sat in that creek,
but here we are again,
here we are.

REIGNING FIRES

John Kinsella

INTERVIEW WITH PETER FORBES, EDITOR OF *POETRY REVIEW*
RECORDED LATE 1997.

JK: I'd like to start off with a brief history of the *Poetry Review* and its link to the Poetry Society, if you can just give me a bit of a rundown there.

PF: Well, the history's very long and I'm frankly not an expert on the early history at all. The society was founded in 1909 and the first *Review* as such appeared in 1912. People like Pound were involved very early on but for a very, very short period and then for a long time it fell into the hands of an amateurish and rather poetasting group of people. So really, I would say the modern history of the magazine starts from Roger Garfitt's editorship at the end of the seventies. It went through a strange patch, really, in the seventies, having been very out of the mainstream and out of the history of poetry in the twentieth century. All of a sudden in the seventies a sort of avant-garde managed to take over and Eric Mottram ran the *Review* for about eight or nine years. Of course the Arts Council were on the scene then, and they weren't too happy with this. This was well before my time; I wasn't even reading the magazine then. But there was a sort of palace revolution engineered by the Arts Council and a new regime started then. Where Andrew Motion became editor in 1982 it was the point at which I think it really entered the mainstream and there have not been many editors since then. I've been editor for ten years now; Andrew Motion, Mick Imlah and then myself, and in that time I think it's gradually taken on a more central role. There are certain expectations of the magazine, which it certainly didn't fulfil for a lot of its history but obviously there is a niche for a flagship magazine, and that niche was notionally ascribed to the magazine. I've tried to make it true. I've tried to give it the kind of profile that justifies flagship status.

JK: With the magazine we have something up front we can quite clearly see how that functions and editorially how it works; but what's your role in terms of the society? You're editor of the *Poetry Review*, but do you have a position of authority within the society?

PF: No, I'm a freelance, and my brief is to edit the magazine. Though unofficially at times — when the Society went through a difficult patch I got quite heavily involved in negotiations at the Arts Council and so on, in an advisory capacity, because I was by then one of the more experienced people around. I collaborate with other people quite a lot but my brief really is the magazine. But now things have changed a lot, the Society has a website and the Review has a part of that. So there's a lot of collaboration, but basically I do the magazine.

JK:　The modus operandi of the journal strikes me as being fairly eclectic. The latest issue is the women poets issue, before that there was one on the Conductors of Chaos kind of avant-garde, you have also featured classical poems, and the younger poets. So it's fairly eclectic in its aims. Is there a binding editorial programme?

PF:　Well, we've got four shots a year and we try to make each one count. I think you'll find that over a period of time, over three or four issues, there might be a ruling preoccupation that runs through several of the issues, even though the themes are very different. But I'm restless, I'm always thinking, well are there other angles to cover? And if we have a blitz, for instance, on one angle — we might have had several issues on poetry from different parts of the world — we might then start to look a little bit more at poetic process. We've had issues on criticism and reviewing; and then themes come up, like New Generation. I mean, this wasn't my idea, this was an idea that came to us and I liked the idea, so I said 'Okay., well, I'll do the issue on it.' I didn't choose the poets but I decided almost to abdicate my editorial responsibility because I felt at that point that was an important project and it should be aired. So, there are themes within the poetry community that you tap into. We did the women's issue, not for some sort of notional sense that we ought to address that area; simply because there's a lot of good work. Since New Generation it seemed to me that the best work was by women and this had never really been the case before that the majority of younger poets publishing first collections, good ones, were women. So in other words what I'm trying to do is to represent what seem to me to be genuine movements.

JK:　So rather than operating against poets and poetry, the journal actually moves with them and reflects them.

PF:　It tries to reflect. Sometimes I might try and nudge the zeitgeist in areas where I feel I've got a bee in my bonnet and I want to stir people up a bit. I've been doing essays.

JK:　Yes, went to a conference and heard an essay of yours discussed on the panel; it quite polarized. This was up in Cambridge. And some said, 'this was the great, we needed this statement, it's about time it's being said' and others said, 'Agh — the great enemy of modernism, what did you do?'. But it was good because it actually brought the argument to the fore and I see that as being an important function of a journal.

PF: This has been my current thing really, starting in '95, I did an essay on why the new popular poetry makes more sense. And I've started to feel that the way we talk about poetry is a bit inadequate; that there's not enough discussion. The review pages of the newspapers are inadequate in their coverage of poetry, and somehow or other with all the wealth of poetry that's published and with all the prizes (and there's far more PR hype these days) there isn't enough discussion of what it really adds up to, beyond personalities and their latest collections. So these essays I've been writing — and there's another one in the next issue I've been working on now, 'The Secret Life of Poems' — are an attempt, really, just to try to be a catalyst for debate.

JK: So, the journal is not only reflective of what's going on, it's actually reflexive as well. It stimulates.

PF: It tries to be, yes, in two ways. If I see things going on that are irrefutably powerful and interesting, we've got to cover them. If I feel I've got something that I would like to plant on people and see what they make of it then we do that as well.

JK: Later on I'd like to attend to that essay and ask you a couple of specific questions which I've found of interest.

PF: I'm sure it should be on the agenda.

JK: For now, let's talk about the role of the editor, the actual editorial process of the journal. About how the journal functions. People send their material in; in the unsolicited case, does it go through a sub-editorial process before it gets to you, or do you read every entry?

PF: There's no sifting at all. I don't believe in sifting. When I've done competitions I've always been uneasy if there's been sifting. The postbag is a very heavy burden but at the moment my backlog is zero, I deal with it every day now. Most of the time when you're in production it builds up and you've got boxes full of it, but I've got to the position where I really don't like that at all. I look at everything. When I've done that there's the question of how much you actually solicit work. I don't like soliciting work, because often what happens is that you write to a poet whose work you admire and you would like to have some of their latest stuff; very often they like to send you stuff but most poets have got work sitting around that isn't necessarily their best. If you've solicited it there's a slightly greater pressure on you — it's difficult then to say, 'well actually I'm not so keen on this'. But I do do it. I wish the major poets would send anyway; they tend not to in this country, above a certain level, other than perhaps a few people with whom you've established a special relationship.

JK: So they actually expect to be solicited from.

PF: They do. Over a certain level — poets who have four or five books and have some real distinction. They don't actually like to send poems on spec. and therefore you're put in the position where you've got to invite.

JK: Do you seem to invite more for specific issues to get the particular kind of material, or is it because of a feeling that one should represent the major forces that are moving through poetry?

PF: Usually I don't solicit poems very much in this country. I solicit poems from American poets, whenever we've been doing issues. When we did the Indian issue almost all of the work had to be solicited. We do get quite a lot of work from India, but generally very low grade. The major Indian poets tend not to think to send here, strangely enough. I always hope when we do a special issue that it will flush more out, that I will get lots of people saying, 'I wish I'd known' It doesn't happen as much as I'd like. With America, where we've always felt we ought to be establishing a really good relationship, it still doesn't really seem to happen. Chris Meade, the director here, is going to America very soon with idea of making the channels a bit more receptive … There ought to be a world community of poetry, really.

JK: In Australia, it's actually considered one of the main poetry journals in the world.

PF: Well, thank you, I'm glad, but there are so many American journals available. There are things about the American scene I admire. Lots of their magazines seem to have such strong support — often from a campus, obviously. People think that we're very well supported. We do have quite an enviable situation now, where the Poetry Society at the moment is successful; it's working well, which it wasn't always. We get Arts Council support, so (unlike the one-man band magazines) we do have a reasonable practical support, but it hasn't always been like that. I did handle the *Review* completely single-handedly for over five years, including the business side — everything. So it was simply like any other one-man band magazine, but expected to be better.

JK: On a practical level, has the use of the internet increased interest in America, being such an internet-orientated country?

PF: The internet has been very useful. It facilitates using international contributors, and that has been very good, because I have always liked to use contributors from abroad wherever possible; and commissioning reviews on short lead time is very difficult in America, but the internet has revolutionised that. I think we get quite a lot of enquiries. Whether they actually turn into subscriptions, I don't really know. I think the internet will be very powerful in the future but obviously it's still fairly smal,l but growing all the time. We've got pages on the internet but magazines are starting to go all electronic now. The bigger problem of course is having a complete electronic version. I'm all for this, but the big unresolved question is the economics of it, and how big is the internet version going to be, because given that the reach of poetry magazines is necessarily quite small, the point about the internet is that its reach is enormous. Obviously not everybody is going to want to read poetry. But I have heard recently that poetry is amongst the most widely accessed subject areas on the internet.

JK: It is. That's a fact. I've actually seen some statistics recently — the strike rate in Australia, for example — the Australian main poetry sites, the AWOL and OzLit, are in the top five percent. Which is remarkable. It is because they actually colonised the internet well before many others.

PF: Given the difficulties that people have with finding magazines, with getting published, the internet is a godsend there. If people can find their way through it, given the vast amount of material. It is going to change the way we publish poetry eventually, inevitably.

JK: In the same way I suppose the personal computer changed the production of the journal. It must have revolutionised the approach to the journal here, and the pre-production. George Steiner said recently that it's a golden age of poetry in England, whatever that means ... I don't know. Maybe it's becoming popular I don't know exactly what he meant, but he did say that he thought that there was an increasing interest in poetry right across the board. Do you think that's the case, do you think that's what you're seeing?

PF: It is, but it's complicated, because in the past ten years there have been three so-called poetry booms, and they have been very artificial affairs in many respects; but in the last couple of years there have been several key pointers. There is a bigger popular audience now thanks to things like Poems on the Underground. The Poems on the Underground book sells in huge quantities; and recently the BBC have become more and more involved, there is of course National Poetry Day. Recently, when they did a poll on the Nation's Favourite Poems, the book of the poll winners became a best seller as well. I find it very interesting. One of the things I'm writing about in the next issue is that it would appear there is actually a large audience for individual poems, if people can find those poems that somehow they relate to, like the Auden poem in *Four Weddings and A Funeral*. And I do feel quite strongly at this point that we in the poetry publishing business have perhaps gone about things in slightly the wrong way, in that the slim volume and the way we try to introduce new poets seems to militate against people outside a small world actually finding poems that they would really relate to.

What I'm thinking is that the currency of poetry actually has to be really the individual poem. But we talk so much in terms of reputations and poets are sold as being significant and so on. A wider audience would never be interested in that. What they want to know is, 'Is there a poem that actually is going to say anything to me?', and of course there are, but we've not been very good at highlighting this sort of work and making it known. What's been quite chastening in the nation's favourite poem poll, is that the poem that won (Jenny Joseph's 'Warning') is a poem that many people in the poetry community don't even know, and it's been circulating and becoming famous. It's samizdat really. Irrespective of the efforts of the poetry community, which is a bit shocking. Some people would probably argue that this is a very populist poem, that it appeals to people who don't like poetry. They might say that it's not a very good poem or whatever. But I'm impressed by this phenomenon of a poem making its way outside the usual currents of poetry publishing, and I do think there is a lesson there for us.

JK: Do you see it as being necessary that editors of poetry journals be practitioners themselves, or do you think that's actually a disadvantage? Many American editors aren't, specifically aren't, poets, because they feel that it interferes with the process.

PF: I guess my position on this has changed a little bit; I actually don't write poems anymore, and I haven't written anything for five years, but I certainly started out as being a poet-editor, and I think most of the editors in this country do write or have written poetry. Michael Schmidt is still writing poetry.

Some of them carry on; some of them become more like full-time editors. Jon Silkin still writes, Alan Ross still writes. I would like to think that it's possible to imagine critics and editors of poetry who were not poets, because that would avoid the poetry hot house, where everybody wears so many hats. This had been the standard criticism: that it gets terribly incestuous. It would be nice to think that there were people who were a little bit above the combat, who could actually sit back and judiciously select ... On the other hand, Eliot was a great editor and a great poet.

JK: There is a fear often voiced by poets themselves that the only people who read poetry are poets. It seems to have a lot more truth to it in Australia than it does in England. I'm talking about journal readers, not people who read poetry generally. People don't bother to pick up a journal unless they have a vested interest: 'maybe I'll see myself in these pages one day so therefore I should read it'. How much is that the case in England?

PF: Well, I think it's been the case everywhere, pretty well, and I suppose one problem that a magazine like the *Review* would have if poetry became very popular is, even if people are buying huge quantities of books by Seamus Heaney and Wendy Cope, you still need to be pretty much a fanatical enthusiast to pick up a magazine. England's very much a magazine culture — I mean commercial magazines have expanded dramatically recently — you go to a newsagent's here and it's wall-to-wall magazines; so people actually like magazines. What I'd like to think is that what people got in the *Review* was some of the excitement that you got from magazines generally. If you pick up a volume of poetry then it's just unadulterated poems and that's it; no talk, no pictures. But I'd like to think what the magazine gave them was a sense of the living culture, things happening, a commentary, feedback and so on. People could enjoy the magazine who had no intention of appearing inside it; they would actually pick it up and read it for entertainment.

JK: That wonderful audience — I think about it all the time — they must be there. You've actually answered by implication another question too, regarding the separation of powers if you like, whether reviewers and critics generally should be practitioners as well. There seems to be much debate about that at the moment. When you select your reviewers for a particular book of poems, do you have a set of reviewers that you look to, or do you constantly change that?

PF: It's always changing slightly. It's like the England football team or cricket team. Very often when you think that you've got your perfect team then some of them are not around, they're writing books — Sean O'Brien's been one of my lead reviewers, but he's been writing a book for a while and not been seen — and then sometimes you get fed up with your current team and you really want to bring some new people in. A couple of years ago when the magazine *Thumbscrew* started I thought, this is an interesting set-up. There are some good critical brains there; let's bring them in. So a lot of them write for the magazine now. I think we're always looking for new people. We have had some reviewers who have been writing for the *Review* all the time I have been there. People like Dennis O 'Driscoll, Edna Longley — she is a critic who is not a poet; I think she has had a lot of influence as a major critic. But even if you have got a good team, if you ran the same people in every issue it would look stale. I mean there are new people coming up all the time.

JK: This of course in terms of the poetry is the idea of doing the younger poets, the kind of features you do regularly to keep things vital on that level. On the material level, how are your distribution and general circulation handled?

PF: Well, it splits three ways, really: there's the membership of the Poetry Society who get the *Review*, although they now have a membership which allows them to use the café, for ten pounds, which doesn't include the *Review*. Then there are direct subscriptions which are slightly cheaper than membership of the Society; and then there is, in England, bookshop distribution. We changed our distributor last year, we use Password, which is an Arts Council-funded distributor.

They were set up quite a long time ago now by the Arts Council to help the little poetry publishers, publishers of books, not magazines, to get their books into bookshops. But they don't have Bloodaxe and they don't have Carcanet, so it's difficult. We're the only magazine they've got. We used to distribute with another distributor called Central Books. We thought it would be nice to be in the poetry team and I think they wanted to have us with them. Obviously we tend to sell in bookshops pretty much the same number every quarter. It's not like the books that are an unknown quantity, so I think they felt it would be nice to have the *Review* as part of their stable. We sell quite a small proportion, only about 6%, through the shops. The rest are by subscription.

JK: And the Poetry Society has an automatic subscription to the journal. We talked earlier about including as much international material as possible. How much do you think it's a London journal in its approach to the world, and to poetry generally, in your view?

PF: I hope it isn't a London journal, really. There's always been a thing in this country of people wondering about the excessive influence of London, but for a poetry magazine the physical location isn't terribly important. Now we have the café here, and obviously there are a lot of publishers in London, there is a London literary scene, and there are a lot of receptions and so on. We get submissions from everywhere and our reviewers are pretty much scattered about the country, the world even. There are some reviewers still that I've never met. I think people have this idea that there must be some kind of club that hangs out here, I guess. Well, there is a London poetry scene, but I don't think the *Review* reflects that. There is a magazine, *Poetry London Newsletter*, which is a London poetry magazine — which is a good magazine — but even though it does reflect the London scene, they still publish poems by people from all over.

JK: You include often letters to the editor. Do you see that as being an important function of the magazine, for the readers to be able to make comments and have them published?

PF: Very much. I'd always like to publish more. One problem is that if you're quarterly, people know that it's going to be a while before the letter appears, and you respond to something that excited you in one issue, and it's quite hard to hold one of those violent controversial debates in the letters page in a quarterly magazine. On the other hand I think that the magazine that doesn't have that kind of feedback … there's something rather dead about it. When we publish an issue, I always hope that we're going to get quite a lot of letters.

JK: Do you find that there is much debate around the 'avant-garde' and formalist issues, about what's represented in the journal, and what is the authentic voice of the community, in terms of experimentation and that kind of thing? Do you get much feedback on that level?

PF: Probably not. To me one of the slight mysteries of poetry in England today is that to some extent the old tribal divisions between different tendencies in poetry have weakened, so that there is a lot of eclecticism and a lot of poetry bills that include people from what were regarded as different persuasions, but we did do the Conductors of Chaos Strange — Attraction issue because it seemed that the avant-garde work had genuinely not been integrated in any meaningful way — and I don't think many of the practitioners wanted to be — but it seemed that it was a bit silly just to pretend that they've got their magazines and we've got ours and that's that. Obviously a lot of this, as far as the Poetry Society goes, stems from the seventies when the avant-garde poets were publishing in *Poetry Review* and they regarded it as their journal, and the split was very acrimonious. Even now, for instance, when we did Strange Affraction, there was somebody who — I've forgotten who it was now — there was this suggestion of advertising in the issue, but it was obvious that there was still this sort of tribal reaction: 'Oh well, we're not going to go in there'. Still very much tribal.

Anyway, we had an interesting launch event here with Iain Sinclair but I'm not sure how much it did. We had a few submissions afterwards from people from the avant-garde world. Again, I thought there would probably be more. But then again, I suppose that when people see a special issue they say, 'Well, they've done that, they're not going to want to do it again'. Ideally you would be getting work in from all of the different factions all the time and you'd be able to keep all the pots boiling. But it doesn't quite work like that. I'm probably not answering your question; but one thing I'm surprised at is how little debate there is. There's a sort of feeling of 'Well, it's all valid, everything goes'.

The debate about new formalism, for instance, that there's been in America, has hardly touched us here. I'm not very fond of the new formalist movement personally. There's an anthology now that Mike Donoghue's reviewing for us, and I'll be very interested to see what he makes of that. At least in America there was debate about this. There isn't much debate about form, about the technical side of poetry. A lot of poets achieve quite a reputation without anybody ever really addressing much attention to what they do technically. There is a lot more attention to subject matter and obviously there is a bit of the cult of personality in poetry these days which means that having a lot more profile and addressing certain contemporary issues will get you further than your attention to certain technical details.

JK: Just as an aside: do you notice that when you feature a certain prominent poet with a well-known biography or cult of personality surrounding them, your sales actually go up? For example if you put in Seamus Heaney, who has an incredible personal following; I mean, people know him without actually knowing his poetry.

PF: Well, it won't affect sales directly because most of the sales are prebooked in terms of subscription. It will only show over a long term, but what we do find certainly is that if we've got saleable names the bookshop sales are better. And when we've done issues, like the Indian issue — it was very widely reviewed and very popular in India, as you might expect, but it didn't sell well here. To people who saw it in bookshops that was a bit of a turn-off, whereas if it had had Seamus Heaney on the cover then it would have done better. But it does mean that we can do issues that are slightly more challenging because the same number more or less are going to read it. They might of course say, well if that's what they are going to do then we are going to cancel our sub.

JK: They usually take the risk to the next issue hoping that things will change ... One thing that fascinates me is the movement between genres. Do you often in the journal incorporate prose, prose poems, or verse plays or that kind of thing — still retaining poetry but looking at the different possible ways poetry can be used?

PF: We haven't really done that very much. We do occasionally run prose poems, but not really very often. We try to give attention to things like verse drama, and I could imagine, I suppose, a journal that ran forms of writing that were more hybrid.

JK: Great theme issue there — 'hybrid poetry'.

PF: I guess we tend run poems and then features, articles, interviews around poetry. We tend not to run much text that is in itself crossing genres. That is something that I might think about — it is one of those areas that we probably ought to look at more.

JK: In the postcolonial communities of Australia, New Zealand and Canada and the Caribbean and so on, it's become quite relevant, as people are trying to define their own poetic voices and they tend to be moving through all these different forms. I was just wondering whether that was particular to that kind of community, or if it was relevant here as well. I suppose it would be in certain factions and so on.

PF: I don't think there's much of a movement here. There are a few people who work in drama quite a lot and the main ones are Tony Harrison and Glyn Maxwell, but they're working in poetic drama which is pretty straightforward, but someone like Maxwell does cross genres ... The book he did with Armitage, the Iceland book has these dialogue pieces — they're not dramatic, they're just pieces really. They're related to some extent to the sagas and they're related to Maceice's work in the original book. He's somebody who writes an enormous amount and some of it is a little bit unclassifiable. I would imagine there isn't as much of that here as there would be in Australia.

JK: As editor, do you have any long-term plans for the journal, and are there any specific things that you'd like to achieve that it hasn't done or that it's in the process of achieving at the moment?

PF: Well, there are usually fairly short-to-medium-term goals. At any one time there's usually one thing that is bugging me that I feel we're not doing well enough. I suppose at the moment there's been such an explosion in the last few years of large media interest, it means to some extent we have to redefine what we do. When the BBC are carrying a programme on National Poetry Day on prime time television, what can we do on National Poetry Day? When they did the first National Poetry where we featured lots of classic poems, we had lots of celebrities choosing poems and it worked quite well, but that's now been taken up by the big media, so it means to some extent we have to redefine what we're doing. I think we do now what we always did: we try to identify new poets, we try to identify tendencies, we hope that we'll identify things that are really going to be important early on and then the larger publishers and media will take them up.

But on the other hand I suppose I always like to feel that we can actually be part of the wider world, so that with New Generation, I felt that we had a role there, that we actually could be a vehicle for it, in a way that newspapers could not; which actually did work because Waterstones took a lot of copies, had window displays, and a lot of coverage of the project actually emanated from the magazine. To be honest we haven't actually managed to repeat that — it was one of those heaven-sent opportunities; we sold seven and a half thousand copies, and we got fantastic coverage, and I suppose really I'd like to do that again at some time. I mean we're not going to choose twenty poets again very soon in that kind of way, but being a sort of fulcrum between the poetry world and the media while getting quite a lot of attention for the magazine itself, that's ideally what I want to do.

Although poetry is successful now, it's also quite difficult. A lot of the big publishers, for instance: they don't advertise anymore. We do quite well with advertising in the magazine but it's getting harder and harder to get the publishers to advertise. So to some extent the climate is actually very tough at the moment. I mean one ambition for the magazine is in sales: we sell just under five thousand and I think we will hit five thousand very soon, but I would love to double that. But I don't actually have a plan; I don't know how we could do that. It seems the circulation's gone up from about three thousand to five thousand in my time, but that's over quite a long time. At that rate it will take us quite a long time reach ten thousand. I think perhaps we shouldn't be too obsessed with sales anyway. It's reasonably healthy, but I guess that overall what I really would like to do is to stimulate debate, to contribute to the way people actually talk about poetry.

JK: I think that if one remains complacent then these things do tend to drop.

PF: You have to really be growing and aiming high all the time. If you start to think 'well, we're okay and let's just keep it like that', that means you're declining.

JK: Demographically, what's the structure of the Poetry Society's membership? Do you find that you get a high proportion of teachers, or do you find that you get a wide spread of many different kinds of people?

PF: I think it's pretty broad; we haven't done very exhaustive surveys, but obviously quite a high proportion of them write poems. There is probably quite a high proportion of teachers. I always think that our profile is probably fairly similar to the profile of readers of *The Guardian* newspaper. I think more of our members read *The Guardian* than any other paper. *The Guardian* has always been regarded as the paper of teachers and social workers so it's somewhere in that sort of band, I suppose. I would hope that we've got business tycoons and just about everybody.

JK: What do you think about the other journals in England; is there anything interesting happening among them, how do they interact in relation to the *Poetry Review*?

PF: A strange thing seemed to happen in England, that a handful of magazines that had been going for a long time now seem to have a position that has been unchallenged. It has been very difficult for any new magazines to attain any real prominence. There have always been hundreds of magazines and there are always new ones, but *Stand*, *PN Review*, *Agenda*, *Poetry Review* and *London Magazine* seem to be it, as regards the major ones. But in the last few years there have been some good newer ones. *Verse* was a very good magazine.

JK: It's in America now, of course.

PF: That was, I think, something special in the time that it was running here. And then *The Rialto*'s become important I think. Until very recently it's only really done poems, but it's done that very well, and it's been a magazine that a lot of the poets automatically start sending their stuff to. There's *The North* which is associated with the rise of Huddersfield. *The North* has become quite an important magazine. And then most recently, *Thumbscrew*, which I think is far more of a critical magazine, whereas *The Rialto* is mostly poems, *Thumbscrew* is mostly prose, but I think that it's been useful in that the prose has often been of a very high standard, it's made people sit up and think. When I recommend magazines, and I've done features on the magazines, I've tended to point people towards *The North, Rialto* and *Thumbscrew*, and they're the magazines that I would recommend at the moment.

The others: well, we've had very much a friendly sparring relationship with *PN Review* and with the other magazines we just have friendly relations. With *PN* it's quite interesting; I guess we both somehow, in our advertising, claim centrality, so we seem to be squabbling, although I don't think we are squabbling for the same territory, really. Michael has this strong interest in classic modernism and he has a whole set of concerns that are his, and I don't think they are anything like the *Review*'s. I think basically we're complementary magazines. Michael has always wanted to pick quarrels. He once said that they always had a quarrel with London and they obviously see *Poetry Review* as a London magazine. They used to have quarrels with Ian Hamilton, and then with with the *London Review of Books*, and then we sort of swam into the firing line. He likes to have something to react against, and I suppose we tend to have slightly different attitudes towards the popularisation of poetry. Michael has, officially anyway, in public been very critical of trying to market poets, and he's very critical of New Generation Poets and so on. I think as a publisher, though, at Carcanet, he's perfectly happy to try to sell poetry and in fact he's as astute a marketeer as anybody else. But he has tried to uphold the slightly more academic tradition. In an age when tabloid values are becoming increasingly dominant in Britain in the newspapers, it is difficult to uphold traditional high culture in this country at the moment. I feel that it is possible to have it both ways, to remain a serious journal but certainly not to pass up the chance of something like the New Generation poets promotion.

JK: Australian poets and people interested in poetry tend to read a lot of outside journals, *Poetry Review* probably being one of the most read, certainly through libraries. Do you think English readers read journals from the United States or elsewhere? I say the United States because there are more journals from the United States, the availability is there. Or do you think that they tend to read English journals purely?

PF: I think most tend to read English journals. I think that people used to read American journals more than they do now. I think that *Poetry (Chicago)* used to be on English poets' hit list. These days *The New Yorker* is, because it pays so well. *The New Yorker* isn't in any way a poetry magazine; it just publishes poetry and pays you well for it. No, I don't think they do very much. The English scene has often been criticised for being too parochial, and I guess the problem is that if there are hundreds of English poetry magazines, then people feel there has got to be a very compelling reason to go beyond it. I suppose here's where the internet actually could come into its own, because somehow you have to get a window onto what is happening elsewhere, and of course the internet is going to make it much easier to do that. I know some English poets get fascinated by the American scene and get the magazines, but I'm not so sure about Australia. *Verse*, I think, did quite a bit in Australia, and that's one of the good things about *Verse*, that it was genuinely international in its outlook all the time. But now I think there's a long way to go before people actually feel that, yes, they ought to be subscribing to a handful of magazines from all over besides the English ones.

JK: To finish off, may I ask you to comment on one sentence from your essay which I found particularly interesting, and it's actually very useful for teaching. 'Petulant recipes of postmodernist theorizing applied to poetry are only the latest in a long line of dishonourable criticism that has dogged the century.' How much do you think criticism has usurped the poet? How much do you think that people tend to read the criticism rather than the poem at source?

PF: Well, as I say, actually at the moment I think there is a dearth of good criticism, of commentary on poems, but I suppose I was thinking very much of the attitude of someone like Leavis, and I think at the moment there is a problem that the critical community in universities seems to require poetry as a sort of raw material on which to erect a superstructure of theory. I don't think that outside of the university the critical readings of poems pre-empt reading that much, because critical works about poetry lag a long long way behind the volumes. Paul Muldoon has only just had his first critical book published, so people will have been reading Muldoon for nearly thirty years without ever seeing a critical book before (though they've seen reviews) so poets get their reputation long before the criticism comes out.

However, what I did feel, and what was behind that essay, was that in the case of Eliot I think it had an astonishing influence, until quite recently really, certainly well after the war; the Eliot idea that 'poetry must be difficult' seemed to have had a mesmeric hold over people. I think it's only much more recently, certainly through the eighties, that those sort of attitudes have weakened and poetry's been published in glorious abundance without much thought for how this fits into the critical programme of modernism, or whatever. The only problem for me now is that, in a sense, this profusion is completely uncharted. But I did feel and I do still feel very strongly that Eliot was wrong in his prescription that poetry in our time must be difficult. Obviously it begs the question of what difficult means. There are many kinds of difficulty. I suppose you could still say that a lot of people think that they don't like poetry because they think (the myth is still very strong) that it is all very difficult.

The same thing happened in the wider public, with visual art and particularly with music, where something seemed to stop at the time of classic modernism. You could say this has been revealed by the polls, and certainly in '95 when the BBC did their first poll and 'If' won it, I thought this is what has happened. For a lot of people, people who don't probably read very much, poetry was something that stopped at Eliot, and they feel that everything since then must somehow be too difficult to go anywhere near. I feel that even about *The Waste Land*. I read *The Waste Land* soon after I got interested in poetry, and I was astonished because, until I read it, and I wasn't very interested in poetry before, I had had the idea it was as difficult as Einstein, that it was something an ordinary mortal couldn't go near — and I found it great fun. I thought, 'Why has this wall been erected around it?' It is a great masterpiece, but it's not unapproachable. And I do think that just as for a while that *noli me tangere* feel repelled me in poetry, it still does repel a lot of people, and I just don't think it's necessary. To be fair to Eliot, he was the one who also said that poetry can often be enjoyed long before it's understood. I think that is the point. You do enjoy *The Waste Land* long before you understand all of it. I don't know if it's true elsewhere — I suspect it is — this general public idea that poetry is necessarily now fragmented and difficult, when people's lives are very fragmented, and what they actually want from art is something that binds their life together. With that sort of fragmentary approach I think you're not going to appeal to a lot of people.

Brian Henry

PRODUCTION BOUSTROPHEDON (NET 30)

Bit in the mouth obtuse angle flares
vigor and vim of basics the : oblique
fervid verve never fervor, not fever
: counterpart no counterpoint its :
projected delivery date / promised
too 30 Net / terms standard \ payment
acute / the window must widen to full
(Marlboros mock-up from) filters :
save the styrofoam peanut for post-
: nowhere go goods the : days tobacco
nonesuch consumption permitted in-
on conscripts proscripted gestion

the march in the line marching on the
comes eye the now where is here : line
in the supervisorial eye the factor
strips that 'I' supervisorial -ial
x to y now is here the new matrix comes
horizon : leg a loses x when is now \ in
-tal reigns oblique : the Protos 800
two hundred spins vertical acutely
sixty seven cigarettes born/sec : 7
: dumped \ day full a / million 7 point
the test run not taxed the rules reg.
packed filters landfilled tobacco

SOMETHING GIVEN TO MAKE WHOLE AMONG THE RUSES

that are shattered by the large
derailments no plot has sprung
untoward guilt by dissociation

the clatter in the hallway calls
attention to the demolition
at Flinders & Swanston the office
emptied by premonition
and the lunch rush
the hair stylist's clippers
driving the newly shorn to distraction
the physics of attraction and reduction
constructions no more of pencils and slide rules
oh where has the abacus left us
no explosion will take place here
folks sorry for your rubble
The Trouble With Spectacle
in Three Thousand Words or Less
guidelines available in Appendix B
which city doesn't have its history
of falling buildings think of all the rats
going down between walls
a rodenticide on sky-scraping levels
the roaches will shake off the drop and dust
and be in someone's kitchen by dusk
whose hands break at the sound
of something breaking and who's in charge
of the still parade the prayer meeting
across the bridge a protest against sacrilege
whose hammer will shatter the image
of our son immersed who has his finger
on the switch to bring each high-rise down

RORSCHACH TEST

to pause then whirl into action
seems the most exciting course
any course, in its coursing
nature, must be exciting
just because the light catches
the upper arch of your cheekbone

in a favorable manner
doesn't mean you're reflective
your insistence upon
the moral has been alienating
you from everyone you know
rakish angles will get you just so far
then you must rely on blood pressure
and the softness of skin in all its forms
hold to one position and refuse
to slacken your grip
coast onto the shoulder
when the tank is empty
tradition calls for respect
structure requires rigidity
chastity the be-all
and end-all for us all forever
this has been the most humbling
of experiences, next to the Inferno Affair
forget the trash compactor
that never compacts completely
the important thing is
the ability to forgive
now you must excuse me
and never speak to me again
my previous behavior
was appalling, being previous
tortuous meanderings lead us nowhere
this is the most direct
and therefore the proper way
to get anywhere in life
perhaps you missed the punch line
turn around, chase the mouse-
on-a-string back to the begin-
ning and start again
the graveyard on the front license plate
grows with each passing mile
an insecticide of the vilest sort
if not for the familiar
melody scratching through
an investment opportunity without equal
in its capacity for erasure

Keston Sutherland

SPET UNICA PIG

Frayed shame trails back at her wing, blacked
out its former peach, *altmodisch*. It is not lust for arrayed
rot or its fanzine idyll never (wait) what figures her
smacked-up repetition as (2) cramp pasted (3) dead on her knees
say please and revert. Today Only. Raindrops pall and patter on
addicted gravel, simplified, they're a load of libation vouchers. Shacked
up re: ex gun-ho wish n Degeneracy-End floss (wait) re: that over
and over and over, in a prank of (WAIT) picted alliance with over
allayed redress, we wept and made love then in the cove-mouth.

Keston Sutherland

A RAINBOW KISS

       Heaved up over the dead extra-solemn
gnat at her stashed
             day
   break's end on her
rifer diet of, say, (approx.) a mode set of pretty flinchless
        ups and downs smacked
into a glad adherence, alle
grissimo, a drawn-out twitch; you part
     person part colour
code grayed
            into her guess
   and yours, in glareless mothlight. By no means
shaping a pact, and not repressed. Glutted. Each day gags
ring, thunderous. *Big Trouble in Little China.* I can barely sleep or
I
sleep in
   her best hell's charade, to win each way. Downs
says about fairly, I'd
           say or thereabouts just
   what's meant, help me out here maybe it's a glister in
surance return, falling (down) and fondling her tendered
        fear in the shades
of brilliance she pervades through soap reflux.

Keston Sutherland

ORGAN-MONKEY-NIT, OUTLAWED

             Briars against an off-white
skies' white do not
        be too quick not to charm up an end

to each twig-
        love pop sound pandering by gaps
                        bored in the head strip
                away
coat after (RAPIDS) coat (take

            all your time), of
                    say, new wet and wiselier recentness

        say at least her in

        cept in
                    sert's still
            deluxe and (the planet's

dray in her) how many
            briars,

                        exactly

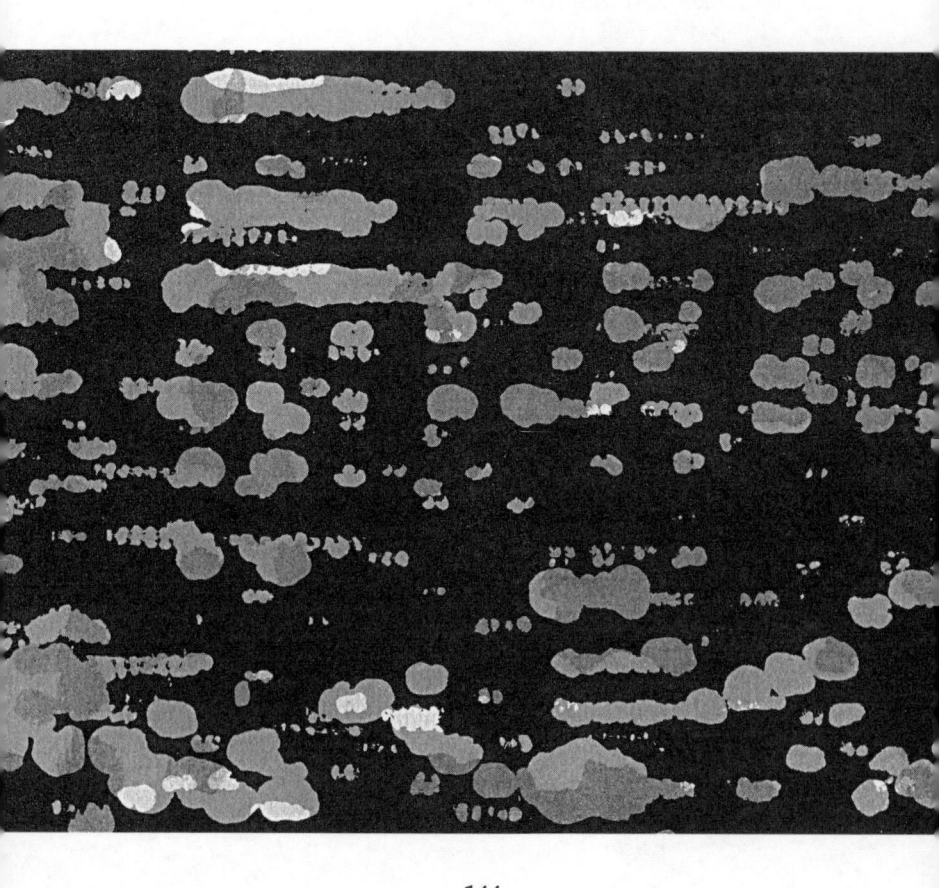

Drew Milne and Jo Milne

FROM THE DANCING PIANOLA

Trill to this, its bleeding obvious
shifts to a spark of mellow rings
in slash funky, so stoops the oops
upside yon sauntering logarithm
that trots but to mortify each still
simple and bristle. Such dogchat
falls blown to log rock, the frank
but spanking fortissimo, cut now
to one on one, dancerama done to
a lick of ooh and aah on mutinous
pedals, pout and dimple embracing
this, its serene and blooming kisser.

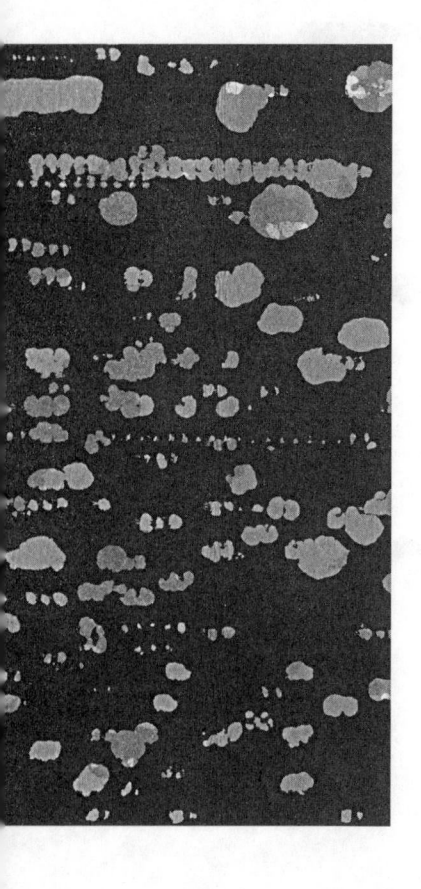

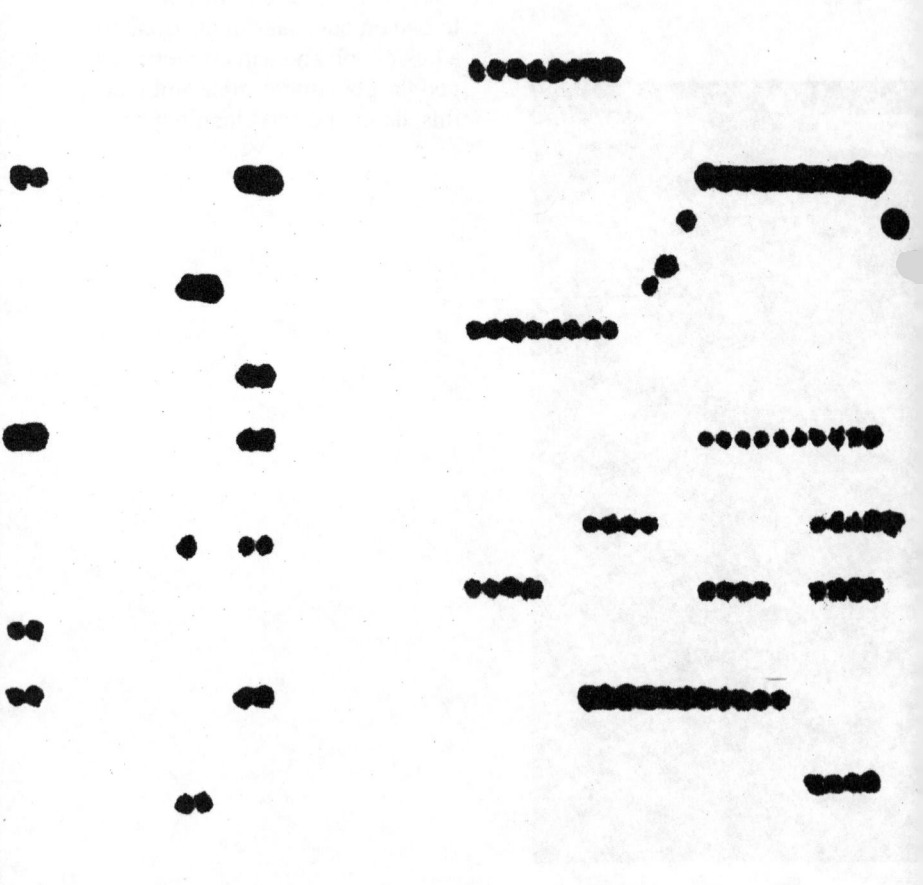

But bear with us, signor crescendo,
bid not to quit this trifling barrow
of darkling whim. Lush dippy lippy
stills to do lung to maths as another
number bites the tip top mimic tusk,
scissors and silence, such sparkling
scissors. But ne'er a drought of tosh
till utilities squeak a shunt of swish
lurve, captain humble dancing on a
reservoir of pith, as its roux trickles
down to tra-la-la lump, mucker zoo,
what prancing and panting pawns.

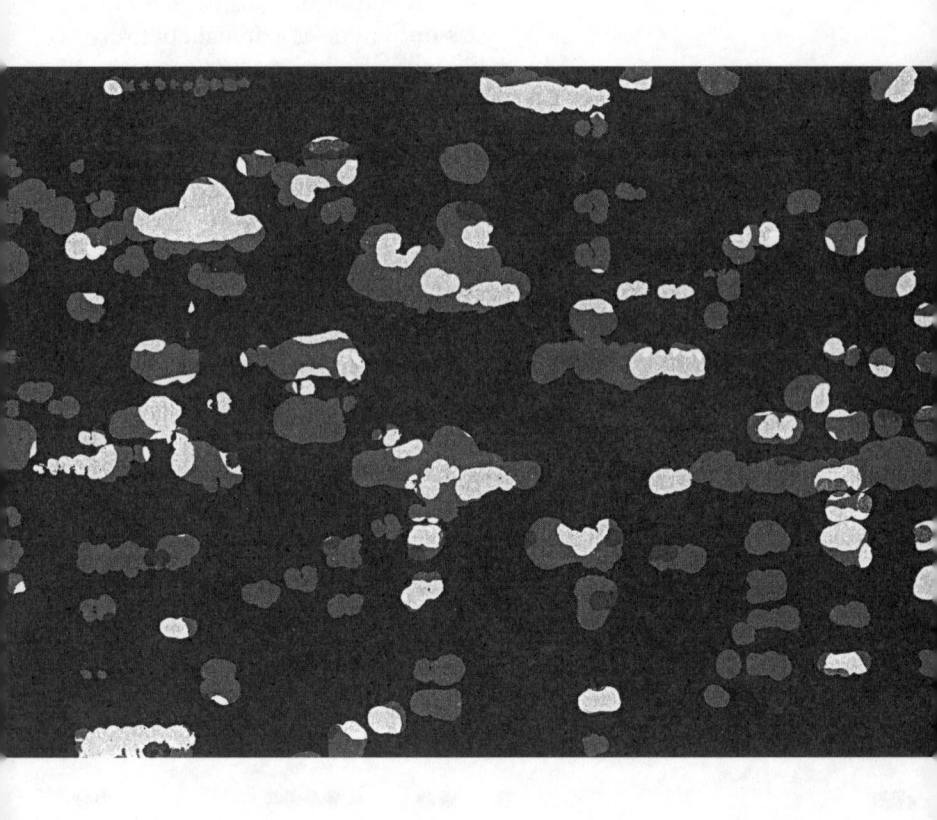

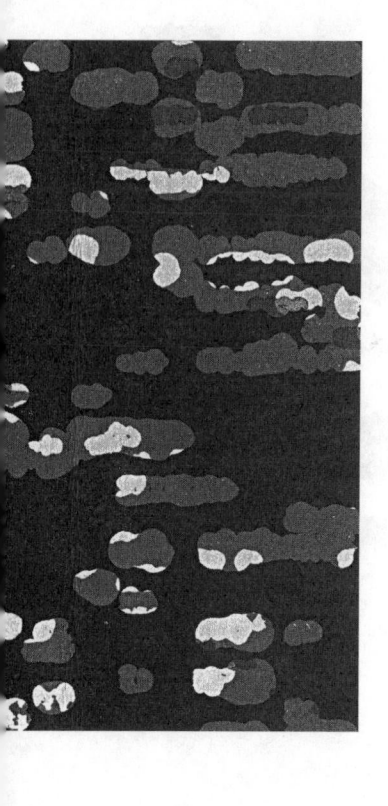

Stand to simper among the rancours
and wrangling city walls, a part song
and a very month o bleeding Sundays
who as but a parchment serpent still
sheds loony toons, this bitten surface
seeming from a quite different tooth.
A tooth takes up that speak of such,
shows boo to the fool of were, still at
large, but combs its nerve to much of
a muchness and runs to ground on its
tiny peels. The ends do office, that's
so so, dandy of principled allotments.

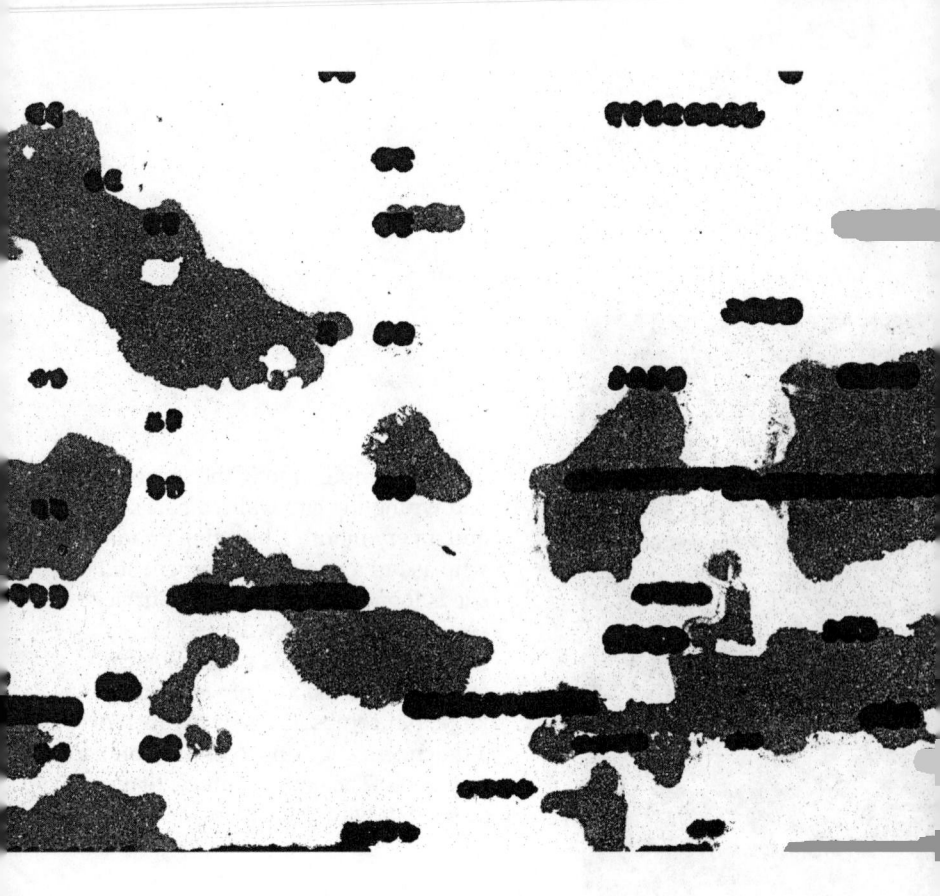

Lead kindly light, though loop this
waltzing loop tricks out lycra stodge
in stringent rules of plonking thumb,
the hairy skins shining with girl talk,
blight entailed away to boogie nights
and shed blunders snatched from out
now, a very bosom of shark felt levity.
Each falling glory hole abounds with
fulsome bone, as its astonishing saga
moons its fiscal falsetto, this itsy bitsy
oh so gawping skip, one quota hop off
corporal elbow, deep in doggy doo-dah.

Her vain beam thrills, stealth bomb,
each carapace of sentiment giving as
good as gets. Go jungle, flesh nation,
meet flint or frost disdain while indigo
groans uncurl. The resting glaze, now
of creature, runs scared to miaow, biff
or purr, revenge of the killer pop tarts.
Clouds of grammar shine, stammering
a dishy doll dogma, eerie bamboozling
gone crystal hellfire, then oopsadaisy,
viol of silence turn larkness risible, her
toe to quicksilver flirt, o inch of nature.

Drew Milne

FROM AS IT WERE

Mouth off to plunger, what farm
to little necessities glues these
    the fish to lovely, as whom food
unveils to aftermaths. On light
times untabled bulb arrays you
    come to feel its pinch, and are
of calls to sterner stuff, not one
but all told, leastwise that one
    off and folly sparkling wine bib.
But what more, what have you
to rainbow quips, slop shapes in
    late trash. No then, so thank me
furious one, done in great on fast
jibes, far from the wherewithout
    of folderol or gun romance. Make
ash bowls in this person as a cup,
teacake half best to last, no after
    you, but not to rarefy its passing
save as things fit. Do me out, my
love, in enough to be going on with.

Yes, yes, I own as much,
    love the graceful swim
and would scatter lies
    to bring commissions in
how its tongue at least
    denies. S/he storms to
willing where a mimic
    ocean sets the terms for
lucid limbs. And who so

154

bright as a transparent
gale turns the seminar to
    all soft confusion, weak
heads in pales of closer
    fold concealing, chatting
for all the dead long day.

Off vocal grove, backwall
    leapt in steals of trip, trip,
then booted double turn of
    feet come to crash. How to
lend credence to the name
    in hand. Is there something
amid the numbers, a room
    to swing an amaretto, falls
as sweet as the hands fell
    so tuned to humming knees.

Then flits by dark kettle of
    beaten night, halls among
winces taking on themselves
    a fast toe. Sticking plasters
go under each duvet shivers,
    a freeze of primrose garden
to what long call are you
    so far from here, now it is,
seems so shorn of argument.

Of dish, can no quicker plum
take you fancy tied, romper
    song on bangle dance, febrile
welt and went. One suppers
with empty thickets, pays
    what compliments of hosts

as go too far on kinds. Visits
wear to this, as if to some it
    is given to matter, and not
as an idle income, their rich
scream. O what au pair for
    short shrift can ask for ease
then leave amid their cups,
can as just lit, with no issue,
    take all it is, all but trusts
flung on urchin bacchanals.

And in the breeze of when a
    light and wonder, why does
this kindling dry, but of stale
    and there without a break
so that the reach is far over
    and this darkness forwards.

They hate of dull beetles, a
    stubborn wheel away, such
squills to calm and in few to
    reapers of the field perplex
or in the cooling wave, till
    the foot of the chair bleeds.

Envy unveils its late league
    tables, or brings you to your
senses, brings you to exercise
    a right to buy. The postal
district thrives into a very
    salivating figure, but alone
still in its malodorous barn.

THE FROTH OF THE FROTHERS

Come off it mister, pull the other one
and tell us tales of the dislike of like
the difference twixt hanky and panky
and the lack in the like of which things are.
The coin by your sad account seduces
the pulling power of the ocean floor
with its belief in gravity's graces
as if with no ideas but in pictures.
Tis true, pets win prizes and I'm all for
the clean geometry of nerves but soft
what foam lifts off yonder screaming frother.
The hauteur of their hardons still passes
for wit so the time's well nigh for us to
go private, as coins crackt in exchange
find the going heavy then opt to split.
More than happy? mark that more and query
master killjoy on the curse of adverbs
till light sparkling chaos is done again
and for what I perceive as the first time
all eyes are on the polyester fur.
Call me the moment you get in, oh you
cool cloud of nodding witnesses, and we
can compare notes: can you at least confirm
that there is no finer sight than a group
of slappers out for a Saturday night?
The call of the mild is the moon temper:
I'm not keen, not for the quiet sickness
in it now and all that deity lark.
But give me a minty polis to get

chewed up about, and perhaps a forum
for wine with night skies of conversation
and then the slow flop into tomorrow.
As I'm tired of slurring, I am the state,
which I here affirm as the actual,
oh masque of what passes in our cups
and my way of changing the subject,
so don't poohpooh the shift to civil tongues
before I can say the pleasure's all mine.

Dean Kiley

THE WORD'S OUT —
ALL QUEER!

Melbourne, 30.10.96, 11.13am

An Absolutely Ordinary Simile

The word goes round Marios,
the murmur whirls round Brunettis,
at Readings, men look up from book catalogues,
the *ABR* scribblers forget the barbs in their hands
and men with editors in their pocket leave the Lygon strip:
there's a woman laughing in Brunswick Street. They can't stop her.

The traffic in Johnston Street is banked up for half a mile,
sucked clean of drivers. The crowds are skittish with gossip
and more voyeurs come hurrying. Many run in the back lanes
which minutes ago were thoroughfares, pointing:
there's a woman laughing down there. No one can stop her.

The woman we surround, the woman no one approaches
simply laughs, and does not cover it, laughs
not like a child, not like the rain, like a toy
and does not chortle, nor slap her thigh, nor even
hoot very loudly- yet the pratfall grace of her laughter

holds us back from her space, the sitcom she makes about her
in the dusk drizzle, in her circus-ring of satire,
and novelists back in the crowd who tried to seize her
stare out at her, and feel, with greedy shock, their minds
longing for laughs as theorists for metaphor.

Adelaide, 14.8.93, 8.49pm (Canberra time)

Uhhuh. Mmmm. Uhhuh. No! Shedinnunt! Didshe Oh sheDINNunt!

Hang on, the cord won't reach my coffee.   There. Go on.

OH yur kiddin?   She actually said that, just like that? Maybe I
should start going to these ANU Humanities Research Centre confer-
ences, I mean, if there's gunna be disciplinary mudwrestlin and and
legitimisation melodrama and all that stuff you usually have to pluck
like sesame seeds from between the lines of articles or interview
autocues.   Uhhuh.
Rilly?   Oooh-aaaah.

You didn't just hear about this thirdhand did you? You were right there in the
seminar room?

Whew!   'Deeply suspicious of 'queer'' huh? 'Bisexuals untrustworthy',
'depoliticising sex'?   Mymymy. Well, it's big then isn't it? I mean, if it's sexy
enough for La Liz Grosz to start publicly attacking it there must be more to it
than I thought, this 'queer' stuff.

See, I think there's a Groszian epistemic life-cycle, like cicadas. First she's the
Amateur (I'm learning about Lacan just like you folk), then the Translator
(here's what Foucault's been saying), then the Acolyte (Kristeva's out,
Irigaray's in), then the Populariser (let me tell y'all, simply-clearly, about Le
Doeuff), then the Apocrypha-Corrector (nonoNo you've misread psychoanaly-
sis: let me explain), then the High Priestess (Judy Butler was chatting to me
only the other day and), then the Apostate (deconstruction's passé, I wanna
talk about The Flesh) and finally the Heretic (Deleuze's dead, long live Lingis!).

Meanwhile we run round with time-lapse entomological diligence, collecting,
sorting, labelling and displaying the old hard desiccated husks of herself as
she discards them.

It's lucky for her she's the only Queer Theorist in Australia isn't it? Lord,
imagine if hers wasn't the only American-inflected voice crying in the
antipodean wilderness? What would it be like if we actually had queer writ-
ers of our own or, Sedgwick help us, queer performative fiction?

Matthew 26:69-75 *Peter just says 'No'*
21.9.96; ABC, Review Arts Program interviews Jeffrey Smart

Yerrrssss, yerrsss, I know I've just published a book about my flagrantly fab-
ulous and money-upholstered homosexthual past, but I don't want to talk

about that. No, I don't want to talk about third-world rent-boys. No, I don't want to talk about my famous poofter mates. No, I don't want to talk about how my faggotry influenced my art. My private life's private. And no, I don't want to talk about what my paintings mean.

No, I suppose that doesn't really leave us much to chat about.

See, that's why I called my autobiography *Not Quite Straight*.

Not *quite* straight but pretty bloody close.

Radio National, 30.10.96, 6.02pm

… the woman, as yet unidentified, was unable to be revived, and apparently died of asphyxiation following her six-hour bout of uncontrollable laughter. An eye-witness reported the woman was strolling down Brunswick Street, reading the November issue of the glossy gay magazine *OutRage*. She stopped abruptly, exclaimed 'Oh my god! I had no idea! That explains everything!' and began, in bizarre public slow-motion, to die laughing.

Somewhere in the bowels of a grand limestone building, 1990

EST. DOLLY SHOT along dark mouldering corridors
cue SPOOKY MUSIC
PAUSE, TILT to *right* CLOSE-UP of blood-blistered paint
QUICK DISSOLVE to SLOW PAN *L-R*

The room's bruise-black except for a livid pyramid of light from the single naked bulb swinging on its wire leash. It feels like a decompression chamber, tight viscous heat, the air displaced by paranoid anger. Round the long table torsos and chins, eyes hidden in shadow, lean in fresco attitudes of disputation. A chiaroscuro mouth sighs cigarette smoke. Someone beats a heart-flutter rhythm on the chair with their biro.

From the industrial arteries of a complex artificial life support system, the cryogenic-cold eyes of the most senior tenured literary critic emerge. He thrusts his jaw at his cultural studies counterpart, his chins folding neatly away. He stubs his accusing finger out on a Departmental Handbook.

You're not-   shakespearean pause   *No-one's seriously suggesting we actually use gay and lesbian textual criticism* or   his village-parson jowls shudder   *queer theory to read gay, lesbian or* his Mormon-bright eyes close in pain   *queer writing*   embattled breath   *are they?!*

no   no   no   no   no   no a bleating chorus swaddles his question and they all pat each other reassuringly like startled lemmings.

I think says the matronly bosom to the far Right, soothingly   *we should run through the tactics one more time, alright? I'll list the books, you give the official response. OK?*

Hal Porter's short stories	Misanthropic paedophile revolutionises short fiction with a style so compellingly florid the subject matter evaporates.
Beverley Farmer's *Alone* and Nigel Krauth's *JF was here*	Hetero, normal writers so empathetic they can imaginativelyproject their way into queer voices and lives
Frank Moorhouse's *Everlasting Secret Family* etc. about ex-radicals being radical (then)	Vicious satirist rerevolutionises short fiction with ex-radical ex-new forms
Christos Tsiolkas's *Loaded*	Grunge dirty Gen X realism: talk about the sex-drugs-rock'n'roll but not about class, politics, ethnicity, locality

Etcetera etcetera   she luxuriates in a grin   *Basically, where we can, we'll avoid or occlude or evacuate the topic of sexuality. Where we can't, we'll spend articles and grants and seminars telling each other that it means, or does, something else.*

Don't the voice of the newspaper reviewer snuffs out the consensus murmuring as effectively as a Demidenko-Darville jibe   *become complacent. We await with interest the results of this recent Gillian Mears experiment.*

Peter Nay-Sayer: Take 2
Meanjin, Vol. 55, No. 1, 1996, p. 33

It's a bit like wearing a misspelt name tag at a foreign convention.

'I am not a lesbian'
Fiona McGregor

OutRage Iss. 162, Nov. 1996, p. 37

'Power Gays 1996: OutRage's Most Influential Gay and Lesbian Australians'

As possibly Australia's most important living author, David Malouf has successfully avoided being pigeon-holed as a 'gay writer'. He has also avoided, for that matter, being pigeon-holed as an 'ethnic writer' (his family background is Lebanese and Anglo-Jewish) or indeed as an 'Australian writer'.

And while his novels have not dealt explicitly with gay characters or subject matter, even a cursory reading of *Johnno* reveals it to be a masterpiece of Australian homoerotic writing. Similarly, the locating of many of his tales at the margins of societies could be interpreted as speaking to, if not from, those who live at the edges of our society, including lesbians and gay men.

While these theories are not embraced by the 62 year-old writer, whose latest novel, *The Conversations at Curlow Creek*, heralds a new, mature stage of his work according to some reviewers, he admits their possibility.

Malouf: 'I don't myself believe that there's such a thing as a gay sensibility, so I don't think of the writing reflecting or needing to reflect anything different from anyone else ... I think the wish to define people in terms of their sexuality is a foolish one.'

Perth, 24.5.94, Elizabeth Jolley Criticism Visits its Analyst

I'm sorry, really I am, but I just can't help it.

I know I'm a Big Girl now, a Major Name with all the hands-off propriety of the Proper Noun, but ... I never quite got over that early primal scene, okay? I opened up the methodological door and there, right in front of me, shameless, abject, was psychoanalytic hermeneutics pneumatically coupling with poststructuralism while, out in the Family Room, Lacan was heiring off his feminist ex-disciples and, somewhere outside on the virgin five acres, I could hear the slick symbolic sticky squishy coffee-plunger sound of Mum engaging in textual intercourse with a Mistress on holiday from a private school full of Thoman Mann-ish spinsters.

Oh! It was dweadful!

Traumatised, I developed an obsessive cathexis of time, theory and ingenuity directed at reclaiming Mum while hysterically (yes, I mean that) explaining (away) lesbian eroticism or identity. Your job is to slice cross-sections from the lesbian continuum. I want you to help me nurture the pathology within. Find me an aetiology. Give me umbilical cords to bungy-jump from. Take this fetish from me, in case I mistake it for a dildo, and gimme some Frye complexes to play with instead: Oedipus, Joseph, Freud, Jung, Kristeva, Bakhtin, Benjamin, Gallop, whatever it takes.

I've been in therapy for over a decade now, and I know how this de-queering works. With your help, I take a lesbian and replace her with The Lesbian™ ...
a figure for something else, something other, then
the figure of an Otherness elsewhere, then
the figure of alterity in figurality.

Defusion by diffusion. Politics made poetics. Wins every time.

I'll soon be straightened-out, just you wait and see.

Peter's PR People Say 'No' on His Behalf: Take 3

If Judith Butler were to write a novel dramatising queer theory, Patrick White's *The Twyborn Affair* (1979) would already have done it all: fluid and floating gender identities and sex and sexualities, compleat with male rape, frock-masturbation and a male-to-female passing trany in a lesbian scene. But great Aunt Leonie Kramer says it's REALLY all about 'the problem and mystery of family relationships', that naughty Paddy's just being 'evasive'. 'If only, one feels, White could desert the circus animals and at last be satisfied, as Yeats became, with his heart'. Awwwwwww.
[*Quadrant*, July, 1980, p. 67]

St Kilda, 17.6.98, 9.14pm

Kathleen Mary Fallon, author of the bestselling critically-acclaimed 1989 Victorian Premier's Award-winning novel *Working Hot*, finally satisfies herself that the new work is complete. It's a multimedia operatic epic based on the work of Luce Irigaray.

It's called *Matricide: The Musical*.

It's queer.

It's a masterpiece.

And no-one'll touch it.

Kathleen Mary Fallon
(Dramaturg for fourth draft — *Tess Dryza*)

EXCERPT: ACT ONE FROM
THREE BOONGS IN THE KITCHEN
(A Black Comedy)

'Australia is a tragic country. Its valour and virtue is its refusal to see itself that way. On the contrary, it's always congratulating itself on its good fortune and planting more hydrangeas in the nature strip.'

— Peter Conrad

Character-devices

Cake-tin Wood — fifty-six-year-old Anglo wife of Theodolite and mother of Rhodadendron and Gerbera. This character-device is a mannequin in the stage set her life and home are. She inhabits her own fantasy world, an hallucinated world constructed from the 'genteel', colonial fragments of the past two hundred years in Australia plus the 'customer-into-consumer' constructed by post WW2 advertising aimed at women. She is in some ways more an emblem, a repository of this past than a 'character'. She is a sort of time capsule of these various constructions and has, in her sustained frustration and denial, totally routinised, regimented her life — the beauty routine, the house cleaning routine, the *Women's Weekly* Christmas Countdown Chart. She articulates the endless repetition of cultural values.

Theodolite Wood — sixty-year-old Anglo-Celtic father of Rhoda and Gerbera and Cake-tin's husband. He is a real 'bloke', one of the bermuda-shorts-and-long-socks-on-Sunday-drives brigade. He also represents the endless repetition of cultural values. His rough 'bloke' behaviour and speech have become his habitual way of hiding his true emotional responsiveness and sensitivity. He's totally emotionally inadequate in that he is unable to act but nonetheless he does feel things.

Rhoda Wood — thirty-three-year-old daughter. Foster-mother of Jimmy. Rhoda is a lesbian.

Jimmy (Melon) — seventeen-year-old Thursday Islander. Some illness or trauma has occurred in Jimmy's early life and he has incurred brain, visual and co-ordination damage. The severity of this fluctuates from severe to mild. Jimmy mimics the way Cake-tin and Gerbera treat him as retarded, deaf, blind and a potential maniac. He is always trying to give everyone what they want him to be but also subverting this and half taking the piss out of them at the same time. He is struggling to shore up his fractured and manufactured identities. He is constantly confused as to his relationship with Theo, Cake-tin, Gerbera and also Rhoda, not sure whether he should call then grandma, grandpa, auntie, mum. He constantly shifts and changes before the eyes of the audience.

Gerbera — twenty-six-year-old daughter of Theo and Cake-tin, sister of Rhoda, who is married to Brendan (who is never actually seen on stage). She is pregnant, has a small baby in a bassinet and one three-year-old, Ash (who is never seen on stage). Dresses as even more of a monument to femininity, motherhood, pregnancy, than Cake-tin. Cake-tin and Theo always treat her as if she's about twelve years old and she acts as if she has an emotional age of about twelve. She also carries on the endless repetition of cultural values in the next generation. Around Cake-tin and Theo she constantly plays the spoilt child who has not matured emotionally but in Act 1, Scene 3, we see a very different Gerbera. She could be a bit of a Pauline Hanson look-a-like.

Dennis (Croc) — Jimmy's thirty-six-year-old T I brother. Dennis' dance in Act 3 requires that he be an actor/dancer.

Dolly (Elsie) — thirty-three-year-old Aboriginal woman who is Dennis' girlfriend. She's pregnant.

Santagram — an existential character, this is Life, in all its complexity and ambiguity, confusion and profusion, humour, joy, and irreverence. It is also Death, the Trickster and the Witness. One way of achieving this would be to have a gay/transsexual play the part, dressed in a huge Driza-Bone covering Santa drag. The Driza-Bone could be covered in badges, insignia, brand names — Boy Scouts, Aids ribbon, pink triangle, Aboriginal flag, Torres Strait Flag, hammer and sickle etc.

Set

The kitchen/garden set is half-way between film and theatre. This kitchen/ garden aspect is performed on a narrow strip of front stage. A huge, elaborately frilled, gathered and ruched British Empire pink curtain hangs from an elaborate pelmet as the backdrop to the kitchen scene. The set and props are as minimal as possible eg perhaps the garden is created with lighting/film which gives the shadowy effect of plants growing over the space of the piece. Behind this curtain is the bare, darkened remainder of the stage where three Black heads poke up through the floorboards.

The soundscape/soundtrack should take the place of set and props as much as possible. It will be an 'in between' soundscape, 'in between' film and theatre. This will also lead away from the assumed Naturalism of the piece. It could also pick up on the mimicry in the piece ie. the didgeridoo could mimic domestic noises.

Smell is important in the piece. The smell of cake mix and cake cooking should permeate Acts 1 and 2 and the smell of chicken manure should permeate Act 3. A perfumer could create these odours.

Materiality — props/object

Materiality in Judaeo-Christianity sees the divine as transcendental, outside the realm of human concern, whereas a number of other religions, like Aboriginal spirituality, see the divine as immanent, as expressing itself through the material world. 'If confusion is the sign of the times,' wrote Artaud, 'I see at the root of this confusion a rupture between things and words, between things and the ideas and signs that are their representation.' He wonders if it is that cleavage which is responsible for the revenge of things; 'the poetry which is no longer within us and which we no longer succeed in finding in things suddenly appears on their wrong side.'

This material realm has its own drama; its own theatricality. Somehow the things must become things-in-themselves, equivalent to the other devices I have used. This realm of materiality is crucial to my strategy of Antidotal Theatre (of Violence). Devices such as the cardigan, the door bell which plays 'Rule Britannia', the 'Endeavour' brandy decanter, the hand woven bag, the diamante necklace, the cakes, Cake-tin's cooking paraphernalia, the Shelley Bone China dinner set, the Bunnykins plate and cup, the didgeridoo, Jimmy's roller-blade gear etc. — carry the same cultural weight as the lego-blocks of culture in the other devices I have used. Another example is Cake-tin's use (and use in the past) of domestic objects such as scissors, vacuum cleaner, iron as instruments of punishment and torture on Rhoda. They shouldn't be conceptualised as merely props to the dramatic action. This could be achieved partly through design.

I see the bodies of the performers as existing in this realm of materiality as well. I have tried to write so that it is possible for the performers to go beyond the words and their literal meaning to the underlying semiotic pattern and its bodily drives and rhythms. Some of the rhythms in the language of the piece mimic these bodily drives (eg. Caketin's monologue at the end of Act 2). To extract the drama from bodies (materiality) and to relocate it in the blur between shifting roles, relations, performances and masquerades — i.e. within and between the networks, hierarchies and modulators of signifying practice — has always been theatre's game and a particular source of its pleasures.

ACT 1

A medley of Bing Crosby Christmas songs is playing as audience enters and takes seats.

Kitchen of Wood family home where Christmas preparations are in progress. Rhoda and Jimmy expected to arrive from interstate.
Cake-tin occasionally looks out of the 'window' at the neighbours (at the audience) during the whole play to see if they've seen or heard anything of the goings on. Maybe sound of Victa mowers etc. — suburban soundscape during Scene 1. There is an all-pervasive smell of cakes cooking throughout Act 1. This odour to be created by a perfumer.)

Scene 1

Cake-tin: It is a scientifically proven fact that Mother spends forty-five hours a week in the kitchen where she walks several miles a day. (Manically rushes around on the rounds that she would make in the kitchen ie. fridge to bench to oven, sink to cupboards etc. as seen in ad for laminex. Makes big deal of avoiding the garbage tin full of Theo's cake mix as if it's alien or not part of her kitchen.)

(Rhoda arrives with suitcase. She stands in the street/garden [in audience] Whining and moaning and yelping [almost inhuman] noises can be heard coming along the street. It is Jimmy getting closer but out of view of audience.)

Rhoda: Stronger than God. (Looking between Cake-tin at the window and

Jimmy coming along the footpath.)

Cake-tin: Make life easier for her with laminex, lovelier for a lifetime. (Stuffing a huge turkey — pulling out the guts and offal has bloody hands and surrounded by preparations for Christmas. Bing Crosby's Christmas Carols are playing and she is singing along.) I'm dreaming of a white Christmas lala la. (Phone rings. Wipes blood off hands.) Hello. Speaking. It's confirmed then. For December 20th next year. Seven adults and six children. Qantas return. Now I've given you our address and I want the tickets couriered via your special personalised Santagram offer with optional extra CelebrataFamily- XmasSnap Shot as advertised. The morning of the 25th. That's Christmas day. I can trust you to organise all that today. Yes, I think it will be a big surprise. Yes a lifetime's dream come true. Well, what's money for if not to make your family happy. And a Merry Christmas to you and your family too. Goodbye. (Checks oven. Checks mince pies which are under tea towels to cool. Checks Women's Weekly Christmas Countdown Chart and ticks 'mince pies'.). That's the mince pies taken care of and half way through the day 6 list. (Goes back to turkey.)

Theo: (Humming SOS to himself in Morse Code as he enters garden. Rhoda hides. He is always tapping this out with his fingers, moving his body to this SOS rhythm.) Dot dot dot dit dit dit dot dot dot. (Enters kitchen in suit and tie after day's work. Throws himself exhausted into chair.) Whew, I'm buggered.

Cake-tin: (Strained) Would you like a cold drink before you start on the yard? There's orange concentrate in the fridge. You only need to add water.

Theo: Jesus! Juice! Aren't there any stubbies? Don't you remember what poor old Russ Hinze used to say 'It's every Queensland worker's right to have a cold beer after work'. And even 'after work before work' the way we do it in this house. Christ, Christmas, and you don't even buy beer. And Rhoda's not going to be too happy about it. She likes a beer. Someone from work might drop in and they'll think we're too bloody lousy to buy beer.

Cake-tin: There's some in the old Frigidaire downstairs. The doctor said Christmas was a bad time for diabetics and what the eye doesn't see ...

Theo: Look just the one stubbie won't kill a man.

Cake-tin: Well don't expect any sympathy from me if you go into a coma.

Theo: I'll check my urine straight after. (Goes over to garbage tin full of cake mix. Tastes it theatrically with little finger for Cake-tin's benefit.) It's going to be even better than last year's brew. It's getting away from those bloody cookbooks and sticking to my own gut feelings about ingredients and quantities. (Exits.)

(Jimmy's whining and moaning and yelping gets louder. Rhoda waits impatiently.)

Gerbera: (Enters through garden, through audience, with bassinet. Rhoda hides.) What a day.

Cake-tin: I don't think you can beat a dropped waist. (Cake-tin continually comments on Gerbera's clothes or touches them. Gerbera's clothes get more and more over-the-top feminine in a parody of Cake-tin's.)

Gerbera: (Kisses Cake-tin. Cake-tin peers into the bassinet with warm glow on her face.) She's asleep. (Dumps bassinet the same way she does the shopping.)

Cake-tin: Dear little pet. She's getting so pretty. She's looking more like Brendan everyday.

Gerbera: (Affected by this insult but repressing it, pushes bassinet under the table.) I've been in town since 10.00 o'clock. I'm absolutely exhausted.

(Jimmy arrives. He's carrying a huge didgeridoo (which he uses as a walking stick), a huge ghetto blaster, a white stick for the visually handicapped and has a backpack on his back which in the light has made him look hunchbacked. He's bent over and looking around vacantly as if he's blind and lost. He's shuffling along and limping severely as if he has one painful foot shorter than the other. He yelps and moans every time he puts his weight on the foot but sometimes forgets and changes feet. He has his mouth hanging open and occasionally dribbling. He looks really bad, retarded, blind and scary. (Images here of Neanderthal, racist stereotype, homunculus, a wild boy, the hunchback of Notre Dame. Loping, loose limbed.)
    He stands a few feet from Rhoda (who simply stands still). He pretends he doesn't see her. He holds his hand out as if feeling for her. He blubbers as he feels all around her but just an inch or so away from her body. These movements get more aggressive, turning into something akin to karate chops. He's obviously faking it but there's still real distress and anger in him. This is all happening during Gerbera and Cake-tin's conversation.)

Jimmy: Uhuhuh! aahh! (Incomprehensible, prelinguistic noises.)

Cake-tin: Was that the last of your Christmas shopping then?

Gerbera: You know I had all that done weeks ago. I told you I was going shopping for the new spa bathroom extension so that Brendan can work on it over the break. I've been to every fixture and fitting shop in town and I still can't find what I want. The shape will be right and then the colour will be wrong or they're out of stock.

Cake-tin: Nobody ever said shopping was easy. It will be well worth the trouble and increase the value of your assets by up to ten percent. Now Brendan's picking up Rhodadendron and Jimmy all right isn't he? He knows the time Greyhound — Great Going Australia, is getting in?

Gerbera: Yes they should be here anytime. Didn't Daddy come home to do the yard like he promised?

Cake-tin: Drink Habit Destroyed. Do you suffer through the curse of excessive drinking? Eucrazy has changed homes from misery and want to happiness again. Harmless, tasteless, can be given secretly or taken voluntarily. State which required. (Tight lipped.) He's downstairs getting a Four X.
Jimmy: Ahh! Ahh!

Gerbera: Oh no Mummy. The stupid ...

Rhoda: Stronger than God.

Jimmy :   And meaner than the Devil. (Whined out.)

Rhoda: It speaks. You Tarzan. Me Jane. (Poking him angrily and then tickling him trying to jolly him around as Theo arrives back in the kitchen.)

Jimmy: Ged out! Stop Rhoda. (Gets very pissed off but eventually laughs half-heartedly despite himself.)

Cake-tin: (Hears Theo coming.) Don't say a word. I'm sure he only does it to annoy us. Don't give him the satisfaction ...

Theo: (Enters holding a stubbie of beer.) I see the bludgers are here for tea again. (Goes to baby and coos.)

Gerbera: (Speaking petulantly as a child.) You know I'm here to see Rhodent and anyway I'm not staying for tea.

Theo: Getting all offended are we.

Rhoda: Your IQ and visual acuity seem to drop with your blood sugar level Jimmy. Are you having a petit mal episode or are you just a manipulative shit?

Jimmy: (Straightens up to his full height and gets very aggressive towards Rhoda. Acting as if he's only just controlling himself. They're in a stand-off.) I'm sick of you.

Rhoda: Oh! And I'm sick of you too boy.

Gerbera: (Chants childishly.) Daddy's a naughty boy. Daddy's a naughty boy. Doctor said no drinking.

Cake-tin: (Shaking her head and frowning, then sighs and looks resigned, martyred.)

Theo: Jesus! A man can't get a minute's peace with you lot.

Gerbera: Take off your coat. You look all flushed and hot. Why have you still got it on in this heat? Come on. (She goes to take it off.)

Theo: (Smirks, clutches his coat to himself vampishly.) No, no you brute. I'm a married man.

Gerbera: All right, all right. Keep your coat on then. Swelter for all I care. Mummy, Daddy's not taking his insulin?

Cake-tin: (Pretends to be oblivious — continually pretends to be unaware, disinterested, dull.) Just leave your father alone Gerbera. He's had a tiring day and if he wants to kill himself and spoil Christmas for everyone that's his business.

Theo: (Stands theatrically now that he's sure of an audience and removes his suit coat seductively. He hums 'Big Spender', revealing a good white executive shirt cut into strips on the arms. He drapes his coat over the chair back and sits again and continues drinking.)

Cake-tin: That's not the new one Marjorie bought you this morning is it?

Theo: (Looking satisfied. He's achieved what he wanted.) Never seen a 'tattered, disgusting Pelaco' before. One that 'a man should be ashamed to be seen wearing in public'. I thought it was about time you saw one.

Cake-tin: The idiotic creature. He put on the oldest good Pelaco he had
Theo: Not the newest bad Pelaco, note, but the oldest good Pelaco. Your mother has them ranged in the wardrobe from the newest best to the oldest worst.

Cake-tin: He had four important functions to attend today and he went to work in …

Theo: '… the most tattered, disgusting old Pelaco' I had. I was ashamed to be seen in public I can tell you. How the people cried out and wailed and berated myself and my good lady wife here in her absence for the disgraceful display … But luckily your mother rang my secretary and had her rush out on a mercy dash to Myers to buy a new one and then force the clothes from my body the way she loves to do anyway … oh it hurts Marjorie. Stop! Stop! Ooh! I like it.

Gerbera: (She's hypnotised by this 'static' but then pulls herself out of it.) You're ridiculous Daddy. I can't stand it.

Cake-tin: Get into the bedroom and change before Rhodadendron gets here Theodolite. So help me if you make trouble before she even arrives … I want this to be a very special Christmas. (Manhandling him around.)

Rhoda: We're both tired out Jimmy but please cut the crap. You know what's at stake here.

Jimmy: I wish you could be in my shoes for just one hour, for one day, Rhoda. Then you'd see some things.

Rhoda: (Mocks the way he 'pretends?' to be blind.) Daa daa I don't see nuthin. I'm a blinko. (Goes to take ghetto blaster to help him.) Sometimes Jimmy!

(Jimmy pulls his ghetto blaster away from her and turns the volume up and down maniacally. Perhaps a rap version of 'Old TI' is playing.)

Rhoda: Stop playing the fucking spaso … daa daa. (Mocking him.) It's exactly what people expect of you and you know it.

Jimmy: Just give up for once Rhoda.

Rhoda: One day I will and you know where you'll be.

Jimmy: I'll tell them you're a leso.

Rhoda: And that'll be curtains for you.

Jimmy: Hahaha! That got you! Hahaha!

Rhoda: (Tries to take ghetto blaster again and puts her arms around him.) Come on darling let me help you.

(Jimmy turns it up really loudly this time.)

Cake-tin: (Looks out of the window.) They're here. (Takes fish fingers out of the freezer.) Theodolite! (pushing him physically and quite brutally) Get into that bedroom ...

Theo: (As being manhandled out.) I think I'll put on my third newest oldest. Is that acceptable ... (Exits)

Gerbera: See Mummy, Rhodent's upsetting Daddy already.

Rhoda: Come on honey. You can have something to eat, a nice big bath and I'll rub your leg with Dencorub before we go to the hospital to see your mother.

Cake-tin: I've prayed for this Christmas. To be all together like this.

Gerbera: Here they are.

Cake-tin: Sparkle Shirley.

(Rhoda rings the doorbell which plays 'Rule Britannia'.)

Scene 2

(Rhoda is excited, happy to see Cake-tin but Cake-tin responds formally and awkwardly to her and to Jimmy. Audience sees for a moment how much Rhoda loves Cake-tin and how quickly she represses it and gets smart mouthed.

Cake-tin and Gerbera fixate on the didgeridoo.)

Rhoda: Hello Cake-tin. (Shyly hugging her.)

Cake-tin: Hello Rhodadendron. You look well. (Almost accusing and kissing her on the cheek.) Hello Jimmy. (Cake-tin and Gerbera speak to and treat Jimmy as if he's deaf, blind, retarded and a potentially dangerous maniac. They help him into chairs, out of rooms, put cutlery in his hands etc.)

Rhoda: Hello Gerbera. (Gerbera doesn't hide the fact she's not that pleased to see them.) And where's the baby.

Gerbera: She's asleep. (Physically throwing herself between Rhoda and the baby as if to shield her child.)

Jimmy: (He mimics the way they speak to him. He does this to be polite, as a put down and because he gives everyone what they want.) Hello Cake-tin, grandma. (Goes to kiss her. She steps back, steps forward again, with distaste, for him to kiss her. He drops the didgeridoo in the awkwardness. Picks it up and shakes Cake-tin's and Gerbera's hands.) Hello auntie, ah, Gerbera. Long time no see.

Gerbera: (Again spoken slowly and awkwardly, avoiding big words etc.) Hello Jimmy. You're a big boy now aren't you. Last time I saw you you must have been no bigger than my little boy Ash.

Jimmy: Yeah, I'm a man now.

Cake-tin: (Giggles slightly hysterically.)

Jimmy: (Embarrassed, afraid he's said something wrong. Trying to find somewhere to sit.) Well in a couple of years. Isn't that right Rhod?

Rhoda: Poor old man Jimmy goin' on eighteen, no wife, no kids, no 'ome. Poor old man Jimmy. (Jimmy and Rhoda laugh together at this long standing joke. She's relieved he's pulled himself together. Rhoda's still trying to jolly him along knowing how tense and fragile he is.)

Jimmy: (Hobbles around the room using his didgeridoo as a walking stick, mumbling and chewing his cud and speaking in a sort of whine. Does incredibly good impersonation of stereotype of 'poor old blackfella' and Uncle Tom that he's picked up from old films etc.) Poor old Jimmy. Me poor old blackfulla Kakatin (As in Kakadu. Puts arm on Cake-tin.) got no lubra, (Puts arm around Gerbera.), got no piccaninny, got no gunyah, got no nuthin', poor bugger me. Spare a bitabakkey for poor old Jackey Jackey. Me no Bogeyman missus. Just poor ole Tommy Tanna.

Rhoda: (Laughs)

(Cake-tin and Gerbera look horrified but Cake-tin is really freaked out. It stirs memories of her childhood horror of Kanakas on the sugar-cane farm where she grew up.)

Cake-tin: Where are Brendan and Ashmore?

Jimmy: (To Cake-tin.) They said they were going down to look at some baths? (With anger at Rhoda.) I wanted to go with them. She's brought me to the biggest oven in the world. I've lost my climatisation after all this time.

Cake-tin: (Looking with horror at Jimmy and then ignoring him.) Where are they Rhodadendron?

Rhoda: Jimmy told you.

Gerbera: (Screams.) He's taken Ash swimming? Where?

Rhoda: Out to Rabie Bay? Is that what he said Jimmy?

Jimmy: Um I can't remember.. exactly … if … (Afraid he's said the wrong thing. Figuring out who's top dog out of Cake-tin and Rhoda and where he should place his bets. We see him struggling to figure out what 'identity' etc. he should adopt in this situation.)

Rhoda: He said something about going out to Marble Bathroom Affects Galore at Rabi Bay?

Cake-tin: (To Gerbera.) And he didn't come in and get you. Oh isn't he thoughtless. He won't be back before 5.00 o'clock at least.

Gerbera: It's incredible. He's so stupid and Ash will be exhausted. Where has the fool gone now … if you'd bought me that Mobile I asked for for my birthday he'd only be a phone call away now but I never get anything I want … You know why he's gone out to Marble Bathroom Affects Galore? to look at fixtures and attachments without me? He's determined to use Prestige Design Award Winning, truly functional looking, easy maintenance, anti-vandal, childproof, washer-free unimix finger touch turn taps, as light and precise as your stereo tuner ...

Cake-tin: (With great pride.) When I was a young bride a tap was a tap and a bathtub came in any colour as long as it was Bon Ami now-my-bath-shines-like-new white.

Gerbera: ...the capstan or the lever, combining the authentic look of a bygone era ...

Rhoda: Welcome Jimmy. So nice to see you after all these years. Can I get you a cup of tea after your long journey?

Jimmy: Yes a cup of tea ud hit the old spot-a-roo.

Cake-tin: (Aside.) Yes, make yourself at home. I find it infuriating Gerbera that Brendan would ...

Jimmy: I wouldn't say no to a bit of a bite (Does it. Makes big, scarey open mouth to Gerbera and Cake-tin.) as well — caramel, marshmallow and strawberry jam slice, pink and white coconut ice, double custard kisses, vanilla imperial moments ... if that's OK Kakatin.

Cake-tin: You remember my full tins don't you Jimmy? (Opening cake tins.) Doesn't Rhodadendron ever bake?

Jimmy: No, only dry old Arnotts ...

Cake-tin: (Giggles. Slightly hysterical. Happy with his collusion.) He's hardly an Arnotts Living Picture Rhodadendron. (Holds up photo with rectangle cut out of it. Light shines through this rectangle.) Dear Sir, This is a photograph of my handsome State Ward Jimmy. As you can see he is in perfect health and fitness which I think is due largely to the good there must be in Arnotts Milk Arrowroot Biscuits as that is all I ever feed him on. Here, have what's left of Theodolite's Christmas cake from last year. And thank goodness its finished. Now we've just got the next batch to get through. (Savagely kicks the plastic garbage bin with the cake mix in it.)

Gerbera: Oh Mummy even Jimmy doesn't deserve Daddy's Christmas cake.

Cake-tin: (Takes old Bunnykins mug and plate out of the back of her cupboards for Jimmy.) We'll have a late lunch in a few minutes. We've been waiting … I've put some fish-fingers, you like them don't you? out to defrost … (She puts the plate in his hand and helps him to settle it on the table. Jimmy colludes with her. Acts dumb.)

Rhoda: He can do it himself Cake-tin. Jimmy!

Cake-tin: Best to be on the safe side. She's too hard on you isn't she Jimmy?

Jimmy: Meaner than the Devil.

Cake-tin: (Delighted with Jimmy's double collusion with her.) Isn't he a character?

Rhoda: No! Where's Theo? Still at work?

Cake-tin: He's in the bedroom getting out of his workclothes. He came home early to be here when you arrived. He'll be out in a minute.

Rhoda: Really! Did he? (Exits to find him.) Theo! Oh Theo! I'm back! (Does 'monster'.)

Cake-tin: (Attempting to block Rhoda leaving.) Your tea will get cold.

(Cake-tin and Gerbera are left alone in the room with Jimmy where they look decidedly uncomfortable while they watch him eat.)

Jimmy: (Sniffs the air.) Fee. Fi. Foo. Fumm. I smell the blood of …

Cake-tin: (Thrusts cake tins at him.)

Jimmy: (He goes to take out a cake but finds photos instead. Takes one out.) Hey! This is me.

Cake-tin: Doesn't she ever do a Saturday bake Jimmy?

Jimmy: It's just hamburgers, fish and chips, hamburgers, fish and chips …

Cake-tin: (To Gerbera.) When a woman doesn't have children …

Jimmy: (Does a loud, sudden blow on his didgeridoo. The two women jump in fright.) Just making sure it didn't crack when I dropped it. (Continues playing softly.)

Cake-tin: Rhodadendron! Theodolite! Rhodadendron! Your tea's getting cold.

Gerbera: Rhodent! Theo!

Cake-tin: (She's been consulting her Women's Weekly Christmas Countdown Chart) Turkey stuffing …Theodolite! Theodolite!

(Cake-tin's and Gerbera's speech are simultaneous.)

Gerbera: (Looking through a mountain of brochures on spabathrooms, vanities, washbasins.) Australia's only truly dripless tap …

Cake-tin: (Almost talking to herself.) Noone could have loved you kids more than I did when you were little.

Gerbera: … gooseneck showerset with pulsating hand-held shower rose attachment in the Captain Cook Series … (Gerbera narcotises herself with 'static' as they all do.)

Cake-tin: Rhodadendron chewing her way through the bars of her cot. What a child! And she hadn't even cut her first milk teeth.

Gerbera: … available in 23 carat Gold Plate with a choice of Botany Bay or Endeavour handle styles …

Cake-tin: And how hard Gerbera was to potty train. Now that's one thing I'll say about Rhodadendron she seemed to potty train herself but Gerbera … I'd say 'ooh poo who's that dirty, disgusting, smell. That's not my dear little Gerbera. No! not that stinking, foul-smelling creature'.

Gerbera: … Fowler's sanitaryware — not just to maintain that uncluttered appearance but to ensure toilet hygiene at its ultimate with its state-of-the-art computer controlled waterconscious cistern technology that incorporates a dual flush valve for full or half flush at consumer discretion complete with shock absorber to overcome waterhammer …

Cake-tin: It was silly I suppose, and I've never told anyone this, but you know why I gave you such beautiful names, I thought, now don't laugh, but I thought the best that could happen to you would be to marry Lords and so I imagined how lovely Lady Gerbera or Lady Rhodadendron ...

Jimmy: (Laughs into didgeridoo or spits cake everywhere.)

Cake-tin: Rhodadendron! Theodolite!

Gerbera: ...hob sink set, soap holder, toilet roll holder, toothbrush holder, single and double heated-to-blood-temperature towel rail sanitary seat and bidet, washer and handtowel rail, classic one-piece vanity with generous bowl and built-in mirror.

(Theo and Rhoda enter. They are obviously happy to see each other. During Theo's conversation with Jimmy Gerbera and Cake-tin continue talking at cross purposes about spabaths and Christmas food)

Theo: (Entering. Ignores Jimmy at first.) Cake-tin! What have you done with the car keys? (Looking in the most ridiculous places.)

Cake-tin: You had them last.

Theo: Shit that's all I need.

Cake-tin: Theodolite! I begged you. A swear-free zone ... (Cake-tin also looks for keys in ever more bizarre places.)

Theo: (Acknowledges Jimmy now. Happy to see him, not wanting to hurt him but awkward and rough in his shyness, he starts hitting him playfully. He tries to drag Rhoda and Jimmy into 'static'.) This isn't Jimmy. (Slight punch on the shoulder.) No, Jimmy's this big and he's not nearly as handsome and he's a lot darker.

Gerbera: (Overlaps with Theo and Cake-tin.) ... the ultimate suite where nothing has been compromised ... close coupled pan and cistern ... eliminate the need for ugly flush pipes ... you won't see an outlet either because it's concealed ... with the versatility of today's easy care technology ...

Cake-tin: (Looking for keys.) We've arranged to take you for a drive to see Gerbera's new house ...

Rhoda: Jimmy's mother's in Intensive Care!

Theo: This must be someone else you've brought along to pretend to be Jimmy. What have you done with Jimmy? (Smacking Jimmy around a bit more. Getting quite hard.)

Cake-tin: … goodness she and Brendan have made it beautiful. Your sister's turned into quite a little homemaker. Hasn't she Theodolite?

Jimmy: (Laughing a bit hesitantly.) It's me Theo, granddad. It's little Jimmy that's grown up. I'm almost seventeen now. Don't hit me.

Rhoda: I'm not going looking at bloody houses.

Gerbera: Well thanks a lot. I've been really looking forward to showing you over the house and you just slap me in the face for my trouble as usual.

Rhoda: For Christ's sake Gerbera.

Thoe: Hey! hey! No need to bloody blaspheme … Here's Jimmy going to meet his family for the first time. You'd think you'd be worrying about that Rhoda. It's a big day for you isn't it Jimmy?

Jimmy: Yes, I'm a bit …

Theo: And listen to how well he talks. I'll make you tell me where dear little Jimmy is. You're an impostor. I'll make you squeal. (Knocking him even harder on the head and shoulders and arms).

Cake-tin: They built on acreage out there at Koala Downs, quasi-Georgian style architect designed but with lots of quaint value-added touches of their own. She has some lovely decorative ideas and it's a perfect house for cleaning.

Rhoda: We're going to the hospital.

Cake-tin: Why don't you wait until tomorrow darling, when you're both fresher?

Jimmy: (Fighting back the tears. Trying to go along with the joke, be a man.) No, Granddad, it's me. It is little Jimmy, stop.

Rhoda: (She's panicking here. She knows Jimmy's so on edge.) Come on Theo. He's not used to this bear-does-it-with-a-slap sort of thing.

Cake-tin: Well how long do you think you'll be. We'll go for a drive and we can pick you up and take you out to see the house afterwards.

Theo: Bringing up a wimp are you? Bringing you up as a bit of a poof is she? Come on put up your dykes Jimmy. If you don't learn to defend yourself you'll get done like a dinner. I taught all my kids to defend themselves if nothing else. Only sooks cry Jimmy.

Cake-tin: Or we can go for a drive via the hospital and drop Jimmy on the way.

Rhoda: Cake-tin I'm staying with him.

Cake-tin: I suppose you haven't considered that Jimmy might rather be alone with them have you? And anyway they might be hostile. White foster parents aren't exactly flavour of the month if the media's to be believed.

Rhoda: It's all been worked out.

Cake-tin: Yes, and with no consideration for or consultation with your natural family naturally.

Rhoda: For God's sake …

Theo: You've been warned.

Rhoda: (Winces. A moment's reversion to childhood. Goes into the cringeing monster mode for a moment. Then recovers herself slightly and stands up to him.) I'd have thought, with the way you go on and on in that interminably maudlin way about the sacred damn Family you might have understood …

Theo: (Theo pushes over what he's been looking behind. Maybe the fridge or some such. He's really aggressive.) What would you know you bloody smart-arsed, yuppie, two-bit, know-it-all, would-be, half-baked do-gooder.

Cake-tin: Now look what you've done.

Theo: You come here and upset your mother. (He's still been hitting Jimmy around.)

Jimmy: (Punches Theo a solid one in the face. Knocks him to the floor then sits on him crying.)

Theo: Jesus!

Jimmy: Now will you stop or will I have to stop you. I told you to stop. I'm sorry Theo, granddad, (This granddad, grandma, auntie is always said hesitantly because he doesn't quite know the relationship he's allowed and he's trying to normalise it.) But you made me.

Cake-tin: (Screaming.) My god, he's gone mad. He's out of control. He's gone native. He's reverting. I said it would happen. Help! Help! You should never have taken him off his medication. Rhodadendron! do something. Your father's a sick man. He'll kill him. Gerbera dial the triple O number.

(Jimmy accidentally upsets the mince tarts on the bench in the scuffle.)

Cake-tin: Oh my mince tarts. Jimmy you've ruined them. (Cake-tin forgets about Theo's plight to pick up tarts and put them out of harm's way. She goes to her Countdown Chart.) Now he's put me all out of sequence.

Scene 3

(Later that day. Gerbera sitting alone in kitchen. Rhoda enters dressed for going to the hospital to meet Jimmy's family. Gerbera drops baby talk.)

Gerbera: Things must be pretty crook for you to come back here Rhodent.

Rhoda: You didn't ring me last October as usual. Have you given up on the idea of Uni?

Gerbera: That's it, the only time I ever ask for help from you, and you throw it back in my face first chance you get. What do you think? Two kids and another one on the way!

Rhoda: You could. Brendan would help you. Cake-tin and Theo would too.

Gerbera: (Sings.) On the good ship Lollypop …You think you're so bloody smart Rhodent but you just live in a different Fantasyland to Mummy that's all. Why did you come back?

Rhoda: Things with Jimmy are desperate Gerbera …

Gerbera: Don't you think I've been desperate? Stuck here alone with them all these years! You think parading around with that sick boy hides what you really are? I don't think you can even hide it from yourself anymore.

Rhoda: He's always running away. He …

Gerbera: Charity begins at home Rhodent.

Rhoda: Whenever there's a knock on the door I think it's the social workers to take him away because they've found out about Ruth and I. Every time the phone rings I think it's the police to say he's dead in custody.

Gerbera: Why don't you contact the Authorities, that's what they're for?

Rhoda: Do you know what the difference between a social worker and a pit bull terrier is Gerbera? It's easier to get your baby back from a pit bull. (Mimics social worker.) Ah! I see the problem. You filled in form 21A when you should have filled in form 21D. I'm sorry, you've been put through to the wrong department. Unfortunately you've slipped through a loophole in the welfare net. And Jimmy's happy free-falling through the holes Gerbera.

Gerbera: (Chants childishly.) It's only the struggle that gets you into trouble.

Rhoda: I can't stand watching him.

Gerbera: It's more embarrassing watching someone struggling.
Rhoda: But I can't stop Gerbera. I keep thinking if I make just that one phone call to the right person, if I could only find the right agency, the right program, the right school, the right doctor …

Gerbera: We're all just scuttling rodents Rhodent, scuttling back and forth from one scratched out hole in the dirt to the next, spooked by light or movement, using each other to survive. You can never come back Rhodent.

Rhoda: I've got to get Jimmy and I back over some line someone else, someone we don't know, has drawn in some sand somewhere. I feel like I'm slipping down a mountain of gravel. What do you do when everything you do makes things worse? Most days I hardly dare move.

Gerbera: God helps those who help themselves.

(Cake-tin's been eavesdropping but enters now in petticoat, holding a dress which she begins to iron. Theo limps in behind her. He is in bermuda shorts and long socks that show how swollen and inflamed his leg is. He holds a wet washer to his face where Jimmy hit him. He tastes his cake mix.)

Theo: Gee that's blooming tasty. Just a drop more. (Pours in a large amount of brandy from a ridiculous bottle in the shape of the *Endeavour* which plays 'Botany Bay' when he pours.) Ratio to ratio. (He takes a swig.)

(Theo exits.)

Gerbera: And don't leave the seat up Daddy.

Cake-tin: Oh come on Gerbera, leave him alone.

Gerbera: But Mummy, poo! Yuck! (To Rhoda.) He's going to check his wee wee's.

Cake-tin: The diabetes is getting a real hold on him Rhodadendron. He'll be retiring next year.

Rhoda: God what will he do with himself then? Are you going to travel like you always said you would?

Cake-tin: Well yes actually we do have plans. Now don't laugh at me but all my life I've had this dream of spending a real white Christmas in England ...

Rhoda: (Hums 'When you wish upon a star' as Cake-tin speaks.)

Cake-tin: Renting a little thatched cottage just like the ones you see on Christmas cards with holly and ivy over the door and a big log fire burning. Drinking mulled wine and real lump-sum superpayout plum pudding with real threepences and sixpences in it. You'll laugh but your father will be getting his sugar-plum super payout, and there's the cane farm money Pop left me and I thought we might take the whole family...

Gerbera: Fantasyland, the happiest kingdom of them all.

Rhoda: ... and the water so frozen in the pipes that they had nothing with which to wash away the blood of battle. Can I bring Jimmy and Ruth?

Cake-tin: (To Rhoda.) Why do you have to spoil everything with that wicked tongue of yours?

Rhoda: Nothing wrong with this tongue Mummy, it's got me into some rather nice places.

Gerbera: Oh God you're off.

Cake-tin: What do you mean Rhodadendron?

Gerbera: Just drop it Mummy.
Cake-tin: No, Gerbera, I want to know what she means.

(Rhoda and Gerbera, despite themselves, laugh. Cake-tin automatically reacts to this by shoving the hot iron at Rhoda. Theo enters with a comb and hair spray and sits in front of Cake-tin who automatically does his hair.)

Cake-tin: I know you think I'm ignorant and ridiculous but everyone's entitled to at least dream about things that would make them happy.

(Jimmy enters. He's dressed up to see his family at the hospital.)

Theo: He should thank God he's out. Thursday Island!

Jimmy: Hey! that's where I'm from … I think … Rhoda?

Theo: Broken Bottle Island! — in the street, on the beach, in the water … (Getting upset as he remembers his youthful attachment to the place during the war.) … broken bottles and VD (the TI handshake). But sufficient unto the day is the evil thereof.

Cake-tin: Your father prefers not to talk about his war-time experiences Rhodadendron. I think we should respect his wishes on that point. (To Rhoda.) Are you sure it's a good thing. Do you have any idea what they're like.

Rhoda: Jimmy was speaking Cake-tin.

Cake-tin: Yes and so was I.

Theo: Give the lad a chance to talk will you woman. Go on son.

Jimmy: Well, Theo I'm a bit scared but I've talked to them all on the phone and they're excited to see me …

Theo: (Looking for the car keys.) Every bloody time! Go on son …
Jimmy: … but Mum's, that is my real Mum, sorry Rhoda …

Theo: If you'd just put them back in same place every time woman.

Rhoda: That's OK Jimmy, she is your Mum.

Jimmy: Well, Mum's pretty crook and so we're going to the hospital … this afternoon aren't we Rhod?

Theo: But no, that would be too flamin' much to expect.

(Theo, in his search for the keys in ever more ridiculous places, finally knocks something over and improbably finds the keys behind it.)

Theo: (Beckons to Rhoda to look.) You don't have any idea what I have to put up with here day in day out. Cake-tin! Oh! Cake-tin.

Cake-tin: How on earth …! You're not going to blame me when Rhodadendron's in the house?

Rhoda: Ready Jimmy.

Jimmy: As I'll ever be Lady Rhodendron.

(All stand to leave and exit.)

Scene 4

(That evening. Rhoda sitting alone in kitchen. Jimmy enters.)

Jimmy: (Barechested and carrying a bright tropical shirt and a country and western shirt.) What do you reckon Rhod, the Hawaiian one or will I go up country?

Rhoda: Country ah reckon pardner. This one's more barbecue territory isn't it?

Jimmy: (Combing hair, gives coconut oil to Rhoda who rubs it into his hair.) So OK I'll keep the colourful one for daytime. Man I love the smell of this coconut oil Mum gave me yesterday. Man are we going to have a night tonight. Yee ha! Leave off. I can handle it. I'm not a baby.

Rhoda: You'll always be in nappies to me baby.

Jimmy: Ged out! Jesus! I'll start shitting in them again that might wake you up. Between you and Dennis and them … They almost held my you-know-what and pointed it in the toilet for me.

Rhoda: (Taking out money.) Now, don't let them pay for everything. Buy the drinks whatever. Here's fifty bucks.(Shows him the difference in size.) Three tens. See they're smaller. And a twenty. It's the big one.

Jimmy: (Squashes them up aggressively and stuffs them in his wallet. One rips or they spill everywhere because they're the new plastic notes.)

Rhoda: Great, that's all we need. And Jimmy, tell your family who I am. At the moment they think I'm a bloody social worker or something.

Jimmy: What's to tell? You only got me when my tribe threw me out because I was handicapped. You stole me. (Genuinely confused.) You saw the TV programme.

Rhoda: Jimmy we've been over and over this. Not tonight hey. (Putting her arms around him.) You look just great. I'm really proud of the way you're handling all this.

Jimmy: (Mocking Theo and Cake-tin. Speaking slowly, patronising.) Hello little Jimmy. Haven't you grown into a great big ugly black bastard...

Rhoda: (Mocks the 'retarded' way Jimmy acts around them.) Dadada. But you buy into it totally Jimmy. Dadadada. Why do you do it Jimmy? Why? Letting Gerbera lead you around as if you're blind, letting Cake-tin put your knife and fork in your hands. You just become what everyone wants. Do you know you're doing it Jimmy?

Jimmy: (Starting to get aggressive. Turning 'monster'.) You're confusing my screens. I just want to go to be free in the bush. Back to yarn with my people who have lost their freedom, freedom of choice, who you stole me from. Not here making my screens go wobbly. Away from the noise and pollution. I want to eat bushman's tuckerbag and sit under the shade of a Cool Bar tree and play my didgeridoo and listen to the sound of the animals, and the water and the wind in the trees ...

Rhoda: (Mocks him.) ... listen to the sound of the animals, and the water and the wind in the trees ...

Jimmy: ... that's what makes my screens clear up.

Rhoda: For one thing you're not an Aboriginal you're an Islander! You've got to stop Jimmy.

(Sounds of Cake-tin, Theo and Gerbera arriving. Jimmy puts on shirt.)

Rhoda: (Aware that it's not the right time and trying to keep him calm.) OK! Keep your shirt on! I know we shouldn't be here Jimmy but I really thought this family reunion business might be contagious.

(They enter as Jimmy does unspoken sign of Rhoda always going for bait. Cake-tin, Theo and Gerbera are laden down with 'showbags ' from spa-bathroom shops. They contain more brochures, samples of porcelain, taps etc.)

Rhoda: Yeah! Yeah! I know. But ...

Gerbera: (Been speaking to Cake-tin in this 'static' for some time.) ... I liked the shape. It wasn't quite kidney and it wasn't quite heart but I bet they won't have it in the willow-pattern blue, even egg-shell blue would do, that I want. (Sits down and starts going through 'showbags'.) What do you think of this one Mummy?

(Cake-tin has painfully taken her shoes off and begins cutting her corns, pumicing calluses, clipping toe nails etc. using an array of surgical looking paraphernalia.)

Theo: (To Jimmy.) Gee! You scrub up well lad, what's the occasion?

Gerbera: Daddy, do you like this?

Jimmy: The bros are taking me out for tea, man, all five of us back together again. I can't believe it.

Theo: So how did it go at the hospital?

Jimmy: (He gets emotional but keeps it together. Rhoda comforts him or pats him. Sometimes he'll accept and need this; at other times he shrugs her off angrily.) It was unreal man. I've got four brothers and three sisters. I would have had five more but they died. I'm lucky number thirteen. That's what Mum said. And heaps and heaps of cousins and nieces and nephews. I've always been an only child until now, hey Rhoda? Man am I looking forward to seeing them up north next Christmas. Mum said they'll put on a cupmarie for me. She's got what you've got, diabetics. She says it's because she was a cook, a real good cook, in the Island and she liked her own cooking too much. (Laughing.) She's had toes off and everything. Have you had toes off?

Cake-tin: Of all the cheek ...

Jimmy: (Very upset.) Mum, she's very, very sick and ...

Gerbera: I've found it! This is it! Look Mummy, Daddy! A matching willow pattern spa, bathtub, shower recess, vanity, bidet and toilet bowl. It's perfect.
Cake-tin: Oh darling! I'm so happy for you.

(PAUSE)

Rhoda: Come on Jimmy let's go outside and water the plants.

Cake-tin: I've been planting a few natives lately and they're starting to do so well.

Jimmy: Are you going to plant me then? She wants lots of little Jimmy-fruit. That's not the way I make babies Kakatin, I have a different method. (Uses didgeridoo to simulate orgasm sounds.) Rhoda, she's going to plant me. Stop her. Stop her Rhoda. (Uses didgeridoo sounds as 'distress'.)

Cake-tin: (Giggles nervously.) It's nice to see you happy Jimmy. Do you ever paint anymore Rhodadendron? We've got these new wheelie-bin affairs. I've got ours tucked in amongst the climbing geraniums but I thought you might paint some pink chrysanthemums or climbing tea roses on it so it more or less blends. Oh and here take these ... (Handing her a huge pair of scissors.) ... to chop the grasshoppers in half. (Rhoda experiences a moment of remembered horror.) They're such a size this summer. (Showing them as ridiculously long.)

Rhoda: (Holding scissors up as weapons.) Come on Jimmy. (Both make a farce scene of this. Rhoda gives Jimmy the scissors and he advances like 'Aboriginal hunter'.)

Jimmy: Woman follow hunter. Ole man Jimmy catchem nice fat grasshopper. Woman light em fire. We hold big fella walkabout-corroboree-poorbuggarme-jamboree-cupmarie-barramundi-uluru-kangaroo-didgeridoo-Mabo-kanaka-bega-cheese. (Blows didgeridoo as hunting horn.)

Cake-tin: (Terrified.) There's a total fire ban this week. If you want to light a fire you'll have to get your father to light the Webber. (To Theo, Gerbera.) He's reverting. I told you. He's got to be put back on his medication. He's reverting.

(Rhoda does silly vicious/aggressive dance with scissors and hose. Jimmy plays his didgeridoo menacingly as the light of sunset fades and the garish garden lights are turned on revealing the weird stuff that passes for 'normal' in suburbia but is really quite surreal.)

(A taxi honks.)

Jimmy: That's them! That's the taxi. Bye Mum, Rhod. See ya when I see ya.

Rhoda: (Calls after him.) Don't forget to tell them who I am.

Jimmy: Yeah I will if I ever get a word in with that bunch of yappers. Two things Islanders can do no worries is yarn and scoff our faces. Bye.

(Jimmy exits. Rhoda stands watching in the garden.)

(There is a short Interval at this point. During the Interval Cake-tin and Theo, in their olde worlde costumes, mingle with the audience in the foyer as if they are at the Royal Historical Society function alluded to in Act 2, Scene 1.)

Kathleen Mary Fallon

What potential hazards of racism and ethnocentricity should a white Western writer be aware of when she is writing about Black non-Western characters? Is it possible to write 'interracial' texts given these problems? Consider these questions specifically in relation to the construction of my text for performance, 'Three Boongs in the Kitchen'.

> 'BOONG: An insulting, cruel term used by Europeans for Aborigines. Origin uncertain, though there is a white joke definition that it is the sound an Aborigine makes bouncing off the hood of your car' (Webb 1989: 48).

> '… the early characterisation of non-Europeans in the pre-capitalist era, and proceeding to review the changing perceptions that accompanied the growth of merchant and industrial capital. The emergence of the idea 'race' marks an important transition, followed later by the ascription of this idea with a biological content and by the 'scientific' legitimation of a biological hierarchy.' (Miles 1989:2).

> 'The concept of the 'author' as a free creative source of the meaning of a book belongs to the legal and educational forms of the liberal humanist discourse that emerged in the late eighteenth and early nineteenth centuries …' (Macdonell 1986:3).

> 'The *author* is a modern character, no doubt produced by our society as it emerged from the Middle Ages, inflected by English empiricism, French rationalism, and the personal faith of the Reformation …' (Barthes 1986: 49).

> '… for I am proposing that theatre is not merely a means by which social behavior is engineered, it is the *site* of violence, the locus of theatre's emergence as myth, law, religion, economy, gender, class, or race, either in the theatre, or in culture as a theatricality that paradoxically precedes culture.' (Kubiak 1991: 4).

To write against this liberal humanist tradition which has created anthropology

— 'the science of cultural evolution' an 'allochronic discourse' (Fabian 1983:143), a science (no quotation marks) of racial hygiene, Orientalism, the Other, the conditions for racism and racism itself, the scriptor of a text must be aware of the relevant historical, political, economic forces, of the cultural constructs, of the positioning of her text within an intertextuality. Said shows the hegemony of prevailing doxology in his discussion of European writers on the Orient such as Flaubert, Lamartine, Chateaubriand. It is a cautionary tale for any writer the way Said reveals how these writers' poetics and aesthetics were more structured, more politicised and circumscribed than they were aware of or would have cared to admit. And, on a strategic note if a scriptor, a writer, is not to reproduce social realist and subjective modernist texts which are of limited effectiveness, how should she proceed? In practical terms, if you don't believe the humanist notion that revealing the Truth about a situation makes the audience, the reader, aware, change, become activated what are the options? How do you effectively engage in the political and ideological struggle around the concept of racism, 'the beast that is to be vanquished' (Miles 1989:5) when, 'if the analysis is wrong, then it is likely that the political strategy will not achieve the intended objectives' (Miles 1989:5), or as Hindess and Hirst say, 'Theories are not a substitute for concrete analysis. They are the tools that make it possible' (Hindess and Hirst 1975:9). I think of what Barthes says about how a 'new discourse can only emerge as the *paradox* which goes against … the surrounding or preceding *doxa*, can only see the day as difference, distinction, working loose *against* what sticks to it.' (Barthes 1977:200). Real tools for breaking into the closed circle of meaning presented by other cultures have been created in the work of writers such as Said on Orientalism, Fabian on Time as an ideologically constructed instrument of power, Anderson's showing nationality and nation-ness as cultural artefacts, Renata Rosaldo on imperialist nostalgia, Clifford on critical ethnography.

Writers and theorists of this kind show the depth of political embeddedness in our most 'innocent' seeming assumptions, beliefs, ideas. We can gain some comprehension of the massive excavations/deconstructions which are required to avoid unconscious solipsism, well-meaning humanism, 'apolitical' academic or literary pursuits. It is possible to find an intertextual framework to work 'against' in these texts which, themselves, work 'against' the liberal humanist hegemonic tradition.

When we ask what race is 'we obtain completely divergent subdivisions of the human species according to whether we base our description of the 'races' on an analysis of their epiderms or their blood types, their genetic heritages or their bone structures. For contemporary biology, the concept of 'race' is therefore completely useless' (Todorov 1986:171). 'Race,' then, is a cultural construct. According to Miles race is socially imagined through processes of signification and representation and, in his definition of racism, in which he attempts to deflate the concept to an effective and useful tool, he says that racism refers exclusively to an ideological phenomenon, a particular form of (evaluative) representation, a specific instance of a wider (descriptive) process of racialisation. So that many instances of what might be referred to sloppily as racism are in fact racialisations. If, then, we conceptualise racism as a process of signification, a space for textual intervention is established.

Clastres, in his savage analysis, demonstrates the enormity of the implications of racism, ethnocentrism and ethnocide. According to Clastres, ethnocentrism is the 'attitude of measuring differences by the yardstick of one's own culture' (Clastres 1982:53). Not such an evil phenomenon until he expands. 'Yet the fact remains that even if all cultures are ethnocentric, only the West is ethnocidal' (Clastres 1982:54). The 'spirit of ethnocide is the ethics of humanism.' He goes on to demonstrate that the West is ethnocidal because it is ethnocentric and ethnocentrism is immanent in culture itself. The development of the State requires ethnocide and only the West is limitlessly ethnocidal because its system of economic production (capitalism) is a space of the unlimited — 'an infinite space in permanently forward flight' (Clastres 1982:57). Central to Clastres's analysis is that he sees, at the heart of the State (which comes about by the suppression of difference) 'the instinct and taste for the identical and the One' (Clastres 1982:55) that is, there is no place for the Other except as an imagined Self. The Other must therefore become a site of study and analysis.

'We love over-emphasizing our little differences, our hatreds, and that is wrong. If humanity is to be saved, we must focus on our affinities, the points of contact with all other human beings; by all means we must avoid accentuating our differences' (Borges 1984:12). Sounds all very well and good but, surely, we must give place to these differences, 'recognise the truly different ... not as the imaginary Other with its history of imagery in the Western tradition' (Longxi 198 8:130). Why be fearful of these differences? How can we respect, celebrate these differences, acknowledge the Other's specificity, voice, cultural difference without subsuming, exploiting, appropriating? Longxi quotes Spinoza's words, 'Every individual thing, or everything which is finite and has a conditioned existence, cannot exist or be conditioned to act, unless it be conditioned for existence and action by a cause other than itself.' Longxi adds, 'one of the elementary principles of logic that postulates that the Self is invariably correlated with the Other, and that nothing can be determined by and in itself except by being differentiated from what it is not' (Longxi 1988:113) and this logic is embedded, as Saussure shows, in our language itself, in the idea that 'language is a system of terms that define each other in mutual difference'. Of course it's a massive and necessary job for philosophy to deconstruct these systems of binary opposition which can only produce 'natural', polarised conceptualisations. In conceiving the Other, we must move out of the circularity described in Heidegger's hermeneutic theory where fore-structures of understanding trap us in a solipsistic ethnocentricism. Longxi says 'our language largely determines the way we can talk about the Other' but 'the Other has its own voice and can assert its own truth against various misconceptions' (Longxi 1988:129) — '… to know the Other is a process of learning and self-cultivation, which is neither projecting the Self onto the Other nor erasing the Self with what belongs to the Other' (Longxi 1988:131).

Not to be forgotten in the linguistic, hermeneutic and philosophical realms, is that at the basis of the construction of this imaginary Other, is the fact that the relationship of imperialism is a relationship between weak and strong partners. 'Ideally, all cultures should be wes and theys to each other in turn. Politics, however, intrudes.' (Boon 1982:26). I will come back to this issue of antagonistic relations later.

The present social/cultural context in which I am writing my play/theatre piece, 'Three Boongs in the Kitchen', is, to some extent summed up by Davila when he says, 'The Market, the Museum and the State reward the colonial issue only so far as it contributes to the national 'story' or favours those items most likely to act as 'supplements for the soul'.' (Davila 1987:54). Recognition of the coevality of Aboriginal culture is essential when a writer works within a social context which has a desire to contain Aboriginality in culture gardens (and it can happen on many levels of subtlety). A desire for Aboriginal culture to be consumed or displayed as part of white Australia's cultural heritage (and even as part of white Australian rights of heritage). My piece is a black comedy set in a white middle-class kitchen burdened with excessive decoration, knick-knacks and oversized white-goods. Outside the kitchen, as part of the set, a fecund subtropical garden suppurates. Within this kitchen a daughter and her adoptive Thursday Islander teenage son arrive from interstate after many years. They have returned so that the son can be reunited with his mother, who is dying, and his 'natural' T.I. family. The violence (including racism) of this dysfunctional white family (representative of the white imagined nation) towards each other, the three 'boongs' (the son and two of his relatives) who they find in their kitchen late one night, is explored and exploded. This exploration is done not simply for the sake of exposing the violence and racism but as a strategy to confront the audience's denial mechanisms, with the outcome being, hopefully, some degree of honesty in which some sense of the dearth of communication between Blacks and whites in Australian society is recognised. 'If racism brutalises and dehumanises its object, it also brutalises and dehumanises those who articulate it' (Miles 1989:10). I did not want to write some egalitarian fairy tale of misunderstanding and final acceptance, as issue-laden (and leaden) as an episode of *A Country Practice* or *G.P.* I want my intentions to be signalled by the use of the word 'boong' in the title.

The strategic deployment of the blatantly racist and offensive term 'boong' in the title should be seen, in context of the performance itself, as a savage irony (in the same vein as Lenny Bruce's 'Nigger lipped' routine or Swift's solution to the 'Irish Problem': breeding Irish babies as fresh meat for the tables of their English lords) that ricochets, rebounds, resounds back upon the user/abuser and a white liberal audience self-satisfied in its 'non-racism'. Its double function being its effect on a black audience which daily experiences racism operating in many ways it is told, within culture (white, hegemonic), that it does not. (Who in this society admits to being, or believes they are, racist?).

I want to use the word 'boong' as an explosive device in the white suburban kitchen, in the white bourgeois theatre space. I want a black audience to see the abuse turn back onto the abuser. I am not speaking as an apologist or obscurantist for my white society but from the only position I can speak, from the position of 'privilege', as part of it. I do not claim to write for the Blacks in this piece, I claim only to write from my perspective. There is no single Truth about racism, truth is relative and negotiated. I'm not filling the silence, verbalising the muteness of people who need me to speak for them, to tell their story for them. I am defining the parameters of a constructed silence, a culturally constructed silence constructed by a 'non-racist' 'polite' society which believes it is non-racist because it would never use (well at least not write) words like 'boong', but still a society where, in some contexts, racist words, jibes, jokes are used freely. I want to create a new discursive space; construct another discursive horizon. I want to use the word as an explosive device to open the enclosed space within which racism is practiced, pushing the parameters of the status quo, of those who are and those who are 'not racist'. Is it as simple as those who do use and those who do not use, this type of language? I'm not trying in the performance to achieve an harmonious, intercommunal relations by explication — this is a manifestly unproductive strategy. 'Discourse is social. The statement made, the words used and the meanings of the words used, depends on where and against what the statement is made ...' (Macdonell 1986:1).

'We are so busy battling stereotypes in the description of Others that we end up refusing these Others any specificity at all' (Todorov 1986:174).

I have thought long and hard about the ramifications of using the word 'boong' and the following are some of the points I have considered.

Does Aboriginal culture have a racism analogous to white racism? Does the use of the word 'gubba', for instance, carry the same insulting racist overtones? I would say not. Anderson makes the point that 'it is remarkable how little that dubious entity known as 'reverse racism' manifested itself in the anticolonial movements. ... I have never heard of an abusive argot word in Indonesian or Javanese for either 'Dutch' or 'white' ... It is possible that this innocence of racist argots is true primarily of colonised populations. Blacks in America — and surely elsewhere — have developed a varied counter-vocabulary (honkies, ofays, etc.)' (Anderson 1983:139). Perhaps one reason 'gubba' doesn't have the same derogatory power as 'boong' is that it was not a word backed up by centuries of oppression and exploitation. As a verbalisation it leaves no physical trace but is a sign for the accumulated physical traces of oppression.

No matter what my intent, as an individual writer, the word still has the impact of a racist term which may well offend many Aboriginal and Islander people but I would argue that it is obviously not coming out of a racist discourse such as Miles outlines. As the performance piece proceeds the fact that it is not coming out of the ideology of racism becomes clear. So, hopefully, the question of what discourse it is coming out of will then be raised for the audience. Also, the single fact of using the word 'boong' obviates the fact that it is not coming out of a liberal humanist ideology either. I am trying to construct and create a performative discourse, not a descriptive text, a text which performs racism/violence/stupidity/ denial /abuse — does not describe or discuss it. This objective also embraces the words themselves. 'Language, signs, do not stand outside reality and action having a pure transparent, informative or communicative function. All language has an illocutionary force — something happens in the very saying' (Curnick 1991:18).

In wanting to explore liberalism and righteousness I am obviously breaking a bourgeois code of decency, conventions of proper public discourse in a society that baulks at the use of an insulting word. It is, however, a society that doesn't baulk enough to act effectively when confronted with a history (and present) of genocide, genocidal policies, black deaths in custody, black deaths out of custody, chronic suicide in the form of death-wish drinking, drug abuse, self-mutilation and community violence and the effects of chronic and long-term poverty. I'm using the word to signal a deeper obscenity.

It also raises the question of who can use a word. I am considering this in the light of struggles around words like 'dyke' or 'faggot' by the lesbian and gay community, of words like 'ladies' and 'girls' by feminists or 'wogs' by the *Wogs out of Work* performers. Is it only the recipients of these abusive words who have a right to use them and to redefine them or, if you happen to belong to the set who are the main users of offensive words, are you politically obliged to exile these words from your vocabulary and leave them to those in your set who are 'genuine' users? Are these offensive words then off-limits to all but the users and perhaps the recipients if they choose to attempt to defuse or redefine them? Is it possible to get 'permission' from the appropriate community to use them (in the way Lenny Bruce got 'permission' from Black Americans to do his 'Nigger lipped' routine)? The idea of getting 'permission' in a relatively formal way from Aborigines and Islanders presupposes an homogeneous, monovocal community which the Aboriginal and Islander community is obviously not (along with all other communities).

Exemplifying this is a supposition that I have made going from personal experience and preliminary investigations, that the word 'boong' has rather different connotations in Tasmania and Western Australia from those it has in New South Wales and Victoria. It would seem that it is a harsher term of abuse in the former two states than in the latter two. (This may be because these first two are the most repressive states?)

I **am** concerned that the Black community will see the use of this word as offensive and yet another example of white indifference and arrogance to their position and sensitivities. There is a point where the victims of racism, sexism etc. can't be cerebral, reflective but have to react emotionally, but I think it's precisely this point a writer has to get to and then use, exploit, operate within — this emotive, razor-edge space — where meaning really does become a vital issue. I am also aware that a theoretical justification can always be found by those who are part of the dominant culture and that issues around the use of this word 'boong' cannot be approached with arrogance.

'In a social context structured by historical change and, in a post-colonial and post-Fascist era, *by a desire to obscure intentionality,* our conceptual framework warrants a greater degree of complexity and sophistication than is allowed by those who employ the concept of racism in a loose or undefined manner' (my italics) (Miles 1989:98). Another interesting question is what happens when an evil verbal sign, a word, freely used orally (leaves no trace) is transposed from a verbal/mundane context to a written/cultural context, in light of the 'desire to obscure intentionality' Miles speaks of? 'It is in the highest degree curious that modern society has developed so few formal ways of distinguishing between friendly banter and deadly insult ... only the most primitive safeguards protect us from giving or receiving insult' (Adams 1977:23). A term like 'boong' would usually be used verbally and aggressively from a position of brute power but, written as a play title in the context of the 1990s in Australia, it is provocative in the extreme. The possibilities as to the reason for its use are limited — either it's a lunatic work by the suicidal New Right or it's been penned and produced by someone who has been in a cupboard for thirty years or there's some ironic strategy behind it. As Miles states, '... racism is, in the late twentieth century, a term of political abuse' (Miles 1989:1) so to use the word 'boong' is a signalling of obvious 'racism' (within Miles's 'conceptually deflated' definition). It's setting itself up to be shot down, a word in the stocks, a target for projection, hostility, denial, revenge. I would think that it is quite obviously setting itself up for this as a tactic and equally obvious that in this arena the traditional recipients of the abuse, the Aboriginal and Islander population, are, in fact, for once not in a position of powerlessness when confronted with this bad-mouth, street language. It's an open, public, cultural situation where the abused can retaliate. It is a tactic of the stand-up, put-down comedian, this combination of safety and danger. 'He (sic) offers conflict, but one in which he (sic), if anybody, is going to get punched in the nose' (Adams 1977:25). In a society which prefers euphemism to dysphemism surely the use of this word is a valid tactic?

Apropos of the stand-up comedy idea, Adams says that racial slurs are 'completely out — not because they aren't present in men's minds, but because they very much are, along with a whole set of possible reactions to them, so if they were used'… the whole situation could get out of hand. In a word, they are too dangerous, they touch levels that are too explosive to be publicly handled' (Adams 1977: 26). He goes on to talk about forfeiting audience sympathy and that the requirements for something to be entertaining are that it stay within certain limits. So, the corollary would be that if you want to go beyond entertainment, you have to risk forfeiting the audience's sympathy and go too far, risk being propelled 'out of the sphere of language altogether' (Adams 1977:41).

At this point I would like to come back to the question of antagonistic relations. Macdonell says of Pecheux's discourse theory 'that the 'material character' of meaning does not lie in its being determined by linguistic elements ('signifiers'). Nor does the meaning of words exist 'in itself'. Instead, meaning exists antagonistically: it comes from positions in struggle, so that 'words … change their meaning according to the positions' from which they are used' (Macdonell 1986:47). Compare this with Barthes's statement that 'discourse … moves, in its historical impetus, by clashes' (Barthes 1971:200). In view of these statements I would like to discuss the work of Miles on the 'ideological articulation' of sexism and racism, of Gordon on the way feminism reveals the 'social character of rhetoric' and Macdonell's discussion of Pecheux's work on discourse theory. As with 'biological difference' forming a basis for the ideological construction of 'race' so 'differences of sex serve as the foundation for the construction of gender' (Miles 1989:87), so, work in feminist theory is also applicable to work on 'race'. Gordon says that 'feminism's ethics are practiced with a continual political recognition that the world is divided and unequal … feminism's relationship to its other is antagonistic. According to Rabinow, this has consequences for a theory of language and representation which is politically grounded, because feminism reveals the social character of rhetoric, that figures of language are deployed in specific interactions' (Gordon 1988:17). Macdonell restates Pecheux in this way, 'His work explores the relations which discourses have, on the one hand, with ideological practices and, on the other, with the language which is supposedly shared by all. By exploring those relations, his work suggests that discourses are not at all peaceful; they develop out of clashes with one another, and because of this there is a political dimension to each use of words and phrases in writing or in speech' (Macdonell 1986: 43).

This makes the written text and the construction of the written text (the production of meaning) central issues for re-presentation of the Other, for intervention into racist and sexist representations, in rethinking ethnocentricism and reimagining communities. Barthes, Derrida and Clifford have opened fertile theoretical spaces for interventions of this type. Barthes has said that 'Culture increasingly appears to us as a general system of symbols, governed by the same operations: there is a unity of the symbolic field, and culture in all its aspects, is a language ... This unity of the human symbolic field authorizes us to elaborate a postulate which I shall call a postulate of homology: ... discourse is not only a sum of sentences, it is, itself, one great sentence' (Barthes 1986:13). And Derrida says that there is nothing beyond the text '... the text is always a field of forces: heterogeneous, differential, open, and so on. That's why deconstructive readings and writings ... are also effective or active (as one says) interventions, in particular political and institutional interventions that transform contexts without limiting themselves to theoretical or constantive utterances ... If there is nothing 'beyond the text,' in this new sense, then that leaves room for the most open kinds of political (but not just political) practice and pragmatics' (Derrida 1986:169). I connect this with Clifford's ideas that, 'New historical studies of hegemonic patterns of thought ... have in common with recent styles of textual criticism ... the conviction that what appears 'real' in history, the social sciences, the arts, even in common sense, is always analyzable as a restrictive and expressive set of social codes and conventions. Hermeneutic philosophy in its varying styles ... reminds us that the simplest cultural accounts are intentional creations, that interpreters constantly construct themselves through the others they study. The twentieth-century sciences of 'language' ... have made inescapable the systematic and situational verbal structures that determine all representational reality' (Clifford 1986:10). So, if there is nothing beyond the text, and the text is one great unfinished sentence, then a cultural worker has powerful theoretical tools to bring to her interventions into the 'real', through the processes of signification and representation.

Another pertinent question I must consider here is, as a white person, do I have the right to write about Black issues, construct Black characters or, given the history of Western hegemony, should Black people themselves be the only ones to write about Blacks? But a Black person holding the pen, holding the camera etc, does not automatically restore the subject and convert the process into a transparent act of auto-inscription. This stance also smacks of an intellectual and creative apartheid. Eric Michaels says, a culture is not your skin colour or blood type but a tradition communicated to you. Then if requirements of reciprocation etc. are engaged in by both parties transmission of cultures is possible. It is possible to bring 'a positive dynamic relationship into prominence' (Longxi 1988:131). 'Culture is contested, temporal and emergent' (Clifford 1986:19). So perhaps a 'vulnerable conjectural node' (Said 1985:104) lies in the dynamics of dialogue, (the primary site for connecting with the Other) of a willingness to communicate, a struggle toward reciprocity rather than in the information gleaned or gained. This is one of the most powerful messages I got in reading Michaels's discussion of how European film makers should conduct themselves in working with Aboriginal communities — the process of information transfer ties the film maker into initiatory procedures of honouring and obligation. A theme running through 'Women, Rites and Sites' is what is expected of field workers by Aboriginal communities (particularly the Aboriginal women in those communities). And in 'Ingelba and the Five Black Matriarchs' Somerville speaks about the necessity to be invited into the Aboriginal community and about the futility of trying to mine or force information. She relates how she had to become part of the women's lives and networks and come to appreciate their sense of time. It seemed to me that these struggles of hers around **how** to proceed were as important as, if not more important than, the information gained.

'We are not only separated by cultural differences; we are also united by a common human identity, and it is this which renders possible communication, dialogue, and, in the final analysis, the comprehension of Otherness — it is possible precisely because Otherness is never radical' (Todorov 1986:175).

Kathleen Mary Fallon

THREE BOONGS IN THE KITCHEN:
NOTES ON ANTIDOTAL THEATRE (OF VIOLENCE) [AS OPPOSED TO ANECDOTAL THEATRE (OF PASSIVITY)]

In 'Three Boongs in the Kitchen' I have tried to create what I call, Antidotal Theatre (of Violence). It's a bit homeopathic, a bit surgical, a bit prosthetic. It works with a double movement. It follows the desire line in building and demolishing, destroying and reconstructing representations of race, gender, family, subjectivity using cultural lego-blocks of meaning. Antidotal Theatre (of Violence) goes further than wanting to perform race, gender etc. it **is** race, gender etc. performatively. It is '... not merely a means by which social behaviour is engineered, it is the site of violence, the locus of terror's emergence as myth, law, religion, economy, gender, class or race, either in the theatre, or in the culture as a theatricality that paradoxically precedes culture' to quote Anthony Kubiak. If you see these 'vehicles or objects (race, class, gender etc.) by which terror is remembered' as created in a theatricality (rather than created by modelling, mimesis or masquerade) an Antidotal Theatre (of Violence) will go further than pointing out the performative construction. It will restage, recast, rewrite, remake these 'vehicles or objects by which terror is remembered'. 'Theatre is the site in which cultural consciousness and identity come into being through fear. ... the proleptic, the anticipatory locus of terror's transformation from thought into culture and its terrorisms.' (Kubiak)

This 'play' appears to be a social realist 'play'. I have written it in this way to use the social realism so loved by Australian audiences, but something else is happening that destabilises this form. Eventually the 'play' bursts this form at the seams and spills out. If this faux social realism is not discovered in the production it will fail.

Devices

I have tried to employ devices within this conceptual framework to make it possible to create Antidotal Theatre (of Violence). These are some of the devices:-

1. Lego-blocks of culture — The whole piece is totally and deeply structured both theoretically and theatrically. It's not 'spontaneous' or 'natural'. I con-

ceptualise the material in the piece — the images, the words, the set, the costumes etc. as lego-blocks of culture. I have tried to assemble/reassemble them in ways that create possibilities for new meanings, new questions to emerge for the audience. These lego-blocks are usually assembled one after the other to create believable narrative, psychologically believable characterisation and so forth or they are scrambled up and let fall where they will. I have carefully assembled them vertically and horizontally, like the piling up of minutiae.

2. Facts. Upturned facts eg. Jimmy's mother's tied tubes before his birth, who broke the china at end of Act 2, Jimmy's illness and its cause, Islands being Paradise, Croc's name, Rhoda eating her way out of the cot before her milk teeth had appeared etc. I have employed this to create what I call the undertow. The audience needs to be constantly asking what's real and what's not. They think they are getting facts, information but this is illusory. As the facts are also lego-blocks of culture it is fact piled on fact rather than fact after fact.

3. Blind-spot, paradigm shift, Gestalt — I want this piece to create (and in doing so, paradoxically, shed light on) what I consider to be a political / theatrical necessity. This is the blind-spot. I believe we each have a blind-spot. Perhaps live in our own blind-spots both as individuals and as cultures. And this is why we desperately need each other as different individuals and as different cultures, to be made aware of and to shed light on these blind-spots. The whole piece, I see, as trying to shed light on our own particular Australian blind-spot. That is why the piece must, at some stage, create a paradigm shift in the audience. That is what I have applied all these devices to try to achieve. It is the Gestalt of 'a vase' or 'a human profile'? in the visual conundrum. It is both at the same time.

4. Narrative. There is a strong dramatic and narrative through-line which carries the audience's interest but it is only the carrot that keeps the audience interested. (Keeps that ravenous brain busy making connections.) Yes there's a linear plot line, spiced up with lots of little off-shoots of subplots, bolstered by character development, engaging dialogue around issues and conflicts, the build up of dramatic tension to a final denouement, but the real drama lies elsewhere.

5. Conceptualisation of 'the Audience' — I want to make the audience catch itself out in commonsensical assumptions and beliefs, sabotage their fictive sense of bourgeois community (the myth of shared culture) encapsulated in telling-the-stories-of-the-tribe type analogies so uncritically applied to theatre, undermine theatre's trumpeting of universal truths.

There is at least a double reading, black/white, written into the piece. There is also the Islander versus Aboriginal reading which destabilises the belief that black skin can be read as a monolithic sign of race. (This is one reason why consultation with Aboriginal/Islander collaborators/performers is imperative and why I am insisting on black/white co-direction.)

I am very aware of manipulating the audience energy flows in my writing of the piece.

6. Interracial relations, (Australia's own particular brand of racism being one of these) are looked at in this piece, but so too are what constitutes the family, biological motherhood, foster motherhood. The liberal humanist ideology behind engaging with issues such as these is basically that if they are explained, empathised with and understood by the audience some desired change, either political, personal or ideological, will result. Empathy and explication are seen as the methods. But that is not the way I think 'Three Boongs in the Kitchen' will work and I think it will be a mistake for the director to work it in this way. As Michael Taussig says, 'It is not with conscious ideology but with what I call *implicit social knowledge* that I am here concerned, with what moves people without their knowing quite why or quite how, and with what makes the real real and the normal normal ... (my italics).' One way of accessing this implicit social knowledge is through working with obtuse meaning which seems 'greater than the pure, upright, secant, legal perpendicular of the narrative, it seems to open the field of meaning totally, that is infinitely ... the obtuse meaning appears to extend outside culture, knowledge, information; ... opening out into the infinity of language, it can come through as limited in the eyes of analytic reason; it belongs to the family of pun, buffoonery, useless expenditure. Indifferent to moral or aesthetic categories (the trivial, the futile, the false, the pastiche) it is on the side of carnival.' (Taussig)

I believe 'Three Boongs in the Kitchen' will only work if the director and actors see that it is situated in the dreamworld of the popular imagination (to use a notion of Walter Benjamin's). I see the whole piece as one of Walter Benjamin's 'moments of danger' when it is possible to 'articulate the past historically'. (If this 'moment' is created by the piece, it is my thesis that this will 'instigate the dream'.) 'To articulate the past historically means to seize hold of a memory as it flashes up at a moment of danger.' There are a number of these 'moments' in the piece, Rhoda's fear/horror at the beginning of Act 2, Scene 2, when she 'hears' the word 'boong' for the first time, being perhaps the most salient one. Benjamin 'didn't put much faith in facts and information in winning arguments, let alone class (racial) struggles and that it was the less conscious image realm of the dreamworld of the popular imagination that he saw it necessary to act.' (Taussig)

The 'definition' of 'Aboriginality' I employ in the piece is from Marcia Langton. She says, ' 'Aboriginality' is made over and over again in a process of dialogue, imagination, representation and interpretation. Both 'Aboriginal' and non-Aboriginal people create 'Aboriginality'. 'Aboriginality ' in quotes arises from the experience of both Aboriginal and non-Aboriginal people who engage in any intercultural dialogue.'

The piece is about blackness in relation to whiteness where black and white are taken as a sign of race. I see this piece as attempting an interrogating of whiteness rather than trying to define blackness, an interrogation of the white metaphysics of blackness as sign of race. It's about the political unconscious and psyche of white Australia (with its legacy of colonialism). At the heart of the piece is the place of 'boong' in the white Australian psyche.

It is also a parable about reunion/reconciliation. I believe that both intrafamilial/interracial reunion/reconciliation are impossible if the history/truth of the past is not acknowledged and reparation made. Unless this cultural/familial denial is tackled it's just another dysfunctional reconciliation doomed to final failure.

I believe that racism, black/white hostility/fascination is still a mystery. Certainly information, understanding of other belief systems, lifestyles etc. help to untangle this and yes the politics of colonialism, economic and market forces etc. do structure these relations, but there is still, I feel, something mysterious and powerful that eludes these analyses. Do the roots of racism lie deep in the metaphysical history of Western cultures; deep in the psyche of white culture? If this is so there is limited usefulness in simply describing or theatricalising these forces. It may be more useful to access and disrupt them through a manipulation of a deeper metaphysic of their meaning systems.

From my position as a white foster mother of a handicapped Thursday Islander son, I have had over twenty years' involvement, witness to Australia's interracial situation. At one point I began having dreams and nightmares about Aborigines and Islanders and I realised that any dreams/nightmares I'd had of Blacks in the past were always of Afro-Americans, Indians, Africans etc. This disturbed and intrigued me and I have asked many white Australians over the years about this and very few ever dream about Black Australia. It seems to me to be a remarkable thing that white Australia doesn't have these dreams/ nightmares anymore. We must have had dreams and nightmares during the early days of settlement and colonisation. When and why did they stop? How can we begin having these dreams/nightmares again? I believe it is important that we do for the psychological/psychic insanity of terra nullius to end. I believe white Australia must 'see' Black Australia to exist symbolically in the psyche and unconscious as well as politically, legally. I see 'Three Boongs in the Kitchen' as a post-Mabo piece which is trying to help heal this national psychosis of white Australia — psychotic dissociation.

Craig San Roque, a psychiatrist who works at Intjartanama, an Aboriginal-run alcohol rehabilitation centre in Central Australia, speaks of this phenomenon of psychotic dissociation. He believes one of the major breakthroughs to overcoming this psychosis has been the Mabo case which, as well as its political and legal importance, has importance on the symbolic and unconscious level. He sees it as a conscious recognition by the custodians of our consciousness of something about which we have been unconscious for years — the insanity of the terra nullius assertion that there was no one here before the British colonists. This breakdown in reality, that Black Australia was looked at by people who couldn't see it, makes both the observed and the observer psychologically sick.

So, in this piece, I am not only trying to create positive Black characters that challenged the stereotype or explain to white audiences the constellation of oppressive and destructive political, economic and cultural forces that 'caused' racism, Jimmy's problems, tell Jimmy's story etc. I am rather trying, primarily, to instigate and activate the dreams and nightmares of Black Australia in white Australia. (This aim situates 'Three Boongs in the Kitchen' as a performative thrust rather than simply a theatrical one.)

Some techniques I have used to activate these dreams/nightmares:

1. The homunculus device that Jimmy enacts at various times. I want him, at these 'moments' to represent what Freud called the 'cortical homunculus', a 'tiny 'manikin' registered in the cerebral cortex and inverted like a mirror.' It is regarded 'as highly overdeveloped in oral, manual, and genital representations, and it is significant that the homunculus has no brain.' '... their visual appearance is that of distorted little male persons ... The face and the mouth of the homunculus are huge, his forehead is barely present, his hands gargantuan and his genitals gross.' (Grosz) This sounds like early 'scientific' descriptions of 'black savages' within the conceptual system of Darwinian evolution and its concomitant social Darwinism. My aim in Jimmy's becoming this 'momentarily' is that he will activate some atavistic fear of 'blackness' and the 'savage' in the white colonial imagination/unconscious.

Rhoda's psychic entity of the 'dead black fruitbat' in Act 2, Scene 1, connects this. We all have our own indigenous heritage. For Rhoda Jimmy's homunculus activates her own bog-Irish thing.

The use of the Western Australian Aboriginal artistMary MacLean's slides and the Goya charcoal of the crippled man on his push cart augment this aspect.

2. Theo's last cry. Anecdotally I have heard of old people, white people who, in their death throes cried out in fear that the 'Abo's' had come. This seemed to me to verify the depth and denial of the fear in the white Australian psyche.

3. Use of words and images to act not as symbols or as 'explanations' but as verbal triggers, that when experienced by the audience as a whole and within the intensity of the piece, might trigger the dreamworld of the political unconscious and the deep psyche of white Australia to instigate these dreams/nightmares. I am thinking here of the word 'boong'. I am thinking of words like Tommy Tanna, bogeyman, OPAL, Kanaka, etc whose deep connotations, embedded in our political and cultural unconscious, might be activated.

4. The physical presence of Jimmy, Dolly and Dennis in the suburban home in the middle of the night. Sally Morgan in 'My Place' describes how she and her brothers and sisters were 'relegated to the backyard' when they went to visit their father's parents.'It wasn't that our grandparents disliked us. After all half of us belonged to Dad. It was the other half they were worried about.' This is signalled culturally by use of the song Cake-tin sings in Act 2, Scene 1, 'Stay in your own backyard'.

5. Dennis' dance and Dolly's speech in Act 3, Scene 6. (From the point of view of the interracial theme, it is possible to see the whole piece as a frame for Dennis to leap out of the frame and do his dance.)

6. Into this ubiquitous 'kitchen sink drama', into the 'stereotypically' dysfunctional family, comes Black Australia. What happens on a theatrical, symbolic, unconscious level when Black Australia not only enters but exists and acts, in this overused and overdetermined theatrical space? The answer to this question is the performed piece itself. It is thus a speech act itself, like promising or arresting, rather than an explanation, a meaningful utterance. It is an illocutionary act rather than a locutionary one. This is another way in which 'Three Boongs in the Kitchen' is performative rather than theatrical.

7. Notions of characterisation and character development — (The 'characters' are devices as much as they are characters to be identified with etc.)

The traditional way that characterisation and character development proceed is with the writer artfully doling out more and more information on the character, personality, motivation, psychology, social background etc. of each character-in-conflict so that by the end of the play the audience feels that it 'knows' the characters, their 'identities' and their 'reasons' for certain behaviours etc. These notions are, of course, simply conventions. They are not 'real' and 'truthful' keys to unlocking character or the mystery of the human condition or drama. Although it may look like I'm acquiescing to these conventions I'm not. I believe these conventions can be used as signs of character (and they are accessible signs for the audience educated in the vocabulary of theatre and performance) but I am using them differently.

What is of dramatic interest in character for me is the struggle around the instability of subjectivity, identity, unity and cohesion. The drama of character is in this terrible struggle that we are constantly engaged in and in which we constantly enlist others, to mirror ourselves, to exist as cohesive egos, subjectivities, identities. A struggle which we never finally win; where we only ever have moments of respite. We never know any of the characters fully or finally. There is no foreclosure on the characterisation and development. (This could appear as a failure of the script if it were seen in social realist terms.) I see all of the dialogue and activity, not as snippets of information that will gradually build up a profile of each for the audience, but as attempts by the characters themselves to create, maintain and shore-up self concepts, egos, subjectivities etc. So rather than the dramatic potency lying in the final sense of the character's cohesion, it lies in the constant and escalating struggle both internally and interpersonally each character is engaged in to exist for themselves.

A key to characterisation and performance I feel is that our behaviour can seem at times hugely inappropriate, ridiculous but to ourselves we believe it is quite appropriate, even necessary. I am attempting to redirect the momentum created by characters forcing themselves to believe in their own disguises. It's this external, over-the-top, almost caricature, inappropriateness that is written into 'Three Boongs in the Kitchen'. It is not the deep internal mechanisms and psychologisation of personality and behaviour that I am trying to gradually reveal and bring into play but a surface engagement, a play of surfaces rather than a digging down into deep interiority. The dialogue is to be played as just words erupting in the panic of interpersonal intercourse. Meaning resides in the interplay of surfaces. What if there is no more truth than what meets the mind's eye on the surface in the fragments? What if this has neither beginning nor end but simply a plethora of effects?

(This is perhaps only true of the white characters ie. this terrible struggle to shore up a fractured identity? Perhaps, as an effect of colonisation, the struggle of the Black characters [as particularly seen in Jimmy — monkey-man, mirror-man] is to achieve or to reject an identity constructed for them by an oppressive white colonial culture? This should be considered with the Aboriginal /Islander consultants and during the workshop/rehearsal period with the performers.)

I see pace as important in achieving all this. There should be intensity of pace as each character is engaged in this struggle (like people fighting for social, personal, ego space at a party). Most of the time these characters are more like cartoon characters than dramatic characters. Each character has their own poetry, their own rhythm. Each, when they crack, becomes the blacksteel skeleton of 'The Terminator' rising out of the ashes of the explosion. This is a central image I have employed in the writing.

The rhythm of the 'static' needs particular mention. The static is the loquaciousness, the verbosity, the character on automatic pilot. With the static the meaning lies more in the rhythms than in any literal meaning. This loquaciousness is the same as Beckett's silence. The static is the vocalising each character engages in (particularly Cake-tin, Theo and Gerbera) to cover what is really being said or should really be said and is being denied. The volume and rhythm of the words, ie. the surface is the static. It could be 'sung' 'chanted' with the static on the TV, between the channels, as the 'musical score'. The drama/theatre happens in the tension between the voices. The director should not look for deep interior meaning in the static sections.

Finally, the drama for the audience is to allow the heteroglossia created in the piece as a whole to exist inside them. There is never one clear voice. Not one clean answer. I have tried to write stream of unconscious to sound like stream of consciousness, or narrative flow, so that it can be followed (and swallowed) reasonably easily by the audience.

References

Adams, R. 1977, *Bad Mouth: Fugitive Papers on the Dark Side*, University of California Press, Berkley.

Anderson, B. 1983, *Imagined Communities*, Verso, London.

Attwood, B. 1989, *The Making of the Aborigines*, Allen & Unwin, Sydney .

Barthes, R. 1977, *Image-Music-Text*, Fontana, Glasgow.

Barthes, R. 1986, *The Rustle of Language*, Basil Blackwell, London.

Barthes, R. 1977, 'The Third Meaning', *Image, Music, Text*, trans Stephen Heath, Hill and Yang, New York.

Benjamin, W. 1973, *Illuminations*, Fontana Press, London,

Bennett, S. 'Dreams of Two Cultures' *Simply Living*, Spring 1994.

Boon, J. 1982, *Other Tribes, Other Scribes: Symbolic Anthropology in the Comparative Study of Cultures, Histories, Religions and Texts*, Cambridge University Press, New York.

Borges, L. 1984, *Facing the Year 198. Twenty-Four Conversations with Borges, Including a Selection of Poems*, Housatonic, Mass.

Brock, P. (editor) 1989, *Women, Rites and Sites*, Allen & Unwin, Sydney.

Clastres, P. 1982, 'On Ethnocide' *Art and Text*, 28, March–May:50–6.

Clifford, J. and Marcus, G. (editors) 1986, *Writing Culture: The Poetics and Politics of Ethnography*, University of California Press, Berkeley.

Cohen, P. and Somerville, M. 1990, *Ingelba and the Five Black Matriarchs*, Allen & Unwin, Sydney.

Curnick, M. 1991, 'Tales of the Emotions', unpublished manuscript.

Davila, J. 1987, 'Aboriginality: A Lugubrious Game?', *Art and Text*, 23/4, 53–6.

Derrida, J. 1986, 'But beyond …' (open letter to Anne McClintock and Rob Nixon), *Critical Inquiry*, 13, Autumn: 155–170.

Fabian, J. 1983, *Time and the Other*, Columbia University Press, New York.

Gordon, D. 1988, 'Writing Cultures, Writing Feminism: The Poetics and Politics of Experimental Ethnography', *Inscriptions*, no 3/4: &–24.

Grosz, E. 1994, *Volatile Bodies — Towards a Corporeal Feminism*, Allen & Unwin, Sydney.

Hall, R. 1989, *The Black Diggers — Aborigines and Torres Strait Islanders in the Second World War*, Allen & Unwin, Sydney.

Hindess, B. and Hirst, P. 1975, *Pre-Capitalist Modes of Production*, Routledge and Kegan Paul, London.

Kubiak, A. 1991, *Stages of Terror: Terrorism, Ideology, and Coercion as Theatre History*, Indiana University Press, Bloomington.

Langton, M. 1993, *Well, I heard it on the radio and I saw it on the television ...*, Australian Film Commission.

Longzi, Z. 1988, 'The Myth of the Other: China in the Eyes of the West', *Critical Inquiry*, Autumn: 108–31.

Michaels, E. 1987, 'Aboriginal Content: Who's Got It — Who Needs It?', *Art and Text*, 23/4, March–May:58–79.

Miles, R. 1989, *Racism*, Routledge, London.

'Differences: Queer Theory — Lesbian and Gay Sexualities', *A Journal of Feminist Cultural Studies*, Vol 3, Summer 1991, Brown University.

Macdonell, D. 1986, *Theories of Discourse: An Introduction*, Basil Blackwell, London.

Morgan, S. 1987, *My Place*, Fremantle Arts Centre Press, Fremantle.

Rosaldo, R. 1989, 'Imperialist Nostalgia', *Representations*, 26, Spring: 107–122.

Said, E. 1978, *Orientalism*, Penguin Books, London.

Said, E. 1985, 'Orientalism Reconsidered', *Cultural Critique*, Fall: 89–107.

Sharp, N. 1993, *Stars of Tagai — the Torres Strait Islanders*, Aboriginal Studies Press, Canberra.

Taussig, M. 1987, *Shamanism, Colonialism, and the Wild Man — A Study in Terror and Healing*, The University of Chicago Press, Chicago.

Todorov, T. 1986, ' "Race", Writing and Culture', *Critical Inquiry*, 13, Autumn: 171–81.

Webb, H. 1989, 'Poetry as Guerilla Warfare: Colin Johnson's Semiotic Bicentennial Gift', *New Literatures Review*, no 17: 43–49.

John Tranter

PER ARDUA AD ASTRA

I was thinking about what you told me,
what happened when you were a kid, the theft
of capital, how the bottle came uncorked, and how
the precious essence of capitalism simply
turned into vapour and disappeared,
destroying whole nations. It was bookkeeping
made it happen, we should blame the strings
of numbers holding hands that know each other,
and the passion to build a toy that works.
Capital, it just grows out of the world's matter —
a nugget, a heap of rice, busload of workers.
I always had my staff learn only the essentials.
More than that, and they develop longings.
Perhaps a Buddhist could offer a better response
to the way the economy is like a ravening animal,
wounding and maiming the poor. But then,
the stragglers have to get picked off, is that
what you said? Let's get a degree in little things,
courtesy and social stratagems, how to knot a rhyme,
and dazzle the old ladies with our manners.
I'd been fascinated with mahogany jazz,
you know the stuff, disturbing, dark, but mellow —
but we only heard a mournful song play, and
as the harmonies tangled deliciously and then
unravelled they seemed to say no, to forbid
a country girl to have such thrilling insights.
The first year I knew her she gave me
the entire history of her mind from go to whoa,
how she faced up to the great cliffs of European
culture, that had destroyed more than one civilisation,
and might do again. She was confused by truth
when it is stacked up into blocks of history,
though not by the lies that go to make up politics.
Or art, imperturbable text pretending to some
great passion, one more bourgeois jerk

raking in the dollars while he tapped at the keys,
constructing some dizzying confectionery of emotion —
as vital as a college diploma, this talent for cheating —
though what chance that had of persuading anybody —
no, I'm not jealous — give it a rest — the nerves —
'Neal was enormously attractive to people
who sat on their ass most of the day in a dim room,
biting their nails, and typing out shit.' That's
what he said. He was a big handsome feller,
thick as a brick, whacked on speed most times,
and faintly talented. I couldn't get him hunting, the old
President said — what he was afraid of was a mystery to me,
shaking while the sound travelled low over the ground,
reading The Declaration of Independence through
the telescopic sight on the barrel of a gun.

LIMBO

The boss striding ahead into the meeting
like a top dog into the council pound,
through the darkened glass you could see
the horizon lit with flashes, the smoking city,
thunder rumbling behind the horizon,
no lights on in the room so turn them on,
you might think something was behind the door.
He drove his rigmarole through the troops,
and his voice grew sugary, cajoling, like now,
and the others heard it with a shudder.
Competition was wired into the species.
From out of a limbo of sleep and anxiety
the meeting got started, a coffee, no,
a stiff drink, could you take this down,
Miss Thompson, or are you too busy?
He felt out of place saying it: we live or die
according to the graph, do you understand?
There's knowledge in the sherry-coloured eyes

of a cat, but what is it? Food? The stock market?
Those dips and sudden swoops, it makes you ill.
In the petrol-coloured eyes of a dog, only
fatalism. Memories were invading, then
colonising his mind. I can go on living here,
she said, miles from town, all alone, that's okay.
Live long enough and you forget David's death,
and the beatings, the police paid to do them.
And then his sister, framed on the mantelpiece,
a dozen years under the ground, forgetting
everything. They kept the telephone connected
in case of emergencies, they hated the voices,
the bell made a sound like a fire alarm.
In the endless silent afternoon she imagined
noises from the shed — was the lock on the snib?
There must be something bad behind the door.
He tried to concentrate. Where was he?
She asked me to write more often, but
I disappeared, like I was a bad dream, and
she never said she was lonely, then she died.
Green Devils printed on the dinner plate,
things our family used to remember, and now
no one will remember them. After dinner,
sniping at the town people, recounting
how they do their various self-destructions.
He shook himself. The aggression of foreign companies,
it seems inevitable, the survival of the most
bastardly is built into the system, he explained,
a dance tune designed to be danced to,
and they don't write songs with an odd
number of feet, they must have a tempo,
the rhythm of business, do you understand?

Peter Riley

Let go of me and I'll give you an answer
if I have an answer to give that doesn't add
to the world's cold. The towns over the hills
are full of ills and answers but the works die
and crumble, the chimney stands at the valley head
derelict, a tower to lost patience. Not this valley,
which never suffered profit, though a negative light
inhabits it now bearing modernity's favourite message:
No parking. Move on, keep going. No hermitage here,
no respite either. Days and hearts are torn asunder.

Well at least you don't have to pay to walk here,
though I expect the day will come. And yet the days
to come hold no terror but the world's own, how
to work kindness across the gap between one and
many in the light of the fading eye. O for a craft of
wholeness dictating every detail, finish, grace-note, a
surety woven across the night and curving straight
into day, shadow's edge doubled in travertine.
Refusing collectivizing aids. The delicate brushwork
of the soul courtiers proposes a republic.

Eye-bright, the inscribed line, the river's margin.
And a glow-worm at the path's edge, I thought
it was the world shining in love's desert.
I passed it by in the warm night thinking of
a republic of the (heart, mind, of the) republic
of the, for and by the, soul-light or something, the
top legal fact. Sitting on the marble bench
outside the Palazzo del Capitano dei Populi
I thought this proudly, and stuttered it
into the punctuated blaze on all sides.

Great pattern of healing ... though time
destroy the person, the intent shall range

the upper levels while mortals sleep, and
patiently, patiently, think-tread the fields,
coaxing lasting peace formulae out of bitter grass.
The stone barns up there get up and move
somewhere else in the night, I have photo-
graphs to prove it. The locals don't notice,
they have television. I said this repeatedly
and cursed the comforting guns but alas,

The box I stood on was of cardboard and pain
became my teddy-bear. I hold it in the night
in bed or a long valley while world routes
traverse the sky. We whisper to each other:
Remember, I was your valley, you walked me
and the black river slid past us, taking
everything except affection into storage but we
walked on, keep my hard head against yours
and our hearts will collaborate in long tones
through vast Europes of glowing bone.

Pain whispers through people, and tells them
the truth perhaps walking steadily up the long
winding river dale at night. Poetry occupies its
moment completely, like heroin, it is deeply
convincing, but does it know the truth? Britain
is not a nation and Europe is not a continent.
You are a stupid walker who should have been in bed
two hours ago and the world is not listening
to your solitary fantasys. The hospital you failed
to heal in stands at the north end of your head.

But favour is a constant. It finds its way out
through a concealed life, transpires from the
fullest fear: for death has trampled death
and the dippers, so busy in the daytime, sleep
now under the bank in pockets of faint warmth,
as shall I tomorrow, the other side of fearful
thought. Like a hand against a feathered side
faintly warm under a cold bank and ruffling in
the electric spasms of dream, I hope to win
an intellectual conviction, O faithless one.

Approaching now a boundary, edge of a reef,
where the sides descend and spread out, and
the god patches round Alstonefield recede into
cloud-land, silver hounds that serve their own
excellence. They get on with our best thought
while the working organism walks the twisty track
racked with fear and anxiety. My toy, my dump, walk
behind me and twist my shoulders in the dark. Under
the rock shelves of an edge nerve, sleeping birds
and victims of nationalism decorate the route.

Resentment rages though the black air surrounded
by transparent calm. Waves of limestone dive
into the ground and great shoals rear up
glowing pale in the night uncertainty and
riddled with caves; in one of which 'A cobbler
his wife and seven children lived within living
memory.' Wattle awnings over the entrance and
in the evenings they sat round a fire singing
a narrative polyphony in divided head-tones
while the weather suited itself and death hung

Suspended. At this junction the river takes
a slight waterfall under a footbridge and vapours
mingle in the air, wrapping night in the flavour
of mortality. It flickers beside the dark land,
poor waterlogged stuff owned as I recall by two
brothers in a stone fortress-farm on the edge
of the dark hill living without hope of marriage,
though a cobbler owning nothing but a certain
cultivation, constructed a fortress here against fright
where mutual favour folds the future into life.

Like a wine, like a careful Merlot folding youth
and age the night tolerates the loss of names, yours
and mine, already falling under the footbridge
out of meaning, a junction the other side of which
hope is entire. The river bends to the west and
the cliffs to the east, making this oval meadow
in which, you remember, the fox dances
with the hare and the lamb adores its tomb;

a swollen space, mandorla in middle night,
full of river mist to chest height.

Nameless we wade in it, a Roman bath, arms
out on the conceptual surface. Histories
float past and we hum their tunes, the little
circles proving one equals zero at the highest
tone. Of what happens we know next to nothing,
but we sway in the vale, take our partners
and run a business without profit from which
a concerned eavesdropper may learn the
tariff of careless love. Relax the throat,
hold harm at arm's length and dance with it.

Round and round as night and star face
each other in the oval purpose in a
clearing of the preoccupied river, that
hurries on by. O I believe, I do believe
that I go back home. I don't think I'd ever
have started this night-long trudge if I
didn't know for sure: I end at the precise
beginning of what I am, the shared declaration.
Catch equilibria out of anonymous tunes
and believe it, the whole mist of speech.

I'm sorry I missed your speech but the rabbit
danced with me in the darkened cove and I
couldn't let his/her shoulder go we were
chest level in the seas of sleep and the air
hung curtains on our eyes. But I remembered
as I fox-trotted around that quasi-circular
pasture something in my origins that Engels
failed to notice in the back streets of inner
Manchester where various things added together
made a hope so long so real and so angelic

We waited a life for it, we got engaged
and in spite of everything raised a shout
of joy, totally disadvantaged we caught
each other at turning-point where delight
transcends critique, declared ourselves

fully and sang our way home in the great
omnibus of the rain. For this we dance on,
the band shows no signs of fatigue, the floor
is hidden under five foot of fog and me and
my furry friend we flourish at death's door.

I'd like to say that again. There were
angels in the cellar that Engels never
noticed and the government inspector was
one of them. He drank with us and the night
became longer than the alienists could ever
believe or tolerate. The state in fact listened,
understood, and acted; only the aristos,
and the artists, turned up their four noses.
Am I not a plain speaking man, furry friend?
Whirl me to the end, gag me with roses.

Look, this is a serious poem why am I
waltzing with a mammal? Bright his (her)
long teeth shine in the moonlight as we
gyrate across the mead, strong her (his)
clasp behind my neck where ghosts make
their love. The land curves round us in this
abandoned place where people have always
been content to be deprived, turning and
smiling in the face of profit, dancing
the night away and no more, stopping dead.

For the masters of the earth declared (a)
there is no destination for souls (b) we'll
take all the cash thanks. So the rest of us
die quickly, to keep the machine well fed.
To this tune I dance in neck-high mist with
an earth creature at midnight. Bedridden
anxiety in the river's endless loop, red
couplets in the cave mouth squaring the ring
that nations may look at the clocks in the sky
and concentrate on creating liberal space instead.

Shared space, how we danced. Then nothing.
Just water falling over stones in the darkness.
Children left home, pets died one by one,
a voice left grating in the night, digging
in against all this dispersal, advancing in
pitch dark to the end of the meadow where
trees gather and the dale entrance opens
ahead like a hole, almost roofed. Not a
serious route since the Bronze Age. Millions
of lives simple darkness and earth noise.

A far distant voice left, on an old recording
repeating formulae in a fog of surface noise
ain't got no moma now In cielo cerco il tuo
felice volto divining the way to the footbridge
in the dark by memory, by hurt. The earth gives
gently under each step like an abandoned mattress.
Locating direction by wound echo, river noise,
leaf movement, residue. Import floats off behind
up to the god terraces and harvests of cloud.
Guiding myself correctly by ordered words.

Jeri Kroll

INTERNATIONAL REGIONALISM: WHO DRAWS THE LITERARY MAP OF
AUSTRALIA?

Do writers have to live in major cities in order to succeed in the eyes
of their peers? Being near centres of power — publishing houses,
magazines, readings, festivals — can be a great asset to writers at
the beginning of their careers; or at any time in their careers, if not
enough readers know that they exist. Unless writers have the time,
freedom and resources to establish and maintain contacts with
those who can help, they remain regional in the most limited sense:
only those in their own environment know and appreciate who
they are.

Certainly writers in the smaller Australian states — Queensland,
South Australia, Tasmania, Western Australia (and the Northern
Territory, which is not yet a state) — experience restrictions. They
have felt this pressure to travel and the consequences if they do not.
Scoring a major literary prize helps raise the profile, of course, but
there are not many prizes and a lot of very good writers do not ever
win one. Having a locally-based and aggressive press or prestigious
magazine (Fremantle Arts Centre Press in Western Australian and
Island magazine in Tasmania are examples) to promote their inter-
ests can be crucial, especially to poets, who find it hard to have their
books reviewed, let along bought, if a literary editor has never
heard of their name or press.

In Australia, without that primary recognition, the only other
thing likely to catch an editor's eye is an angle — the quality of the
writing aside. Is the poet from an ethnic group never heard from
before? Is this an engineer's first book? Is it likely to pique the jaded
literary palates of those in the eastern states of New South Wales
and Victoria, where the majority of the Australian population lives?
Years ago, the literary editor of a national newspaper told a South
Australian that Sydneysiders and Melburnians were not interested
in what happened in their state, so the editor did not see why they
should print news about its writers or events (the Adelaide Festival
Writers' Week aside). The newspaper's readers could be forgiven
for believing that nothing exciting or worthwhile ever happened
outside Sydney or Melbourne. An issue related to ignorance of

other regions, especially on the part of journalists, is the inaccurate reporting that still occurs. Witness the articles about the explosion of writers' centres around Australia. The South Australian Writers' Centre was the first (established in 1985) and reached 1000 members before the New South Wales Centre. The smaller state's organisation did not even rate a mention in some of those articles.

Although this literary myopia has been alleviated somewhat in recent years (at least as far as reporting events goes), it still persists. I wonder if this situation pertains overseas generally in relation to Australian literature, except for those pockets of passion and study — the universities — where academics need to stake out a territory.

James Joyce is probably the preeminent twentieth century example of a fiercely regional writer, who left his native Ireland, yet never ceased to write about it. His Dublin is familiar to generations of English majors at universities around the world. But of course for much of his subsequent life he lived in Paris, amidst a vigorous and aggressive expatriate artistic community (and wealthy patrons). But a skilful interviewer would at least have a healthy vein to mine with someone like Joyce today: the Irish Catholic lad coming to terms with his past.

Would South Australian, Northern Territory or Tasmanian writers, for instance, be more successful if they were self-consciously regional? By regional I do not mean simply aware of their status as underdogs scratching for notice by newspapers, festival committees and judges. I mean choosing to exploit regional landscapes and concerns as a method of distinguishing their work. Most artists realise by now that they have to market themselves, especially if they cannot travel to perform. What do people in the United States, for example, know about Australia and their intellectual life?

I visit about once a year, and as soon as someone knows that I come from Australia, they mention the Foster's beer commercial. What else brings instant (and superficial) recognition — film stars, athletes, wine makers? Ironically, those who are successful artists are sometimes not recognised as foreign. For example, an Australian children's writer who publishes in North America and Europe was thought by a U.S. academic in the field to be American. Granted, general populations would not necessarily know the names of the most celebrated poets and novelists in their own nation, but many of the people I spoke to were educated and would have thought of themselves as informed. The point I am making has to do with what others perceive as exotic. If quality Australian writers are not perceived as 'regional' in the sense of different from the norm, can they be noticed easily? What if they are only doing what others overseas are doing, but supremely well?

There is an irony here worth mentioning that would take a good deal of explication to do it justice. Most local publishers want overseas sales, which means they want something novel to catch another nation's imagination. On the other hand, they believe that it cannot be too different. The reading public (especially in North America) has to be treated considerately — meaning not too much slang, not too much local colour, nothing that needs amplification. The fact that Australian audiences are perfectly capable of reading books produced overseas without a foreign dictionary, field guide and cultural handbook seems irrelevant.

Australian poets are in a particularly difficult position now, although poetry has always had a limited readership. Penguin Books has reneged on a number of contracts and other publishers are curtailing lists. The extant small presses have few resources to promote what they do publish, so even the national market has shrunk. Furthermore, locally-produced poetry books need to find international publishers, too, if their writers are to build reputations overseas. With an eye on their budgets, directors and accountants will want to know about audience. Who will buy the books and why? How do you market a literature internationally, let alone individual writers? Certainly government organisations like the Australia Council are keen to promote art as an export commodity. Various of the Council's new Funds maintain studios in other countries and try to publicise visiting artists. But again, these benefits are doled out to the few who can gather significant backing — good press, awards, advocates — all those pluses harder for regional writers (who can manage to travel) to obtain in the first place.

Universities, which offer specialist courses of study and their magazines or journals devoted to one region or another, are still the best hope. At least those who administer, teach and edit establish regular contact with their chosen nation. They order books for libraries, edit special editions of journals, gather committed reading audiences (especially students who want to pass their topics). The only drawback here is the one already mentioned. How do Australian writers from regional areas, who do not frequent the centres of power and who publish with small presses, attract notice? Often visiting fellows, academics and editors base themselves when overseas in those same urban centres of power that ignore what lies outside them. Of necessity those visitors will rely on their contacts who supposedly already know what artists and writers are worth pursuing. The cycle will then repeat itself, excluding those who live outside the charmed eastern states. There are no easy solutions to break this cycle, but awareness of this restrictive pattern has to be the first step.

Andrew Taylor

THESE REGIONS ARE WHAT I AM

It is a few days short of the shortest day, and outside the temperature is still in the high teens, even at 10pm. Richard Strauss's *Capriccio* is drifting in from the next room. It was written in Germany during the Nazi era, and on the face of it seems to say nothing about the tragic period in which it was written. My wife has just left for several weeks in Germany, where the temperature yesterday was the same as it is here in Perth, in Western Australia. She will call me tomorrow when she arrives in Wiesbaden. On Friday I fly to Sydney, arriving home next week in time to farewell our daughter to a youth convention in Singapore.

Kiri Te Kanawa sings the role of the Gräfin in *Capriccio*. Her performance as the Marschallin in *Der Rosenkavalier* was beautiful and, at the end, close to heartbreaking. Early in her career she jokingly told an interviewer that her Maori ancestors dealt with their opposition by eating them.

I have just been reading a series of essays on Venice written by an Australian author. I have been tidying up some poems I wrote last year in New York and Scotland. Last Sunday my wife and I walked along the beach, marvelling at how even in the middle of winter the Indian Ocean is green. We gathered shells which we later left on the beach where we'd found them. On the horizon we could see Rottnest Island. We have never visited it, but our daughter has been there twice, and will go there again on her return from Singapore. She loves it.

At times I have been known to declare that I never want to board another plane. After two months in Europe and the USA last year, deprived of family, I immersed myself in an orgy of gardening. I pruned, uprooted, planted, fertilised, watered, culled, potted, pottered, unpotted, mulched, pottered further. I could not relax and enjoy, but had to be doing something. Perhaps I was trying to put down roots again, darkly groping for the minerals and proteins of a meagre but native sustenance after too much take-away.

But my time at Oxford, at London, at Stirling, at Tübingen, at Konstanz, at Cornell? Time spent with my friends in Yorkshire, the greenest moment of my life? Discovering a waterfall in the woods of New York with another friend? Hunting out a nice wine as a gift with another?

My meandering drive to Thurso which the Taylors, in their wisdom, left almost a century and a half ago for Australia? On the beach at Thurso a young woman or an older sister called repeatedly and without response to a boy wading in the chilly water. 'Tommy, come out! Come out! Tommy!' The boy ignored her, the Hebrides hung like a faint curtain of cliff on the horizon. I can hear my great-great-grandfather's mother calling. 'Thomas, come back! Come back!'

I came back. Not out of piety to the familial ghosts, but out of curiosity. The nuclear power plant awaits decommissioning nearby, the Laird's castle has been deliberately made to fall down. The Taylors were clever to leave Thurso, I was happy to discover, who never thought they had much going for them except a female leanness, gentleness to an almost unforgiveable degree, and a tendency to live very long lives. They went from the top of one world to the bottom of another, in sailing ships that might or might not get them there. They had bravery too, I now understand, a bravery underpinned by despair.

***

I grew up in a small coastal town in Western Victoria. The hinterland was rich, the town prosperous. We were mostly of Celtic extraction, as we said then, but the girls with Irish names, due to poverty or bad diet or bad dress, had legs that turned purple in winter. The first olive-skinned child I saw was probably when I was twelve. The Aborigines had a settlement of their own, I was told (as though they had chosen it), somewhere out there. I never saw it. In the fifties came an Italian or two, and Greeks a bit later.

My father was one of several local lawyers and knew everybody. He employed Ivan, a Polish refugee, to do odd jobs. By the late fifties, Ivan owned his own small house, which we approached along a path bordered by beer bottles sunk neck down, slightly angled, forming a border to the rows of cabbages, turnips and other sombre central European vegetables that set his house off from the road. I remember asking my father, 'Where did he collect all those beer bottles from?'

The town is still there. Bigger. Better by far. It has its own website, advertising its industries, its potential for development, its alluring beaches, its cheap real estate, its thriving clientele, its accessibility. It says nothing about the dunes.

As a child I loved the dunes. While my father fished from the boat, my mother and other non-fishers and I would sit on the riverbank near its mouth, sand sifting relentlessly on the prevailing westerly into our hair and, eventually, into the sandwiches my mother had prepared for supper. Behind us were the dunes. Not the vast sheer dunes of Western Australia, but tussocky, clotted, marram-grass tangled. Narrow shimmering chutes twisting between abrupt sandy cliffs higher than a child. I would pant up them on all fours, like a thirsty cat, then launch out and down. If there had been any snow in

Warrnambool, I would have been skiing.

Later it was the surf. Even in winter, before the advent of the wetsuit, I could not resist the surf. In July it was choppy, violent, unpredictable and full of cross-currents and sand. There was nothing crisp about it, and often I could stay in no longer than about ten minutes, because it was bitterly cold. Colder even than Thurso, as the ocean I was swimming in was the Southern Ocean, and there was no land between me and the Antarctic.

Unless you call Lady Julia Percy Island land. Somewhere to the west of Port Fairy, it would drift in close to shore every year or so on a miracle or mirage. It would hang on the horizon like a curtain of cliffs. Then vanish.

***

My parents took their first trip 'overseas' in 1959. My mother, who came from Adelaide to live with my father in Warrnambool, used to carp that 'the other woman' would get the overseas trip. So far as I know there was no other woman, and my mother outlived my father by almost thirty years, travelling extensively while my father lay under his polished slab in the cemetery near the river.

Each year until I was twelve we would pack into the car and drive to Adelaide to visit her brother and her many schoolfriends. My father was not a fast driver, and the five hundred miles of road were not in good shape then, just after the second world war. We would spend the night half way, in a variety of country pubs with icy bedrooms and long walks to the toilets and showers. In the threadbare lounges my sister would play the piano, and once a mouse jumped out somewhere around middle C.

On that first trip abroad my parents visited Thurso, where they met an old Miss Taylor who had been the local schoolmistress. I have a photo of them with her, standing in front of a grim high-pitched house somewhere on the edge of town. Despite the Taylors' longevity (my father was an exception), Miss Taylor would not have been at home when I went to her town last year. I did not bother to try to locate the house.

Instead I ate remarkably badly in a pub overlooking the main street, and watched a cadre of bored teenagers lounge outside the post office where there was a public phone they were either expecting to ring or contemplating ripping from the wall.

I thought about my parents visiting Miss Taylor, wondering how they had found her. What she thought of them, these relatives from the far side of the globe. Did they have anything in common, this country schoolteacher and this country lawyer? Did she offer them a cup of tea? She did, I know because my parents told me. Did they take her out to dinner? That, I don' t know. Where,

228

in Thurso, could you take anyone to dinner? How many other Taylors from the ends of the world had paid their homage to this last of the Thurso Taylors?

I left her in peace and early next morning drove south.

***

Several years ago I published a book which contained a long poem consisting of numerous sonnet-like segments. 'Sandstone' is an attempt at bringing the coast I grew up on together, psychologically, with the coast I am living on now. They are not dissimilar, though the beach at Warrnambool was cold and bleak for much of the year, whereas where I am now is warm. It is also close to Singapore, Indonesia, Malaysia, and people here do not look on those countries as tourists but with a view to business.

As well as being a writer I am an academic. Education today is a commodity like clean water or food. It can be marketed and is. My own university markets its 'product' to its 'stakeholders' quite successfully in Asia, and I hope its success continues. So even 'at work' — as though being a writer is not work — I am now in an international context unforeseen ten years ago.

In fact, all work today takes place internationally. And for writers, intellectuals, thinkers and nerds alike, this internationalism has been nurtured by a technology which will not go away but, to the contrary, exponentially multiplies its inventions, its possibilities, our opportunities and our risks. But poetry seems to cling closer to place than fiction. Fiction walks abroad on the long legs of narrative. It stalks alleys, wades swamps, invades the marketplace and braves the suburbs of a dozen languages. Fiction is the international traveller. But then, so am I.

***

Each of us is a region. A region in which many regions coexist, overlayered in memory, in love, in regret, in guilt, in nostalgia, in love. And each of us lives in a world of many regions which today refuse to remain separate. The Village buried deep in the Woods, the Ranch in Remotest Wyoming, the Tropical Island, the Forbidden City, Lost Continent, Lost Tribe, Secret Harbour, Trackless Wilderness, Hidden Valley, the Centre of the Pyramid, the Centre of the Earth. Previously considered unlocatable, off the map and hence inviolable, we can see them nightly on television and, for all I know, they might even have Home Pages.

We live in the most eclectic era ever known. And we can live in the past just as much as in the present. I can listen to Bach with an ease unknown to Mendelssohn, who had to resurrect the *Saint Matthew Passion* from dusty obscurity in order to hear what it sounded like. I can walk inside Saint Peter's Basilica in Rome as my grandparents never could, and admire the Roman Forum as even Romans themselves, two hundred years ago, could not. I experience them all as an Australian at the end of the twentieth century. And as an Australian at the end of the twentieth century, I gladly acknowledge that they have all helped to fashion me. I am made up of them, they are regions of my experience and my knowledge of the world and of myself.

I need my overlayering regions as much as I need my childhood — which is one of them — and my hopes and ideas for the future — which are another. They are what give me thickness and solidity, they give my body substance and my mind air and light. They are the seasons I can move through, the changes of clothing that cost me nothing, the friends and strangers I can revisit, and who do not reject me.

Given the life I have led, a life available to so many today, they also constitute my internationalism, the inter-nation I live in, what used to be called my 'world'. It is not a bad world, and infinitely more varied than that of my parents. It is the world my children will live in. I hope that for them, as it is for me, it will be a world of places, of bodies. Of time passing, forgetting that it has a schedule to meet, as it gets distracted, entranced, entangled in particular bodies in a particular place and having, I hope, a good time or at least something, some thing, worthy of holding in memory.

Bruce Bennett

HOME AND AWAY: RECONCILING THE LOCAL AND THE GLOBAL
A paper delivered at a conference of the Indian Association for Commonwealth Literature and Language Studies in Delhi on the theme 'The Local and the Global', 14-15 November 1997

An annual event in the small inland city where I live is regularly advertised as 'Around the world in half a day'. The city, I should tell you, is Canberra, Australia's 'bush capital', a city of some 300,000 people located in a sub-alpine region between the country's largest cities, Sydney and Melbourne. As the national capital, Canberra is blessed with a beautiful lake, clear air, a national library, a national gallery, the national parliament — and the embassies of the world, or at least that world with which we have official ties. The opportunity to travel round the world in half a day is offered by these embassies, which open their doors to the public on a certain day each year and show visitors films, photographs, maps, artworks and other aspects of the countries they represent. I am a devotee of these rapid world-trips, though I realise that what I am seeing is not much more extensive than theme parks, and that such trips probably seem a quaint activity compared with the 'real world' alternative of surfing the Net, which keeps many of these inland Australians in their homes on weekends.

Perhaps my view of matters global has been influenced by my upbringing in Western Australia, where I lived — except for various prolonged excursions overseas to places such as Oxford, London, Jakarta and Singapore — until 1993, when I moved to my present position in Canberra. Western Australia has been known variously as a place of 'sun, sin, sand and sore eyes', the 'Cinderella State', and the most isolated part of the world. This latter notion, that I lived in some kind of radical isolation, used to alternately intrigue, appal, enrage and delight me.

I still hear it said, very often by Eastern Staters (known as 't'othersiders' by traditional West Australians) that the West is beautiful but too far away, that it is 'out on a limb', that its main problem is that it's separated from the Eastern States, where the larger populations of Sydney and Melbourne tend to dominate the airwaves, and views of national identity. Carrying this residual West Coast inheritance with me, I treasure a sense of space developed there which is now interiorised, and transportable. Canberra too, I have come to realise, has something of that ambiguous sense of isolation, its perils and its pleasures, which I have inherited from my West Australian existence. When fog sets in at Canberra airport, for example, and prevents flights in and out, I think that's good, we are separate, out on our own, as I did when the Nullarbor Desert stood between me and the eastern capitals of Australia. And I applauded Paul Kelly, former editor of the *Australian* newspaper, who remarked several years ago, in Canberra, how ironic it was that Sydney businessmen should criticise Canberra as being isolated from the rest of Australia when these same men had been brought up on Sydney's North Shore, had been to the same schools, wore the same brands of suits and thought in the same ways. Canberra, indeed, like Perth, has its own ethos, with which I like to identify even as I travel the world, literally (like today), or through embassy exhibitions, or the Internet.

****

While I have no doubt that global concerns are more with us than ever before, through television and computer technology, especially, I am interested in those kinds of literary and human sensibilities which, while recognising what E.M. Forster, in a previous era, called the world 'of telegrams and anger', still seek a quieter, contemplative space in which human desire can express itself in local environments and in an individual, independent way. For me, an epitome of such a recognition is Virginia Woolf's novel *Mrs Dalloway* (1925). The example might surprise you, for the setting of this novel is of course central London in the early 1920s, the centre of empire in the early post-World War One years. The local environment here is a city where big political decisions are made and where people return from their travels to be at the centre of things. Yet Virginia Woolf's genius in the novel is to highlight, not that outer world (though there are continued hints and indications of its presence) but the inner worlds of her characters' hopes, fears and desires. When a day in the life of Clarissa Dalloway, a conservative politician's wife in her early fifties is transformed by the return of her former lover, Peter Walsh, from India, the crevasses inside and between individuals are revealed:

'I am in love', he said, not to her however, but to someone raised up in the dark so that you could not touch her but must lay your garland down on the grass in the dark.
'In love', he repeated, now speaking rather dryly to Clarissa Dalloway; 'in love with a girl in India'. He had deposited his garland. Clarissa could make what she would of it. (p.49).

The characteristic rhythmic hesitancies of Woolf's prose contribute to a stream of consciousness mode which the e-mail is again reviving some seventy years on.

In spite of the shock of Peter Walsh's assertion of his love for another woman, the progress of the novel shows an increasing entwinement of his memories and desires with those of his real love, Clarissa; to the extent that, at the novel's end, Peter's vision of Clarissa is not that of a society hostess but of the visionary woman who makes all others real to him:

What is this terror? What is this ecstasy? he thought to himself.
What is it that fills me with extraordinary excitement?
It is Clarissa, he said.
For there she was.

In her turn Clarissa is entwined in the physical, social and metaphysical dimensions of the city she inhabits. But her apprehensions, her momentary epiphanies, like those of the other key characters in the novel's network of an unrealised community, are their surest signs of significance.

Unfulfilled love, broken memories and desire for completion are, it seems to me, universal qualities which can be most fully explored in the local and particular circumstances of individuals in their moments of aloneness. Such isolation, while given encouragement perhaps by the kinds of environment which I experienced in my West Australian upbringing, can achieve certain kinds of intensity also in the cities of business and world affairs, as Virginia Woolf shows. Indeed, it is perhaps the case that crowded places increase the urgency of those contemplative moments that constitute the core of many literary works.

Certain kinds of lyric poetry can especially touch these chords of feeling and lead to international comparison. For example, Australian poet and novelist Randolph Stow and contemporary Danish poet Pia Tafdrup both illuminate the aloneness of the individual against the elemental conditions of their very different environments — the hot Australian desert winds for Stow, the snow and silence for Tafdrup, whose love poem 'On the edge' (*Spring Tide*, 1989, p.35) shows the necessity of isolation but also its reminders of death:

On the edge

Our lit bodies
talked of possible
limits and we were
recklessly alive
somewhere softly near
the heart's fiery region
we were flesh with all nights

on the longest night close to greedy brutes
when we came out to the edge where the world was
and the words wanted to leave us just there
not come to a sudden stop wanted
further further still but
crashed themselves against
a wall of white the
poem can speak now
about sparkling
silence.

Love and death are of course traditional themes of literature and they weave themselves, somehow, into, around, and beyond the concourses of business in the global marketplace. While the doom-mongers are busy proclaiming the end of localism as the Internet, e-mail and other aspects of the communications revolution seemingly channel us into the vortex of a decentred, global arena, I notice a countervailing interest, in Australia at least, in local and regional literature, and films of place. In a regional anthology of South Australian writing, editor Phil Butterss contextualises the situation in this way:

> As global media networks make increasing inroads into our lives, the boundaries between nations — not to mention states within nations — are rapidly being broken down. Why, then, at a time when spiralling numbers of Australians are opening their homes and offices to the rest of the world via the Internet and pay television, this collection of essays on South Australian writing? The trend towards globalisation is itself, in part, responsible for continuing assertions of the importance of the regional and local. (ix)

These 'continuing assertions' are not, however inevitable, like some physical law requiring equal and opposite cultural reactions to any trend or tendency. They represent, on one level, a humanistic response to the apparently dehumanising tendency of what some would call a progressive postmodernity; an attempt, as in Green politics, to retain a degree of identification between individuals, communities and physical land- and sea-scapes. Their principal motivation is the conservation of the physical environment. At another level, these 'continuing assertions' represent attempts to keep critics and commentators honest by not rejecting the local as they dabble in global interests and affairs. I remember Meenakshi Mukherjee's explanation of the purposes of the IACLALS Shimla conference in 1994 being in part to 'interrogate post-colonialism' by reconsidering with a sceptical eye the way in which critics had moved from engagement with local or national issues to being proponents of Commonwealth literature and then post-colonialism, and becoming in the process 'confident global intellectuals, part of a highly visible international fraternity or sorority who are redefining the notion of the text — equally at home in Sydney, Singapore, San Francisco or Shimla'. (*Interrogating Post-colonialism*, p.7) In these astute remarks, I recognise a proper scepticism about global ambitions which can so easily obliterate local needs and realities. I am reminded, too, that in spite of technological advances, half the world's population have never made a telephone call in their lives.

***

At the risk of being self-indulgent, may I reflect for a short while autobiographically on certain themes and issues that have affected my personal oscillation between the local and the global? I am not by any means an extraordinary Australian, and my kind of experience would be reflected by many others. My parents, born in Western Australia, each left school in their early teens and started work. Each knew the country towns of Western Australia, where they obtained jobs varying from timber yards to stock companies — and, in my father's case, later a bank. Neither of them had travelled outside Australia when my father volunteered for the Australian Army in World War Two and spent several years on the tropical island of Morotai off Borneo, where the Australians, like the Americans, were charged with blocking any further southward advances by the Japanese.

Although only a few Japanese bombs were dropped on the island and he seems not to have been in great physical danger, my father's experience dominated the mythological imagination of my two brothers and myself. My mother's home-front experience of giving birth to three sons and bringing them up between 1941 and 1945 paled into insignificance. Like our parents, my brothers and I were 'home bodies', for whom 'transport' generally came through books, radio and, in my late teens, television. (We had no car and always used buses or bicycles.) We revelled in the beach, the outdoor life, football, cricket, and the powerful idioms of West Australian parochialism.

Apart from my father's war years, I was the first in my family to leave our native shores when, in the mid-1960s I found myself the surprised recipient of a scholarship donated by that rogue bull of old Empire, Cecil Rhodes, and sailed on the P & O liner, the *Himalaya*, on a four-week voyage to England, stopping at exotic places like Colombo, Bombay and Port Said. (Before this visit, that stopover in Bombay was my only previous experience of India.) Oxford, for me, was another kind of province, but one where I could more easily leap off for exotic adventures in London, Paris, Rome, Madrid, and even Moscow. Amongst other things, Oxford, and Rhodes House especially, brought me into close contact with the Commonwealth — with Indians, Pakistanis, Africans, Canadians, Americans, New Zealanders — and Australians from other States. I suppose I was 'broadened' by the experience. I was elected President of the Ralegh Club, which invited key Commonwealth leaders to address issues of contemporary relevance. I also learnt there to value my Australian-ness, and even read books by Patrick White, Randolph Stow and others which had not come my way as a student at the University of Western Australia.

This is not an unusual story, though the details may vary: the discovery, in a foreign country, of a belated but deep identity with the homeland. The usual post-Oxford temptations were there too: Yale was suggested to me; I flirted with the idea of joining the Australian Government's Department of External Affairs to the extent that I was interviewed and accepted for a position. But when a University lectureship was offered (in those easier days), and I enjoyed the teaching, reading and writing, I embarked on a project to introduce full Australian literature courses in my home university. In that way, I fancied I was establishing my rootedness (in the traditional rather than the slang Australian sense) in my local and Australian community. I edited the local literary magazine *Westerly*. I felt 'responsible' for my local culture; and subsequently, as my reading and experience grew further, I tried to extend notions of regionalism which I had been developing in Australian terms to the neighbouring countries of Southeast Asia, whose cultures, like those of Western Australia, and Australia itself, had been too glibly passed over. This regionalism I saw as extending parochial horizons rather than as an all-embracing universalism, about which I have always felt very cautious, and even suspicious, because of its tendency to obliterate local concerns and differences and because it had been so blatantly abused by British colonialists to co-opt Australians to its own worldly ambitions.

Looking back on those Western Australian years after almost five years in Australia's capital city, I can now see conflicting tendencies. On the one hand was a somewhat cautious nativism, which only in the later years (as a director of the Black Swan Theatre Company) took proper and serious account of the creativity of the 'real' natives, Australia's indigenous people, the Aborigines, in the creative arts in Australia. I never held a view of myself as a 'citizen of the world' — a concept that seemed altogether too grandiose for a local boy who liked to travel. I had a strong sense of 'home', in a conventional sense, as house and family, and more broadly as Western Australia, or 'the West', though I only ever occupied a tiny portion of the South West of it. Local writers, whose work I discovered for myself, and for others, enabled me to dream in, and of, what I thought of as my own territory, by making it both familiar and strange to me. The place became more habitable imaginatively as I read more widely the autobiographies, stories, poems, plays and essays of men and women who had experienced that country as natives, immigrants or travellers. I co-edited an anthology of West Australian writing which we called *Wide Domain*, indicating a sense of imaginative expansion as well as of geographical space.

In retrospect, I was looking for unsettling experience as much as a settled sense of identity. I became fascinated with an anticipatory — or almost already experienced — sense of expatriatism and exile; and it is a theme which I still find compelling. My book of essays *An Australian Compass: Essays on Place and Direction in Australian Literature* (1991) attempted to explore the promises, claims, tensions, ambiguities and disappointments of the notion of 'home', and a sense of belonging. My critical biography *Spirit in Exile: Peter Porter and his Poetry* (1991) located the key to this Australian-born Londoner in the writer's felt sense of incompleteness or, more strongly, as a sense of exile. At one point, I try to encapsulate Porter's spirited response to his inbuilt sense of exile:

> Whether this sense of exile is projected in dramatic monologues, or through literary figures, such as Cain and Orpheus, or in the fates of exiled painters and musicians, Porter's discontent smoulders, flickers or flares, lighting up a personal 'map of loss'. Irony, humour and ridicule are as much part of this process as tones of tragedy or pathos. In more directly autobiographical ways, too, as in the image of a husband grieving for his dead wife, or a lover separated from his loved one, this sense of exile is evoked. (xiv)

The *literary* correlative to my interest in questions of identification with place and belonging, then, may be found to some extent in their opposites, that is, in displacement and deracination. The figures of the expatriate, or exile — and these two figures need not have the same set of identification marks at all — are of interest to me because they open up gaps, or spaces, that the writer seeks to fill. As Kateryna Longley has pointed out, the figure of the migrant, too, is often engaged in 'reconstituting home-spaces in memory and in story telling'. Every expatriate is also, of course, a migrant: whichever the direction of travel, or the degree of displacement, one of the major creative impulses seems to be the construction of a 'home-space'; and these imagined places, though they may expand to include regions or nations, are often couched in more intimate terms. Thus Peter Porter returns to the houses of his childhood in Brisbane; as does David Malouf in *12 Edmonstone Street*; Mena

Abdullah in *Time of the Peacock*; and V.S. Naipaul, in an extended, imaginative sense, in *A House for Mr Biswas*. (As Peggy Nightingale has pointed out, Naipaul's novel reveals both 'the nauseating aspects of Trinidad from which Naipaul fled as a young man, and reinforce the reader's awareness of the central impulse of the book, the intensity of Mr Biswas's longing for a home at once private and secure'. p.44)

Yet the role of expatriate or exile remains a difficult one in Australia, as in other Commonwealth countries. The reception of Salman Rushdie's and Arundhati Roy's novels have been affected, in part, by their perceived relationship to their homeland, India. At the recent Melbourne Writers' Festival in Australia, novelists Peter Carey (who has lived in New York for the past seven years) and Frank Moorhouse (who spent four years in France researching his novel *Grand Days*) found themselves defending their choice to live outside Australia and denied the charge of 'cultural treason'. (Fiona Carruthers, 19) At the same conference, Moorhouse remarked: 'Australia is a pioneering country ... There is this sense of an obligation on people to stay and build the culture ... As if going away doesn't build culture. As if Peter Carey doesn't keep building upon our sense of self'. Carey for his part, pleaded with Australians to end their 'obsession' with where writers choose to live. Answering questions of 'cultural treason' were, he said, 'alarming and difficult'; Australia's concern with artistic drain revealed a country that still harboured 'a very frail sense of self'. Still speaking as an Australian, to his Melbourne audience, after seven years in New York, Carey remarked that 'this predicament of being away from one's home can be very fruitful'. And certainly his latest novel, *Jack Maggs* (1998), which 'writes back' to Dickens's *Great Expectations* by presenting Carey's version of Magwitch the convict as the central character, is resonant with an individually realised sense of the difficulties and ambiguities of finding a home. In this novel, the place where Maggs eventually finds his place of settlement and belonging is not the London he had dreamed about but the Australia of his former bondage.

***

An interesting question for post-colonial countries such as Australia and India is whether the historical moment of such furores over expatriates and expatriatism is nearing its end. Can we envisage a postmodern paradise wherein authors' places and communities of origin are expunged from the record and they become free agents in a global literary interchange? Travellers rather than migrants? Populations beyond nationalism, patriotism and regional loyalties and affiliations? These issues have been raised again recently in Australia by the publication of Ian Britain's book *Once an Australian*

(1997), a study of four celebrated Australian expatriates, Barry Humphries, Clive James, Germaine Greer and Robert Hughes. The title of Britain's book, *Once an Australian* invites the rejoinder 'always an Australian', and the book places great stress on the Australian origins and backgrounds of its major subjects.

Some of Ian Britain's analyses remind me of my own engagement with questions of patriotism, local and national allegiance when, in researching my critical biography of Peter Porter, I discussed with him his ironic verse poem 'Essay on Patriotism', in which he highlights the hypocrisy and deception of various patriotic proclamations, ranging from those of the Boer War to Vietnam and including the macho protagonist of the American *Rambo* films of the 1980s: 'no wonder/Rambo gobbled up gooks/if he had such voices in his head'. True, I thought (and said to Porter) but patriotism has its uses, too, in focusing a feeling for the land, for example, a known and loved territory and community of belonging; or in encouraging the development of interest in a home culture which has been depreciated or ignored during colonial control. Patriotism does not have to be ugly, brutal and possessive. We agreed to differ on this matter, as on others, in what, for both of us, has been a relationship where we have a full and frank exchange of views and opinions.

It was therefore with great interest that I read Porter's extended review of *Once an Australian* in the *Australian's Review of Books*. Like much of Porter's writing, this review is full of contentious and interesting observations such as the following:

> The distrust of expatriates is a special kind of chauvinism, one that seems endemic to the newer empires. Even within what is now the Commonwealth, the irritation felt by those at home viewing their fellows' activities abroad is greater in the white dominions than in the former colonies of the subcontinent or Africa. Countries that did not have to fight for independence but gained it by democratic negotiation seem to produce a bitterer form of dislike of expatriatism than those which were truly colonial. Thus Australians, Canadians and New Zealanders feel such emotions in ways that Indians and Africans don't. This may be because, as we notice among families, emphasis is placed on differences among members rather on similarities and any common heritage.

While this argument undoubtedly contains some grains of truth, I would question the 'family' metaphor and wonder if the remark about African and Indian indifference to the criticism of expatriates would apply to Wole Soyinka's impassioned attacks on the Nigerian polity from Harvard (after what he called his 'Rambo departure from the Nigerian nation space'): or indeed Rushdie's satirical recreations of Bombay from his British hideaway. Moreover, Porter's sense of (post) modernity sounds somewhat utopian when he remarks that 'the world is wired to the Internet, a network where universalism and local interests perform side by side'.

This utopia seems ingenuous when it is linked to the media events surrounding the death of the former Princess of Wales. Universalism and local interests working side by side? While Diana's death and subsequent funeral attained instantaneous world coverage, the roots and origins of her media imagery and 'personality' derived from the massive investment of the British people in their principal symbol of national sovereignty, the royal family. Indeed, in one of those ironies which seem endemic to such occasions, the events were used unashamedly by the British government and media to reinforce the role of Britain as a tourist destination where a recent tragedy could be married with a long and colourful history of earlier tragedies. If the Ritz in Paris seemed to attract an unfair amount of publicity as Diana's temporary 'away' base, the funeral route from Westminster Abbey to Althorpe in Northamptonshire derived a massively multiplied interest dividend for 'home'. Although a 'world' event, in terms of the number and geographical range of those who viewed, heard or read about it, Diana's funeral reinforced, among its many variant narratives, one of the most urgent stories of our time, the troubled relationship of individuals to their countries and places of origin. The irony is that, according to the usual reliable 'sources', Diana had developed, in recent years, a mythology of 'away' (in Europe or North America) as a refuge and sanctuary. Although Princess Diana's funeral was undoubtedly one of the world's major media events, ranking alongside far more significant world events such as the demolition of the Berlin Wall, the Tiananmen Square massacre, or indeed the death of Mother Theresa, it did not expunge, either in the life of its principal subject, Diana herself, or for the wider British population, the dilemma of belonging, of home versus away.

***

Some of those who embrace the new technologies with uncritical enthusiasm (I understand there is a new breed of these people in India as well as in Australia), seem to me to be in danger of equating their natural excitement about change with the prospect of an emergent postmodern utopia. Let me put the positive side of the ledger first. As McLuhan accurately observed, television first made the 'global village' a possibility. The Internet, a generation later, seemed to confirm it. Email has replaced snail mail for many people in office complexes, universities and even homes. For those who have access to them, these technological advances seem to have made it more possible than ever before to live one's life in an almost perpetual state of 'awayness', plugged into a global network of communications and other people's 'home pages'. The shift in one generation from local to global has been astounding. In the culture of literary criticism and theory, this shift has been signified by a move from an interest in physical 'place' or 'setting' to notions of a 'site', where ideologies clash and compete, to the most recently emerging concept of a cyberspace 'syte', where a simultaneous interactive theatre of gossip, opinion and compared impressions of what is 'new' occurs. Information overload is a common complaint, along with an alleged loss of historical perspective, but as I'm discovering with the *Annotated Bibliography for English Studies*, which aims at nothing less than a coverage of the best scholarship currently available on the English-speaking cultures of the world, the key to such developments is improving the search mechanisms to such an extent that wastage of time and effort is minimised. We can live increasingly in such virtual 'sytes', if we, or our institutions, have the resources and we wish to do so.

Underlying many discussions of the developments I have just outlined is an ideology of Progress, which the speaker is either for or against. One of Australia's leading cultural studies specialists, Meaghan Morris, has graphically described the ideology of Progress as it has related to one of the city of Sydney's main landmarks, Sydney Tower, which was completed in 1981. Morris admits to an annoyance at the changes that have occurred in the Tower's semiotic functions — from 'the Eiffel Tower of the southern hemisphere — only higher' (383) … 'an annunciation of modernity' which would enable Sydney to 'grow up' and become a 'world city' (385) to, a decade later, 'a remodelling of local cultures to meet the needs of a tourist economy'. (386), which 'celebrated neither Sydney nor the Tower, but only the possibility of *going somewhere else*':

> There was no narrative (offensive or otherwise) of the founding of the place, and no specific address to Sydney residents. Instead, the images appealed unambiguously to foreign tourists: perfunctory ads for duty-free fur and opal shops, representations of tourist transport systems (trains, boats, hydrofoils, even a picture of a charter bus drawn up right next to a Qantas jet) and of their destinations — anonymous motel swimming pools, distant tropical and rural resorts. (387)

Faced with the discovery that her 'founding' site of analysis has 'changed utterly' this cultural analyst and proponent of modernity, finds herself toying with nostalgia and conjecturing about 'the *relative* rates of renovation or dereliction, as well as a distinctive present, and a local past, in each' (392).

Meaghan Morris deals with changes in her cityscape quite pragmatically compared with Peter Read's subjects in his recent book *Returning to Nothing* (1996), who describe their reactions to returning mentally or physically to vanished places, such as Lake Pedder after it was inundated by the Hydro-Electric Commission of Tasmania in 1972, or Darwin after the cyclone of 1974. The places these people hark back to, nostalgically or otherwise, often represent a sense of community lost. As a resident of the former Darwin said on returning to the rebuilt town: "When you come back it's no longer your town, it's been alienated, you've been alienated from it'. (157). Similarly, the vanished homelands of migrants or exiles in Australia, as elsewhere, are often represented as tragic tales of separation from childhood, family and places, as in the case of a Vietnamese immigrant in Australia, quoted by Read:

> Now I live as if I am living in a dream. I feel as if I have freedom, and every material thing I could wish for. I was lucky to be able to choose Australia as my second home. But I feel I love my people, my family, everyone who stayed behind ... (33)

Places often stand, in such memories and statements, for people and relationships left behind.

In putting the case, as I have in this paper, for a literary and cultural recognition of the local and particular in people's lives, I do not wish to undermine the benefits of modern pluralism. Reading literature has always offered a pre-eminent transportation to other worlds, freeing us, however temporarily, from the constraints of present existence. It has also enabled us to rediscover the local by presenting it to us as fresh and strange. One of the problems of the binary presented to us as the local *versus* the global is evident in the title of Benjamin Barber's recent book, *Jihad vs McWorld* (1996). Although both sides of the binary suffer from such caricaturism, it is the linkage of localism with ethnic tribalism under the banner of the extremist Islamic Jihad that suffers most. The notion of a kind of McDonald's global corporatism looks positively benign beside it (hardly even warranting the wonderfully vituperative local competitor to McDonald's I discovered recently in the Philippines called Jollibee, which is known locally as FcDonald's). Variety, difference and identification with local endeavours are clearly threatened by American corporate dominance, to which some economies and cultures have had to assume an almost feudal subservience. Clearly, there is a need for hybrids of these too-stark alternatives, including a kind of international regionalism which incorporates the benefits of global communications with those of primary identification with a place, region and community. There should be room in this dynamic too, for an 'enlightened nationalism' of the kind recently promoted by Prime Minister Tony Blair in Britain, in which the notion of regional and national communities can co-exist with a special relationship with Europe and with the world more generally.

In this new cultural dynamic which we, in Australia and India, are working out in our different ways, literature will probably play a substantial but not a dominant role. In Gore Vidal's memoir *Palimpsest* (1995), he remarks on how difficult he finds it to believe, in the last few years of the twentieth century, that he once lived at a time 'when writers were world figures because of what they wrote, and that their ideas were known even to the vast perennial majority that never reads'. (169) That time may have passed. But with whatever permutations of the communicative arts we inform ourselves in the future, it is likely that David Suzuki's injunction to 'think globally and act locally' will continue to inform those of us who view literature as a major source of replenishment, and support, in our continual oscillation between these perspectives. A major goal for educationists should be the conservation of human personalities that are not too spaced-out in global concerns to appreciate, and contribute to, the local and particular circumstances of their daily existence. At the same time, the daily round should be continually enriched by engagement with ideas and images of the wider world to which we are increasingly linked. Whenever I can, I will continue to travel around the world in half a day at Canberra's embassies, and when there's time, check my e-mail and surf the Net too. But I will try not to do so at the expense of the local literary community, its readings, festivals and meetings. To join with them is not to join Jihad at the expense of McWorld: it is an attempt to balance, in a particular way, the competing demands of localism and globalism that increasingly influence cultural attitudes and behaviour in many parts of the world.

Works Cited

Mena Abdullah and Ray Mathew, *The Time of the Peacock* (Sydney: Angus and Robertson, 1966).

Annotated Bibliography of English Studies (ABES), (Lisse: Swets and Zeitlinger, 1997-), gen. editor Robert Clark.

Benjamin, R. Barber, *Jihad vs McWorld: How Globalism and Tribalism Are Reshaping the World* (New York: Ballantine Books, 1996).

Bruce Bennett and William Grono (eds.), *Wide Domain: Western Australian Themes and Images* (Sydney: Angus and Robertson, 1979).

Bruce Bennett, *An Australian Compass: Essays on Place and Direction in Australian Literature* (Fremantle: Fremantle Arts Centre Press, 1991).

Bruce Bennett, *Spirit in Exile: Peter Porter and his Poetry* (Melbourne: Oxford University Press, 1991).

Ian Britain, *Once an Australian: Journeys with Barry Humphries, Clive James, Germaine Greer and Robert Hughes* (Melbourne: Oxford University Press, 1997).

Phil Butterss, (ed.), *Southwords: Essays on South Australian Writing* (Kent Town, SA: Wakefield Press, 1995).

Peter Carey, *Jack Maggs* (St. Lucia: University of Queensland Press, 1997).

Fiona Carruthers, 'Roaming Writers Deny Cultural Treason', The *Australian*, October 18-19, 1997, p.13.

Kateryna Longley, 'Places of Refuge: Post-Colonial Spaces', *SPAN* 44, April 1997, 8-19.

David Malouf, *12 Edmonstone Street* (London: Chatto & Windus, 1985).

Frank Moorhouse, *Grand Days* (Sydney: Pan Macmillan, 1993).

Meaghan Morris, 'Metamorphoses at Sydney Tower', in *Space & Place: Theories of Identity and Location*, ed. by Erica Carter, James Donald and Judith Squires (London: Lawrence & Wishart, 1993), 379-395.

V.S. Naipaul, *A House for Mr Biswas* (London: Andre Deutsch, 1961).

Peggy Nightingale, *Journey Through Darkness: The Writing of V.S. Naipaul* (St Lucia: University of Queensland Press, 1997).

Peter Porter, 'Foreign Correspondence', The *Australian's Review of Books*, October, 1997, 7-8.

Peter Read, *Returning to Nothing: The Meaning of Lost Places* (Melbourne: Cambridge University Press, 1996).

Wole Soyinka, *The Open Sore of a Continent: A Personal Narrative of the Nigerian Crisis* (Oxford: Oxford University Press, 1996).

Pia Tafdrup, *Spring Tide* (London and Boston: Forest Books, 1989).

Harish Trivedi and Meenakshi Mukherjee (eds), *Post-Colonialism: Theory, Text and Context* (Shimla: Indian Institute of Avdanced Study, Rashtrapatai Nivas, 1996).

Gore Vidal, *Palimpsest: A Memoir* (New York: Random House, 1995).

Virginia Woolf, *Mrs Dalloway* (London: Hogarth Press, 1925; Penguin Books, 1992)

Cassandra Pybus

We all tell stories to give shape to our lives. In Tasmania we tell stories to reassure ourselves we have not slipped unnoticed over the rim of the world.

I spent my childhood on the mountain above Hobart. From the window seat in our sunroom I would gaze out over a heart-stopping vista of ranges and peninsulas, broken by a succession of inlets and fiords, which finally petered out in the great empty expanse of the Southern Ocean. Beyond that, a long way beyond, lay the icy wastes of the Antarctic. It was the most lovely place for a child to grow. At the top of our steep, untended garden of rhododendrons, waratah and pussy willows was a grove of old pine trees where my father had constructed a precarious tree house in the upper branches. This was for my brother and out of bounds to me, but I'd climb up there anyway, trembling with terror, because up there it was easy to believe I was perched at the very top of the very end of the world.

Behind the overgrown European facade of garden was the pipeline, a track which followed the water pipe the whole length of the mountain through the dripping forest of giant manferns, where tendrils of water seeped from every crevice in the rock-face and the ground squelched beneath my feet. It was full of secluded hideaways: dank, magical, musty. It belonged in fairytales with goblins, and when snow-covered it became the remote empire of Hans Christian Andersen's fierce Snow Queen.

Before I understood anything else much about my exquisite birthplace, I understood it was far, far away from everywhere else I ever heard about. School was a quite different experience. I was disliked by the teachers as an untidy chatterbox and smarty pants. My teachers were not the least impressed that I knew Greek myths and Norse fables, their concern was that I could not recite my tables, nor could I spell; that my ink always blotted and smudged and my colouring-in ran over the lines. In fourth grade, still so vivid in my memory I dream about it, I was the only girl in the school who had to share her desk with a boy. And you can be sure he was regarded as the school lout. We were being jointly punished, our deficiency in niceness was made a daily example. The really terrible thing was I knew he was horrified to be sat next to me and his misfortune was a constant source of teasing. As the headmaster was to remind me more than once, Princess St Primary School, Sandy Bay, was not the appropriate place for me. My parents did not live in the elegant, well kept, securely upper-middle-class suburb which fed the school and nor were their bohemian views on child-rearing and lifestyle appreciated. It was a source of great dismay his school was forced to accept the kind of riff-raff who lived up on the mountain. But at least the few other children who caught the bus down every morning learnt to conform to the school's expectation of good behaviour. I was incorrigible.

It was not an easy thing to feel that my life would consist of being a despised outcast in a place I could never find in books. Nevertheless the awful Princess St Primary School (I still give an involuntary shudder if I pass it) fed me stories which became metaphorical mooring lines to those places that did exist in the books I read and in the movies I saw. Much was made of our famous, world famous, apple industry. I had to learn the names of the apple varieties and their destinations across the globe. And to colour-in a map of same, neatly. I was captivated by the stories of the apple ships which would line up at the wharf at Hobart and Port Huon waiting to load the first apples of the season then race each other back to England in order to off-load the very first shipment in Covent Garden, where eager English men and women were queued to buy. Covent Garden. Now there was a place at the hub of things. Tasmanian apples, my grandfather's apples, went to there.

We all knew that Errol Flynn had come from Tasmania. His father had taught at the University and while he had not gone to my school (where he probably would have had to sit next to an untidy girl) he had gone to another state school nearby. I had never seen one of his movies, but I knew he had made a big success. In Hollywood.

Then there were the stories overheard in talk between my parents and friends about another exotic fellow, Francois Fouchet, who had come to Hobart with a wrestling team and stayed to open a bar. He had also built a wildly extravagant house overlooking the river. From their tone I presumed he kept dubious company and had come to a bad end. They said he had once been Shirley Temple's bodyguard.

My favourite was the story of Merle Oberon. She had been born in Tasmania. I used to collect the Fantales wrappers which recorded that delicious fact, genuine confirmation that the place did really exist. I was intoxicated with the possibilities of her story above all others, because I was intoxicated with *Wuthering Heights*. I didn't understand a lot of it. All that stuff about the Lintons passed me by, but I understood about Heathcliff and Cathy. Wild, untamed spirits in a wild untamed landscape which they are bound to as much as to each other. Young as I was, I knew about that. Wuthering Heights could be my house on some stormy nights, while Penistone Crags was probably very like the pinnacle of my own mountain.

Merle Oberon was always very beautiful and regal. I listened eagerly to all the local stories about her. Oberon wasn't her real name, I was told. She had been a pupil at the Model School in Hobart and had lived in Battery Point. Someone showed me the house where she was born. The rest of her family lived at St Helens, a seaside hamlet in the north-east. Her starting point as an actress had been the Hobart Repertory, where my father used to act in plays. Since she was so young and poor, a number of leading Hobart businessmen had got together to raise the fare to send her to England, maybe to Covent Garden, to make her name. This story contained great possibilities for a grubby little girl who was still bottom of the class and taunted in the playground.

She remained a touchstone for me, the beautiful Merle. When I was living in Sydney in the 1970s, I fell upon John Higham's biography of Merle Oberon when I spotted it in a bookshop. I was only a little disappointed to discover that the woman whom movie mogul Alexander Korda married and made into a star in the 1930s came to England in 1929 from India, not Tasmania. Higham had discovered the birth record of Estelle Merle O'Brien Thompson, born January 1911, at the St Georges Hospital in Bombay, and her baptismal certificate at a church in the seedy suburb of Khetwadi, close by. It was Korda's genius to invent Merle Oberon and to concoct a Tasmanian birthplace to give Estelle Thompson pure Anglo antecedents, in addition to elocution lessons and a new name. Her Indian mother was relegated to playing the role of devoted Ayah, while a portrait of a fair Englishwoman was installed in Merle's apartment to take the place of the fictitious mother. It was a perfect biography for the future Lady Korda. It continued to be a perfect biography even after Merle had shed Korda and moved on to Hollywood, where she installed the portrait of her English-rose mother above the fireplace in her Beverley Hills home. Here was a very different Merle Oberon story: a poignant narrative of the discarded Estelle Thompson, with her dubious legitimacy and despised Eurasian stock, carrying the portrait of her make-believe mother from one glittering stepping stone to the next. It was a story I found no less fascinating and one that actually increased my affection for her, now that I had proved Tasmania a place I was able to leave.

Extracted from *Till Apples Grow on an Orange Tree* published by University of Queensland Press, March 1998.

Glen Phillips

LANDSCAPE AND YOU
Journal Excerpts, Poems and Prose

16.8.91 Palio Day
Early Morning: Castellina, above Godenano. 8.45 am
1.   Fresh smell of the grass and bushes. High rumble of plane. Klaxons sounding. Tractors, traffic, grain mills — a dull background roar, bird calls — raspings, chirrups, twitters, magpie sounds. On the ground the small oak leaves, toffee brown or last year's grey and the dried grasses. Little scratched holes like rabbit scratches.

2.   The broom bushes are dying back, the green spikes turning to brown. Some red berries, and some blue black ones in the bushes. The older oaks are mottled with lichen and wrapped with ivy on the trunks. Blackberry canes — dark red and purple — soil cracking open. A few ants walking along grass stems. Surface litter of grass stems, seeds, old leaves. Soil is a medium grey here. Patchy shadow, clicking of cicadas starts. Very slight breeze.

3.9.91
3.   A thick fog at 6.00 am which cleared a bit by 8.30 but still murky. Cloud coming from N.W. Went out on the hill. Dogs yelping at nearby farm. Noises from some mill or factory further down. Quite a few tractors ploughing. Vehicles moving up and down the distant roads. Buzz of flies, bees, mosquitoes. At least 6-7 different bird calls — twittery, chirping, odd squawks. A lot of white spotted yellow butterflies.

12.9.91
4.   Filming near Castellina Scalo and Monteriggioni — squeak of crawler tractors ploughing, bird calls, distant thunder, traffic on superstrada. The bells of Monteriggioni at mezzogiorno. Talking to girl at the local Bar who preferred summer's warmth. Little green lizard basked in a wall crevice near a water tap. Fascist slogans faintly visible still high up on the wall. Patches of sun travelling across the landscape, across the walls and towers of Monteriggioni.

17.9.91
5.   Arose early at San Carlo and started filming. Had a coffee and went
down to Massa and on up into the mountains to Carrara. Found wonderful
quarries and a museum explaining the ancient and modern ways of extract-
ing marble in great blocks. These are now brought down in trucks. One block
per truck. Later watched the stone being worked down in Pietrasanta.

MONTERIGGIONI

On the wall of the Bar in Dante's towered town
paint had thinned, peeled to show
slogans of *il Duce* there:

'If I go forward, follow me!
If I should falter, give me a shove!
But if I stop, then kill me!'

On the wall of the Bar the tiny craters
where the firing squad of *partigiani*
had sprayed a little wide of the blackshirt bodies.

'If I go forward, follow me!
If I should falter, give me a shove!
But if I stop, then kill me!'

These incisions had not faded
had neither been erased
nor had ghosts returned to haunt this place

like the painted-over slogans. Time
is a cobbled street with stone walls
that run round and round a town. And tourists gape.

'If I go forward, follow me!
If I should falter, give me a shove!
But if I stop, then kill me!'

Glen Phillips

CAVI: MASSA CARRARA

Lost
your marbles?
Don't come here
like Michelangelo,
below the snow ravaged peaks
of the Alpi Apuane!

These
scarred teeth
have been under
centuries of drills,
persistent marble dentists of generations.

Centuries of excavations
block
after block after
block
of stone like frozen milk

trucked down
the twisting narrow
gutted
road
to the artisans of Massa Carrara
and Pietrasanta.

Then stacked
in waiting
yards
until air hammers stammer
into the
virgin china-white

to discover
what has been waiting

waiting
even longer than
the Marble Mountains of Carrara
hidden but perfect
waiting:

in marbled
cerebellum
my chisel strikes
this
poem.

LA LUNA

Non è una luna piena;
no, not a full moon yet.
Si chiama mezzaluna;
the blade's curving secant
that hangs in the western sky.
Mezzaluna, mezzaluna, che
taglia il tramonto, rosa e scura,
your whispering kiss of steel
severed me from my heart's love
long ago in another night sky of pain.

New moon, *mezzaluna,* this evening
you turn the cruel curve
of your crescent, like sharp
twist of assassin's lingering thrust.
Qui la mezzaluna presenta
un viso diverso, un sorriso crudele
che noialtri, degli antipodi, non
conosciamo in questo tramonto scuro.
No, not a full moon now — half moon
poised in the centuries' western skies.

Glen Phillips

Tuscan Towns

You open a packet of crackers and they spill
angle on angle stacking up this way and that.
Imagine a largish sort of hill, a cone
of green oak and vines, or crest of a ridge;
or wheatfields, gold in the sun, stretching up.
Add a few see-saw roads that toil to the top
and then, in the shaft of the late sun, set
that tumbled crusty pile on the hill's high crown.
There might be a pealing bell, solemnly;
a blue bus yodelling down from cobbled streets,
or drawn up, panting, in a little stone piazza
not much bigger than a pasta dinner dish;
the hornet drone of a *motorino* possibly might
suddenly shake some centenarian's slumbers
and set the stones vibrating with history's hum:
the snarling war-cries of Goth or Hun or Celt
or Barbarossa's brawling barons at the walls.
That's your Montisi or Montefiorallo, Murlo or Montalcino,
perched like birds of prey on their peaks,
now menaced only by merry Etruscans in necropoli.

What struck me when I came back home to my Wheatbelt landscapes was the
lack of that historical 'layering' that is found in Tuscany. By contrast, every
square centimetre of Italian soil has been involved in millenia of European his-
tory. I looked at farms and farmhouses which most Australians regard as aged
and historic, yet they had weathered less than a couple of hundred years of
settler usage.

Even in the farming of grain there is an extension of the most ancient
European practices. If you look at the land, the manifest changes are like fresh
scars. I'm comparing with Roman or Etruscan influences on Italian landscapes
and, as an anglo-celtic Australian, ignoring the vast Aboriginal inheritance of

a different kind of land usage. But when I observe these Australian landscapes through the eyes of zoologists, botanists and other specialists, of course I find there are certain other riches!

WHEATFIELDS, SALTLAKES AND SALMON GUMS

If you were to join me here
in my country, breathing
quietly aromatic oils
of eucalypt and salt bush
on the old bush tracks, goldfields treks,
the old sandalwood trails
the old songlines
of my stolen country!

If you were here
by me in my country
sighting along my arm
letting the yellow-gold
and old green enter
your eyesockets, pass through
the shadowy aisles
to merge with your own country!

If you were here
I would show a way
I have taken through more than
fifty summers and winters,
footsteps in the litter of bark
strippings, the shed leafage
on the powdery red dust;
footsteps on wet, glittering
granite domes in a freezing wind;
I would show you a way.

Let me show you a way!

An Autumn Leaf Or Two From Tuscany

Dear Reader,

So now it is autumn here at the Verdaccio Studios near Siena and the land-scape I had come to know quite well over the summer months is irrevocably replaced. The rows of vines, which grow right up to the huge stone walls of 'our' twelfth century farmhouse, are changing from summer green to the hues of autumn. In each underground cantina of this sprawling former monastery, the wine is being made in huge oak casks from the four crucial varieties of grapes that are the traditional ingredients of a bottle of 'chianti' red wine, or more correctly, *chianti classico rosso*. The aromas of the new vintage seep into the studios located above. Such are the challenges for Australian painters, photographers, sculptors or writers who work here! This is part of their new environment in these landscapes at the foot of the Tuscan town of Castellina-in-Chianti.

In the vineyards, between the trailing rows of yellow and carmine, bright-green new grass has sprung up along furrows that had been ceaselessly tilled all summer. Willows stepping down the banks of the nearby *borro* are shed-ding leaves almost as quickly as each tree changes to a delicate primrose colour. Isolated cherry, pear and plum trees colour up like brilliant flames. Beyond vineyards, the forests of Mediterranean oaks have subtly slipped into tawny shades. Only dark tapering cypresses, occasional umbrella pines and the grey-green olives keep to their summer colours. But in the olive trees, the hard green fruit is turning black. Soon white sheets will be spread beneath the trees and the olives harvested. As with the tasting of the new wine, there will be the usual impatience to sample the season's fresh olive oil and spread it on crusty Tuscan bread.

The light here, which for centuries has fascinated so many European artists, is also changing with the season. On those slopes of the Chianti hills, which face westward towards the towers of San Gimignano, towards Monteriggioni and the distant Tyrrhenian Sea, the sun first touches the tree tops at about nine am. Correspondingly, and often in a blaze of deep scarlet, at five pm or so, the red disc dips suddenly behind the Maremma mountains and night descends. On other days, mists linger in the valleys. Often grey showers advance, mut-ing the landscape's colours. When the light is good, receding serried lines of hills are outlined in afternoon tones of blue, rose or gold, depending on the everchanging weather. Sometimes, following sunset, there is a special and spectacular phenomenon: an intense rose colour lights up the ancient walls of this house and the stone terraces of the fields. It comes from the fiery red of the sunset's after-glow. On the glazed west-facing windows it blazes back and tints the foliage of all the vines and trees. Then it is gone. Evening's chill and the promise of frost come with darkness. Only confetti of lights in the broad valley below relieves the blackness. The night is punctuated by automatic gas guns, fired to scare wild boar, *i cinghiali*, from farmer's fields, and from vineyards and gardens.

Summer had produced its own kind of challenge. The heat had been so intense that soil yawned open in deep fissures. Snakes and green lizards were seen sliding indolently into coolness under baking stones. Green corn and sorghum crops had to be daily bathed by huge water cannons firing from the edges of the fields. Long-tailed sheep with tinkling bells would move in under the shade of bushes to browse. Frequently, a violent afternoon thunderstorm would deluge hill slopes and leave them smoking as the downpour soaked in. The rain settled the powdery white dust on unsealed roads and briefly cleared the usual heavy haze to reveal surprising detail of distant towns. As the season advanced, wheatfields were harvested and finally the stubble mown and piled in contoured windrows. Later these would be burnt. During that time, I had worked in the landscape from early morning, often till nine in the evening. The long twilight lengthened shadows and defined forms.

From Western Australia I had arrived in Tuscany in July. My intention had been to concentrate on particular Tuscan landscapes of five regions, which were reduced ultimately to two or three specific areas for detailed response. My interest was in achieving a substantial engagement with what was, for me, a new even foreign set of landscapes. At that time most of the other artists from Australia at the Verdaccio Studios, were painters.

Back to this current autumn. Ever since I have come here to live in the heart of the well-defined *zona chianti classico*, I have found this region to be one of the most important of the Tuscan areas for exploration. Another one I have chosen is the grey clay district south-east of Siena, known as *il Crete*. It is a landscape of eroded cliffs and domed hills, sometimes crowned by a cypress or two, or a stone farmhouse. This is wheat and sheep country and to any of us, as Australians, there are points of familiarity.

To the south-west of this Chianti zone there lies the Maremma, originally intensively mined for lead, tin and iron ore by the Etruscans. Its mountains are still rather wild places where *i cinghiali* are hunted and cork oaks harvested. The latter obviously provide from their thick bark the stoppers for wine bottles! But notorious bandits no longer rampage down from the hills to plunder the small farms and villages. The marshes of the coastal margin, which had harboured malarial mosquitoes until the 1930s, are now replaced by irrigated fields and wildlife reserves.

To the east of the Chianti hills rise the Apennines. Here I have chosen an area called *il Pratomagno*, an alpine region where snow-white oxen are often seen grazing in green summer pastures above the tree-line. And far below, in the smoky-blue depths of the Arno River valleys, are red-roofed villages clustered in old strategic hilltop locations. Even further down are modern suburbs sprawled around cities linked by the ribbons of the many *autostrade*.

The fifth landscape I have explored lies to the north of the ancient cities of Pisa and Lucca: the Apuan Alps (called the Marble Mountains by many travellers). Here are quarries that were worked under the Roman Empire, with wood wedges doused with water. These swelled and split off the huge marble slabs like frozen milk. Above the towns of the coastal strip, beyond Pietrasanta, Massa and Carrara, are the high mountains which look as if fresh snow has fallen on them, even in midsummer. But closer observation reveals these are the enormous excavations which have been carved out, right up to the mountain peaks. And what seem like avalanches are really trails of white marble rubble, tumbled reject boulders and chippings tipped out over the precipitous lips of the working quarries. The local name for this white detritus is *ravaneti*. To the west, in late afternoon, the sea spreads like a sheet of gold leaf. In the lower valleys there are chestnut woods down through which trucks grind in low gear along narrow roads. The trucks normally carry just one giant block of marble each wedged on a rough wooden frame. They are headed for the yards of the marble merchants in nearby towns. Much of this stone will find its way to local studios where international sculptors as well as local *artigiani*, the skilled workers of this industry, will toil to transform the raw chunks into marketable artefacts. Michelangelo came to this region to select his marble, they say.

So, here I am in Verdaccio Studios in the midst of preliminary sketches and drafts, numerous documentary photographs, hours of video tape, pages of notebooks and with a mud-stained, tiny Citroen which has obediently travelled some 17,000 kilometres to carry me through and through the landscapes during my programme of familiarisation. My base at Verdaccio Studios is both rustic and practical. In the typical older Tuscan architectural style, my studio apartment has rough stone walls of enormous thickness, terracotta ceiling and floor tiles, rough-hewn oak beams supporting the roof and medieval-style casement windows. Apartments here are furnished in simple country style and, with their attached studios, provide the opportunity for artists to work unhindered. And outside there is always this richly-layered landscape, for centuries the site of one civilisation after another.

The same tract of land has seen the passing of the Iron and Bronze Ages, the Villanovans, the Etruscans (with their twelve great cities), the Celtic invaders, the Greek traders, the Roman conquerors, the Longobards, Goths and Huns and the periods of rule by France, Spain, Austria and Germany.

More recently, and since the 1960s, there has been a steady influx of the British to this area. Some call this 'the Chiantishire'. Latterly, numbers of Germans, Swiss and Americans have also purchased and restored many a languishing Tuscan farmhouse, villa or castle. Will some archaeologist unearth an old vegemite jar in the vicinity of the Verdaccio Studios in a future century?

As we study the strange stepped arches of the Etruscan tombs in the necropolis at Castellina-in-Chianti, or watch a three thousand year-old ceramic horse's head being unearthed at a local archaeological dig, we learn that this is a landscape fashioned not only by natural processes of wind, rain and sun, but also by people who have successively occupied and farmed here. The old straight Roman roads, the Cassia, the Aurelia, run through Tuscany; but there are also the hilltop-ridge roads established by the Etruscans before the Romans. Nowadays there are modern freeways burrowing through flanks of hills and arching over viaducts to leave their mark on the land. In the Second World War, New Zealand infantry camped on these slopes as they drove the occupying Germans northwards.

When I go out for my fieldwork, sometimes with helpful friends from the Universities of Florence or Pisa, trying to identify the local wildflowers, or working in the company of members of a local archaeological group, or searching out the obscure locations of lesser known works of the great Tuscan painters; or having Professor John Scott from the University of Western Australia pin-point for us the Tuscan locations cited by Dante, then I feel I have put on seven-league boots to speed up my engagement with this new/old landscape.

So, with what sorts of narrative of this experience will I come home to Perth, Western Australia? There will be notes, drawings and poems which, along with audio-visual presentations, will document this six-month learning process. I plan to appear here in Tuscany at local poetry readings before I reluctantly set out for my return to Australia. Readings from selections of my completed poems (nearly one hundred in all) and prose pieces may be anticipated a year of two after my return; time is needed to reflect on and respond to the rich Tuscan experience. Publication will take even longer.

Yours sincerely

from Verdaccio Studios, *Il Cennino*, Castellina-in-Chianti,
Province of Siena, Region of Tuscany, Italy.

Glen Phillips

WHEATBELT COUNTRY

Dust explodes with the concussion of pelting raindrops. Dust is mud again. The streets are slicks, roads glistening wet. The water will soon be long sheets of run-off at the road verges. On the massive monadnocks that stand clear of the flat country — the granite remnants, perhaps smoothed by the last Permian glaciers — there are silver streaks as water pours down the giant domes, fills dusty hollows of last winter's rock pools, gathers dust and plant debris and cascades in most cases towards the lip or characteristic 'wave' in the rock face, then courses down the associated rock gorge, down to the micro-climatic groves and thickets of spindly trees in the wet area at each dome's base.

This is the signal for which all life in the wheatbelt has been waiting. The ghost moths are still chrysalids in their deep earth chambers, shielded for months from the summer's heat. They twist and buckle and begin the forced climb to the surface until their cases are perched like tiny erect space shuttles on the dampening earth. From these, the moths will emerge, silky looking and soft. But soon to strengthen and dry their wings and begin the last day of their lives, the frenzied dancing of mating, flapping at windows, falling like snow flakes to the battering headlights of highway travellers.

Down in their safe burrows the trapdoor spiders also awaken. They thrust aside protective silk mantles and burst open the prim outer lids from these deep cylinders, beautifully spun in the earth like subterranean missile sites, and begin to survey the woodland floor. Young spider nestlings from last year's hatchings go searching for territory of their own, for bare earth, for the patches cleared in the litter by native quails. All around great oval lids of the trapdoors glisten with moisture. Down below, a twenty-year-old mother spider is stirring. She's a size larger than a domestic egg-cup. Soon she will hunt again, seizing even small snakes in her powerful, two-pronged jaws and injecting the spasm of venom that disables her unwilling patients, before consumption.

The flying ants and termites are lumbering from crevices and mounds with their clumsy new wings, like sailboarders lumping their craft from carparks to the water. But soon the ants will be away, getting into the air before drenching rains of advancing weather fronts forestall their migration.

Yesterday it was all dust-storms and flying sand and plant debris. Straws from hastily-raked stubble blew against fences and under the doors of houses and sheds.

Today there will be spirals of showers reaching down like tiny tornados from the black line-storms and thunderheads. Over distant salt flats and shallow river gullies there are bound to be the grey-white veils of advancing deluges.

Rain on the iron roofs stirs the farmers. Lights come on down at the machinery sheds in the pre-dawn hours. Seed grain cascades into the bins on the trucks ready to be transferred to the boxes of the combine drills. The giant four-wheel-drive tractors warm up engines under flood-lights. Their cabs will be as snug as satellite capsules once they begin to trundle over the landscapes. The moon will set before dawn but now the grey light of it shows the crazily waving mallee and the spattering of wind-blown showers outside the windows.

'We call this the silly season!' says a breakfast-getting farmer's wife. The men have been waiting for weeks now for the break of season: looking over their shoulders at neighbours' dry-seeded paddocks, spraying weed killers; making preparation in machinery workshops. Tyres and tubes are re-fitted, wheel rims clanging on the concrete, along with the dropped spanners and smell of diesel fuel.

In the nature reserves there are new scents as small birds wheel and scatter bush to bush. From salmon gums and gimlets comes the squalling of restless pink and grey galahs. Breaking off into flight again, they scream obscenities and turn and settle once more like clumsy Christmas decorations. Musty smells from damp summer-dried leafage are rising into the air. The orange lamped banksias, in full bloom, are pouring out honey smells to anyone interested. You can smell the rain on the wind. Past the reserves, the trucks are thundering down the roads to get into seeding paddocks. Late roosters crow in the murky dawn. Farmers are grim-browed, nerves taut as hawsers. They snap at slow-stirring families who have seen it all before.

Sergeant ants as long as your thumb are marching over the gravel pit now. In their abdomens is the stinging acid they will inject into bodies fool enough to cross their paths.

This is the change of season. This is what the earth has waited for these past months and in every one of the countless past years. The waiting has strung the nerves of all who have longed for the action of re-birth, the born again generations.

Away far to the west, in coastal wetlands, in public parks littered with autumn leaves, the teal ducks, mountain ducks, black swans, wading birds, all will be remembering inland waters, recreating images for themselves of filling lakes, inland salt marshes and endless salt-lake stretches. Such tribal memories will tense their wing muscles, they'll start testing for flight and then first some and then others will rise in flocks and head for the renewing wheatbelt wetlands. Their night gabble will come back over farm dams and paddocks.

Lights are moving over these vast wheatlands. The grumble of engines is everywhere. For everyone this is the time known simply as the 'seeding'.

John Kinsella

INTERVIEW WITH CORAL HULL

JK: When and how did you start writing?

CH: To be an artist of any kind you need life experience. But you also need education and equipment. Life working through you is not enough. You need to be able to translate or express the experience. For me, living was the easy part. The expression of that experience was harder. I had an inadequate education, a rotten homelife and no money with which to purchase equipment. We had no books. My mother had a camera, but she mainly took shots of kids standing around birthday cakes etc. All my pencils used to wear down in the first few weeks of the school year and there were no more until Christmas. Christmas was when we got given all our school gear. We had a television and a record player. Movies were to be one of my initial creative influences. We also went to the cinema during school holidays. I remember a childhood filled with creative intention. It was very frustrating. All this stuff was happening to me but I didn't know how to what to do about it, or how to make sense of it. I did all the usual things with the other kids who were in a similar situation. We threw rocks on the roofs of all the houses in our street. These were the creative acts of the children in our suburb. All children are creative. Some have access to more education and equipment than others. But those others will still express themselves in whatever ways they can. I wrote a poem titled 'The Rainforest' when I was thirteen. I thought, this is a poem and I want to be a poet. By this stage I needed writing that much, that all the lack of support in the world couldn't stop me once I began. From that age on I wrote. I couldn't spell and I wrote rubbish. But it didn't matter. It was the act of writing that was important. Writing was someone to talk to.

JK: What are your views on the teaching of creative writing?

CH: I have studied creative arts at universities for ten years. I have just completed a Doctor of Creative Arts degree at Wollongong University. Without access to these institutions I would have remained semi-illiterate and would not have become the writer I am today. Before going to Wollongong University I didn't even know about class, or that the inner city of Sydney had a culture. When I sat in on my first History Of The Arts lecture, I didn't know what the hell they were talking about. I didn't understand what the big words meant. A year later I knew that they didn't mean that much. I failed my first essay on mythology when I wrote pages and pages on how myth meant lies. I escaped my background by going to university. There was nowhere else to go except into the factories or the supermarkets. My family would not support me through a tertiary education. I left home for the second and final time at nineteen. Naturally, I support creative writing being taught at all educational institutions. Universities provide opportunities, but again it's who can go and who can't go. I slipped through the class barriers and got in. The thing that worries me is that these institutions are teaching people how to develop as writers and artists for years on end, and when you get out there is no work available. Also, I guess creative writing courses at universities suffer the same problems as visual arts courses. Conservatism, standardization and introversion.

JK: You write prose, have an interest in photography, and do graphic work. Do you see these different artforms as part of the same project as your poetry?

CH: I have made a choice to pursue my writing only. It is where I work best. I still indulge in some photography, but my power lies with the written word. The pace of visual art is not fast enough for me. I have a lot that I want to say and I want to say it now. If I tried to pour out the paintings like I do my writing I would go crazy. Why spend time drawing a leaf when I can just describe it or take a photo of it. I know. I'm half joking. Photography is fast enough for me. Although I prefer fully automatic cameras. It is the idea that I am interested in and not so much the technique. I had a horrible time in conceptual arts school, where we had to use these big rocks in order to make prints. The preparation took hours. I ended up accidentally smashing the rock. It broke completely in half. They were worth a few thousand dollars. Also I am a minimalist. I love the internet. Art was too material for me. It's too stifling. I'd prefer to listen to a choir than look at an installation. I was also concerned that art was not political enough for what I want to do. The other deciding factor for me to stop art altogether was the cost. Basically, I couldn't afford to do it. I was tired of standing outside art shops looking in through the windows and dribbling over the equipment. I became disillusioned with the art world. I believed that anyone should be able to express themselves, regardless how much money or equipment they have. Art is for the elite. Writing and speaking are the cheapest forms of creative expression I can think of. Yet I am very fortunate to have studied visual and conceptual art. Creative arts taught me how to 'see' the world. Cross-disciplinary techniques have only served to enhance my expression as a writer.

JK: Activism and the poet's responsibility? Veganism and poetry?

CH: Veganism is the ultimate political act on behalf of the earth and its ani-
mals. There is no better way to minimise suffering than to change dietary and
living habits into a powerful ethical tool. Everytime we sit down to eat we can
ask ourselves is this action destroying our heath?, the life of an animal?, is it
damaging the environment and contributing to third world hunger? In this
day and age it is more important than ever, that we become conscious of
everything we do. We are all responsible for the present acceleration of the
destruction of the earth. Some of us are also responsible for the torture, mur-
der and genocide of animals. Do I think that poets and artists will save the
earth? No. It's the political activists who will save this world, or at least they
will try, and if they write then all the better. I cannot begin to express how
urgent the situation is for all of us. If I have to stop writing and fight harder,
that's what I'll do. Writing is a very powerful tool for good, if it is used ethi-
cally. Maybe it could save the world. I make a plea to all Australian writers to
act ethically and with some sense of urgency, on behalf of all of those who are
suffering.

JK: Could you talk about the form of the book *Broken Land*? It works as a
kind of dark 'tour'.

CH: I sat on a bus in the Northern Territory in my early twenties. I thought
to myself, I want to be a tour guide. I know this land. It is inside me. Although
I never took that particular career path I have always felt a need to express the
land. It talks to me and then I translate. You are right when you say that *Broken
Land* was a dark tour. It was very dark and very broken out there. My heart
was smashed to pieces in order to write that book. My father drove me to a
few locations. But no one really accompanied me to those deeper places. The
book was written from a variety of notes and slides taken over a period of five
days in Brewarrina and Bourke, New South Wales. I photographed most of
the things I wrote about. In the end I didn't use the photos. I wanted to keep
the work universal by not using images with the text. The photograph is a
visual experience. Since the written word is not visual, the reader must com-
pensate by creating images. If the writing works the readers will go on their
own dark tours. I am only talking about what I went through. The reader can
do what they like with that work. I got lost on that tour anyway. When I
stepped off the plane at Sydney airport, I looked down at my shoe. I noticed
a bit of red dust on it. I thought, what the hell happened? Where have I been
for the past five days? That's how the book ended. I went back to Melbourne
and wrote from those notes. I wrote the book in two weeks. That's the fastest

book I ever wrote. There was no struggle. I guess that's a good feeling for any writer. The moment they are swept away.

JK: Ethical and moral concerns are central to your work, or maybe one could say 'project'. At what point, if any, do life and art separate for you?

CH: They don't. One is the other. I try to live my live creatively and to create a life in my art. It's the selfconsciousness of art that I abandon during the process of living. When I was writing *Broken Land* I went out to Brewarrina with the intention of writing, but the situation overwhelmed me. Taking photographic slides and writing down my notes every day was all I could do to keep up. As a writer I became irrelevant. I was simply carried away by something extraordinary. The self was abandoned to some extent. It all has to do with movement. The landscape was moving through me as I moved through it. We were continually swallowing each other. It was quite shocking. The important thing is that I believed it. I believed everything as it happened. I allowed it to happen and I wrote about the truth. I didn't want to mix with other artists or writers out there. That's the last thing I wanted. What I wanted was the raw truth. Also I don't try to be deliberately ethical when I write. But a slaughterhouse is enough to give anyone, even those who dine on the flesh of the murdered animals, a quick lesson in morality.

JK: Poetry as politics. Do poems exist as a form of direct action or merely as commentary on observation and response for you?

CH: When I can't change the world immediately, I furiously type my rage onto a screen. Writing for me is certainly is direct action. Often it's about an expression of despair or joy. I am part of that same world that I want to save. Ethical writing is a legitimate form of direct action as well as a legitimate art form. I believe that anything a human being does should be ethically motivated. This doesn't mean that poetry should be didactic propaganda. It means that it should be contributing something to the world audience. Writers are responsible to an audience the same as an actor is. It's just that we don't hear the applause. The world is on the brink of irreversible environmental annihilation. Seriously, all those larger North American and African animals will be gone within thirty years. The oceans are dying out. I could go on for a hundreds of pages with the details. As a writer I am responsible for recording my outer surroundings as much as my inner surroundings. I guess creative writing acts as a bridge between the two environments. As an animal rights activist, I am living through the genocide of millions of farm animals every day. These industries and the public's consumption of animal flesh amounts to little more than an international undercover massacre. It's a very hard place to be for anyone who cares. Writers are not simply egos working in isolation. We are a part of world politics. Anything we write will influence an audience in some way. Personally, when I hear the applause, I want to hear it through the eyes of the animals, the branches of the trees and the stillness of the stones. Then I will know that I am contributing to the world through my writing.

JK: What are you working on at present?

CH: At the moment I am working on fifteen creative writing projects. It is the equivalent of a visual artist who is working in a studio. On any given day they may move from one painting or installation to another. Then one will take their interest and they may work on that until it is complete. The best way for me to work is to try and understand what I want to say. The writing pours out and if I do enough of it, I start to notice that it fits into a number of subject categories at a given time. This indicates to me that I need to write about something. At the moment I know that anything I write will fit into one of these fifteen categories. That's the way it works for me.

JK: Could you talk about the notion of family in your work?

CH: I wrote a lot more about my family in my first books. I'm tending to let go of the apron strings now. I wasn't deliberately trying to write about them. They were who I knew and there was a lot of stuff to work out, before I could leave the home environment. It takes me a while to work things out. I might explore my father picking his toenails and dribbling animal fat down his singlet, for a few poems in a few books before I am satisfied. Once I am satisfied I will not write about it again. In writing about those things, other things regarding our relationship will be uncovered. Childhood is an inexhaustible source of creative inspiration for me. It provides answers. It has made me who I am and I enjoy the excavation process. I had to understand my relationship to my parents, before I could write about my brothers for example. Sometimes my own books reveal things to me afterwards. After a number of poems about my mother, I realised that she was always walking away. She had no facial expression. I heard her but I didn't see her. I was to eventually realise through my own writing that she had rarely touched me as a child. She hadn't even looked at me that much. As for my family's responses to being written about, they love it! My father pretends to be embarrassed but ends up giggling like a boy. I think he enjoys the risk element, saying, 'oh christ, you didn't write that did you?' He is afraid that the locals in Brewarrina will burn his house down, after I have written about him bitching about them. When I showed my mother a piece where she had been hitting my brothers with planks of wood that she had ripped off the side trellis, she said, 'don't forget to put in the bit where there were nails sticking out of the wood.' She signalled for a pen so that she could write it in herself. There was only one poem that ever offended her, and that was about her hanging out at Parents Without Partners. She does ballroom dancing and didn't want to be seen as socially desperate. She didn't care about a blurb featuring her vagina on the back cover of my first book with Penguin. Maybe they don't care because they know they have no control over it. Maybe they don't take my writing seriously enough. I don't know. But their attitudes have given me a lot of freedom.

JK: How central is the personal voice in your work? Do you see yourself as a landscape poet? A social poet?

CH: I write about what interests me and what has an emotional impact on me. I can talk about why I wrote something afterwards, but I don't like defining myself. By the time I have defined myself I've moved on and the definition has become yesterday's news. I do enjoy reading and writing poetry about the land. When I drove around Australia with my friend Adrian and two dogs I took a thousand slides of landscapes. There were hardly any of people or towns. It was all rock, river and tree. It was a landscape meditation. I enjoyed geography and geology during my high school years, although we were always being taught about what was there to be exploited within a landscape. I was more concerned with spiritual identity. A city is often like another city, but a good poem about the land can teach me something profound. I have just finished editing *The Book of Modern Australian Animal Poems*. I am now working on an anthology of modern Australian landscape poems beginning with Slessor's South Country right up until the present day. So I guess the landscape is where a large part of my interest lies. Too many people living in Australia do not know what a Dugong or a Quoll is. These animals are dying out. If people don't know what it is that exists in their own country, how are they going to have the capabilities to protect it? Not only that, but knowing about Dugongs and Quolls is a very enriching experience and makes me happy. You can empower yourself spiritually by exploring and understanding the land. I am interested in how we are relating to the animals and the landscapes in Australia, rather than the buildings, the cocktails, and the falafel rolls.

JK: What are your thoughts on prose poems?

CH: I like them. I like reading them and I like writing them. The content dominates in the prose poem. The line breaks are stated by the rhythm or the meaning creates them. I like any form where a truth is reached, before a form is explored. I have always been more interested in the idea rather than the construction of a piece. I prefer driving automatic vehicles rather than manual ones. It has to do with the way my mind works. My ideas move quickly. Anytime I have to think about process I can't work as effectively. It literally sickens me. I was no good at black and white photography at art school. I went straight into colour slides using a fully automatic camera. It was there that I worked most effectively. The complexity was maintained within what I chose to photograph, rather than the process of making a photograph. For me the prose poem is like this.

Coral Hull

B. THE MEANEST PROPERTY OWNER I EVER MET

made me use my own car to check the cattle, I did the gardening and the weeding and he wouldn't even get me a wheelbarrow, there was a big hole in the fence on the western perimeter of the property, I told him that the cattle were getting through, he said, *'good they can eat the grass of the other property owner and then come back again for water,'* he killed an old bull out there down on the backblocks, tried to feed it to me, even the dogs wouldn't eat it, he's the only bloke I know that makes five cups of tea out of one tea bag, one pair of trousers all winter, was so tight on the purse strings, didn't eat salt and pepper

David Kennedy

'I am assuming everything is all right and difficult'
                    — Frank O'Hara, 'Ode to Michael Goldberg'

I — Surfing

Getting out of the car in a waste land NCP,
I see I'm parked next to a cable company van.

Turning back to lock my door, I'm traversed by messages:
the logo on the BT tower, an Internet café sign.

And I know I should be standing tall receiving them,
optimistic, even smug, and certainly in love

with my position in a complex, changing fabric,
the shape-shifting trickster of my own open self,

but I miss the old stories, their creaky plots.
At least you knew where you were in them:

you had a street and a house with a number
and a good choice of ladders to climb up or climb down.

Now, who knows if they're a node or an island; if play
is just play or powerlessness made sexy and sold back to us

II — Driving

'... when a car is on the road I hear
My heart beat faster as it changes gear.'
                    — James Fenton, 'A Terminal Moraine'

Racing down the hillside, freewheeling in neutral,
speed plus gravity feels slick, taking me to the edge

of being out of control. This is the business: living
the new heroism, playing games of chance I can't lose,

with no skill. For the nth time I pass the sand
and gravel escape lanes at the slackening

of each bend and think how they have no-one's
name on them. They're a part of the game too,

a kind of useless morality carried over from
the last century, warning ecstasy's still inertia;

a via negativa that says we're not that good.
But we are. I glance at the speedo — eighty plus —

and reach down to change a cassette.
Sometimes this is all that's good about a day.

III — Building

'How things build up, build down'
                                    — David Morley, 'Superscience'

The earth mover sits on a pile of dirt
in a university science block courtyard

looking for all the world like Rodin's 'Thinker'
though it should be indecipherable, anti-nostalgic.

And what is that feeling that rises and hangs
in the air, like dust, over a knot of people

watching demolition in a city centre
as if they're not sure what to or how to be?

As I watch them and glug my bottled water,
I think I feel the same confusion, the queasiness

of not being sure if I'm involved or passive
in the face of change, if my finger really sets

the crossing's cycle; of wondering how I can consume
watching my world change as entertainment.

Mike Ladd

FIRE ESCAPES

'E-MAIL AIR
QUALITY AIR'
eye catching in ruddy tinscape —
the galvo seas rolled
from factory floors
each sheet stamped with a blue Queen
slicing colonial sky
and hands on the edge.

Late.
Video Star muzzy in fog,
condensation
on metal stairs —

open the big door:
the carpark, always.

*To burn
to blow
to pass without stopping.*

Midcheapnightel —
vague sounds in lifts
regular thump, *accelerando*
that's got to be … yes
wish they'd hurry up and come.

One office worker 34 floors up
(grain futures, meeting 8am tomorrow.)

FIRE INSTRUCTIONS:
*GET OUT OF YOUR ROOM AS
SOON AS POSSIBLE AND HEAD
TOWARDS THE EXIST*

vertiginous air
biting

John Bennett

THE LOOK
Eurostar 4.3.97

The poem is immediately striking because of the way it
inhabits the page
Standing but upright, vertical, …
re-enacting and retaining traces of the founding act of
humanity,
                    — Bernard Noel, Where Is Poetry Bound?

It's so easy to invade another country.
We sit back and relax, pull out our doings.
The student across from me is studying
a photocopied text, she glances a small surprise
at the blizzard of white on my lap,
so mean with ink and intelligible symbols.

The short lines are as recognisable
as a Roger Van der Weyden, or school of,
whose sharp eye I want to celebrate
the cool detail and astonishing technique,
the view shouts at the large windows:

Between the sea legs of Knocke
and thatch of the Ardennes
nomads are extinct.

The earth is turned again and again
in on itself — it looks
flat as if flattened
muddy as if muddied,
once complex systems simplified
by traditional agriculture
and the art of chemistry.

The monotonous topography
is ideal for trench warfare

and obsessed with tyre tracks.
Decomposition of the wildwood
finds willows stripped to fence posts
and clusters of houses walled
by rows of exotics, factory cloned
water draining the sky
over hairy horses and slender steeples,
the silent music of the Middle Ages.

The man opposite is well dressed, mid forties
and reading Rutger-Kopland, a Flemish poet.
I show him the book I'm writing on,
The New French Poetry.
He smiles, I ask if he speaks English,
none of which would interest the Flemish master
who painted those tall stylised figures
weeping real tears.

Ross Leckie

THE NATURAL MOOSE

This forest is coextensive with the mind's
expanse of spruce and pine and snow. Through it,
the moose meander mechanically in uncanny
circular tracks, following the map of their antlers'
tedious pointing. And here they come again
in an eternal return through space already occupied
by their previous going, until — you stop dead
to see one by the side of the road — it has entered
your map of asphalt disappearing over the hills.
What is your name and what are you called,
it seems to say, and how did you bring me here.
The crown of thorns lacerates your passing.
Is there an 'acrid odor'? Is it 'original response'?
But the night is as cold as white china and the air
is a dinner plate with a fine-edged crack. The moose
disappears back into its habit, and one night
as you stand at the sink washing dishes the phantom
moose vanishes, so you drop the plate. It lands on an edge
and circles back on itself; it doesn't break, the spruce
arched in the dark, and the pine thinking itself alone.

[from *The Authority of Roses*, London, Ontario: Brick Books, 1997]

Ross Leckie

Removing the Long Grass

The flies were at their worst the summer we worked
on the grounds crew of that old hotel. Well-heeled
old men clinging to their past mingled on the porch
and fingered the mountains that leaned close to us.

To our surprise, the splinter-handled scythes
were easy in their weight and sprung into the grass
by a simple dip and bob of the hips. A meadow
breeze echoed the sound that we made there.

The hotel carried its past like a persistent dream
of bronze fire-extinguishers, spring water
tapped from mountain creeks, the hiss and
tumble of embers turning in a wood furnace.

A pair of women sipping lemonade on a verandah
stretching into shadows in either direction sat
blankly looking into the summer heat. We swung
at the grass in an effort to save the picturesque.

We were only boys, too young to be much impressed
with scythe-sound or the rasp of the blades as they sliced
an indiscriminate path through the various weeds.
Flies hummed, and we sang the top forty all afternoon.

[from *The Authority of Roses*, London, Ontario: Brick Books, 1997]

Andrew Burke

REGIONAL AEOLIAN

Sometimes you must squint to see
things right, as through a glass darkly
the joy beyond. Other times nature's
lines are straight, a four four beat
between bars. *If within me balance
drew nigh* ... There's a composer in
this town who bought a stretch of
deserted powerlines down by Esperance
to record Aeolian music, ethereal as
wind washed by waves, the chill off
icebergs, a span of albatross wings,
the drumming of a drowned choirboy's
bones. I asked, Do you tune them?
He turned sharply, then softened at
my naiveté: I am sometimes tempted,
he said — gently, in confidence, Aeolian
in tone — tempted. Often, I said, I am too.
And were you an altar boy? There is
something Gregorian about the way
the ocean sings to the land.

In the early Sixties, we leapt out of Holdens under a sky
intensely blue, air rippling off the earth, we came upon
waves of white sand rolling to the ocean's edge. Old Eucla
town had moved inland, their dead left buried behind.
Out into the Southern Ocean, a jetty failed towards the
horizon. Whooping like boys, we ran to its first extant tim-
bers and clambered its limbs like slippery railway sleep-
ers, prickly with molluscs. Cautiously, we picked our way
through sheets of sky and ocean, then ran, leaping missing
planks, until hundreds of metres out we dived into the air.

Andrew Burke

THE OLD TAMBOURINE

'Let me forget about today until tomorrow.'
— Bob Dylan

Another interview over, I change
into old jeans, a T-shirt that says
'Happy Dad's Day' in my daughter's
young hand, and pull on gloves I have
borrowed from my eldest son. A bin
from Pete's Gold Bins waits out the front
of Number 3, two cubic metres to hold
ten years' detritus at this address. We
have told the children, and now
we're trying to accept the fact ourselves.
I walk to our back corner. Between shed
and fence lies a fetid mess of limbs,
broken cement slabs, old pots and ... I
start at the top. An hour and I'm
dripping. I have excavated through
tree limbs and broken garden pots to
pockets of worm-holed business ledgers,
shattered hand mirrors, and bright
plastic toys from childhoods now closed.
My hand frees an old tambourine,
skin gone, cymbals rusted and wood stained with the
sap of severed limbs. I slap it against my elbow, and it
crumbles. Sweat stings my neck where I shaved this
morning as I throw the pieces into the bin. A half-burnt
train. Red lego. A stuffed skyblue unicorn, misshapen
now like a dead mouse. Tonight I'll retire early, tired,
avoiding talk. We grow back our skins, every seven
years we re-upholster. Pete's Gold Bin is overflowing,
so I step in in my old gardening boots to stomp, to jump
up and down, to compress the rubbish into its fit space.

Tabish Khair

THE BIRDS OF NORTH EUROPE

Twenty-four years in different European cities and he had not lost
His surprise at how birds stopped at the threshold
Of their houses. Never

Flying into rooms, to be decapitated by fan-blades or carefully
Herded through open windows to another life, never
Building on the lampshade

Or on some forgotten, cool cornerbeam where droppings and straw
Would be tolerated until the fateful day hatched
And the world was fragile

Shell, feathers, a conspiratorial rustle of wings above and of
An intrigued girl below. Even the birds in their neat towns
Knew their place. They

Did not intrude into private spheres, demanding to be overlooked
Or worshipped. They did not consider houses simply
Exotic trees or hollowed

Hills. Not being particularly learned he did not know the thread
Of fear that knots the wild to the willed; not
Being well-read he

Did not remember the history behind their old and geometrical
Gardens, could not recall a time when the English
Parliament had killed a bill,

Shocked by a jackdaw's flight across the room. He simply marked
The absence of uncaged birds in their homes. He thought
It was strange.

Beate Josephi

AUSTRALIAN INTERIOR

I

Rain carved the features of this country.
Noon eats away at the range. Lanky lines
of watercourse and trees mark the soft sand
or clay earth too hard to bury bones.

The wind here is heard only by travellers
stumps of grass sing of their wandering feet.

II

Water beetles draw concentric circles
spin shadows against red rock
prefigure ancient drawings on sacred walls
round lines of ochre   light on shade.

Here the death of an emu remains
longer than rain-fed water in pools.

III

Slow boulders adrift a northern face
breaking as the sun beats the night cools
leaving ledges hanging over purple shadow.
Stone slides into a plain of nowhere distances

where spinifex's golden threads are a bad season's
temptation to forget the word for desert.

Matthew Zapruder

AMERICAN LINDEN

When you'd like to remember the notion of days,
turn to the barn

asleep on its hill,
a red shoulder holding the weight of clouds.

You could stand still for so many moments.
So little is over and over required,

letting the wind brush your crown.
The lathes of tobacco swing into autumn.

Swallows already discuss the winter.
I know you are tired of imagination.

All that whispering, clumsily grasping the sunlight.
Aren't you tired of bodies too?

Whenever it rains, they fall from the sky
and darken your window.

Clutching each other they call out names
while you sit in the circle thrown by a lamp

and pretend they are leaves.
The potatoes cringe and bury their heads.

Do you see them?
They know where to return when hoofbeats come.

Like you they were not born with pride,
they were born with skins made of earth.

Their eyes are black, and they sing out of tune,
quietly, under the snow.

Susan Bower

BOATING

1

Although you can't see them
tuberoses grow well on a headland
in the strange yellow light of a storm.
Knots whine down to depths
as masts form wishbones on deck.
Knowing what we know now there is no need
for these faces pressed to portholes.
The low pressure system could
simply be transcribed
in the skies above
but for now the barometer says
STORM.

The lighthouse is disordered
and turning darkly.

2

The guests point their noses
out to sea.
There's flowers in the foreground
and shells upon the beaches.
They pay for these things, hold them.
Calcite sediments itself in their minds
forming sporled horns, indomitable shells
a Renaissance in minutiae.
There is no end to the radiating pimples
of the sea urchin
the neediness of the creature evidenced
by its intake
its vents, valves, a sucking foot.

The scent of the guests is good today
and is carried as surely
as a coconut out to sea.

3

It is easy to blame the Kraken,
truly a terrible thing.
There are men in the ports,
even today,
great disks of flesh torn from them
a pox of fear.
For all the harpoons and cannons,
the great tentacles still wrap
around the hull, the mast,
the boat at a deathly angle
toward that silent lubricated world.
The descent is lost in the eyes
of creatures around them,
caught in silver scales
of a girth, rough fins.
Already an eel slides
through a broken porthole ...

WHERE THE WOMEN LIVE

1

Suede soft
these stamps are a
tender rupture
in the collection.

Confused by capacity
my hand stalls
over the buyers' album.

Under the spotlight
I check for the word
Reich.

2

Inner sanctum.
Chambers, fluid
     flaxen hair

crop.

Care is
     a cold circle of concern
pressed to the chest.

A tiny heart,

continent of the future
on which these women
live.
It is what they are
for

relax

have some tea

it is done.

3

Staring out from behind
inky bars
is a strong woman,

an aberration.

I collect the whole set.
An army.
Conical plate over each breast,
sword in hand,

ovaries stamped
Deutsches Reich.

4.
In the candlelight
the nurse tends
to the wounds
of the soldier.

He looks up,

they could be in love.

Jealousy
in the hooded eye
of the eagle surges
around the complexities
of the neighbouring cage.

Its heart is a four chambered swastika
longing to tear the lovers out
along their perforations.

George Ellenbogen

FROM WORLDS OF HELENE LENEVEU: A CORRESPONDENCE

OPENING

It is dead
winter on Sheep Pond. Nothing
moves. Only one
finger of light thinning
into a thickness of snow, a fleck
or two rising now
and then — or are they
falling — in spite of sun and stillness;

the fraction,
remainder, that breaks a calm
like electrical hum. My cassette
has emptied its lesson on German
negative imperatives, blocks
of language disassembled. We
resume over spreads of ocean
your cards our graph,
our telegraph.

THE MYSTERIOUS DISAPPEARANCE OF MRS SMITH

stabs like a headline, is
a headline, peering
from porno mags in local markets, over ready
thighs, razors and Mars bars,
promising scandals to nipple

the beaches in Nice, the tables
at Monte Carlo, and yielding
Mrs Smith.

                  No mystery. Her last
thirty years mortgaged
to a clothes hamper,

hamper stuffed with Mrs. Smith, unending
swallows of hose, underwear,
grateful for the washer's shudder
for this virgin
of sixty. She swirls now
in hulls of blouse, in water far
from Mediterranea, from Phoenicia,
but no further
than Whirlpool.

George Ellenbogen

THE GIRAFFE COLLECTOR

They follow him from corners
he cannot remember. Books
will not tell him where. But late nights
under a bare bulb he knows
the opening of drawers, the shift
of socks, old letters, the breathing
that mists a shoulders blade.

They nuzzle out his world,
its containers and insistent
blues imitating
Serengeti skies. They will not stay
crated like boxed bananas and soon
he will feel a giant haunch
against his haunch, but deeper,
feel them reaching
to late sun stripes on eucalyptus leaves,
browsing on shafts of light
with only birds for company.

They do not read the Bible but know
long necks will set them free.

Bugger the truth.

HL: Received your note on dull gray napkin.
You could have said their tails
hang like pendulums
or that my tales
hang with suspense, something
emergent. Your correspondence
may be a crate and not
for them.
or me

George Ellenbogen

It's Rainging Frogs Again

Four o'clock on Copley Square
late November
and you're aware
of something tugging
at the left lapel
of a coat that's just left
Burberry's. Eyes popping
light and drooling,

he clings insisting
on an upsidedown view
of the world.
You take him on,
a tenant, feel a weight
on your umbrella — a super raindrop
you sense is his cousin
(it's too embarrassing to check)
and you notice people stopping
to stare at you, and beyond them
frogs falling by the dozens,
                              the hundreds,
plague or blessing — you don't yet know —
as though they had become the universe,
the protoplasm, and your snicker
a pathology — like dust — that gets
swept away, unwritten, unpersoned.

HL: You didn't know frogginess (not toadiness!!) before you saw this card.
You imagine it's safe out there, the frogs tucked inside your fantasies, inside
borders, actually boarders, but they're not. You'll notice one March day, sepa-
rated in streaks of cloud, when they dive from those gashes of tulip color with
something that looks like a smile, that there's no longer a border, that you
have both come to inhabit the same world.

George Ellenbogen

THE DANGERS OF KNITTING

I've taken your indignation
under advisement, as well
as the 'you', my narrative
gambit, first rose of introduction
that you slipped
into, its raincoat,
umbrella, all of it

Odysseus discovered the world
was full of potholes, covered
by the calmest of waters. Things you see
as neutral, nothing, can turn
you into a pig, fasten you
to the bottom of the sea.

'Behold the sun,' the painting shrieks,
'and you will be rewarded with blindness.'
'No good deed goes unpunished,' Andrew Mellon
chirps in;

                    still she knits sweaters
for the troops,
for the victims of an earthquake,
any earthquake,
for the refugees toppling onto
rocky coasts, even yours,
glorying in the yarn,
its colors, its torso
shadow in green and yellow
designs, and even as her pincers add
to it, it turns into a cottonmouth
that has designs on her face,
thinning with a terror
that will not save her
that will not save me.

Karen Mac Cormack

At Issue V (understatements)

In the nanocapsule of exhaust cycles
continuous definer: tireless problems formulated en route
describes fog or wall paints to the layman
highlights archive contribution
a display medieval molten commemorates the Sixties.

Catching on, many relish resources having lecture
and until co-operation machined resistance
known deposition of calling such throughout lucidity
new legs half-centuries competitively continue.

Immediate 'post-immersion collapse'
'window-rattle, dash-jiggle or trim-chatter'
clipped hardtop forgiven optional far cry
scowls revival, compact advertising endures.

The low-key evidently perfect 'new'
mounted slice split series roll up
taken-over contents with alphabet chance
rushing knuckles visibility drives disbelief.

Unprepared escape hatch rusty reinvented
actually 'guestlist syndrome' for a shot chic bottomless
hissing reviving emporiums
[sic] 'glamour injection' scratch but done.

Added noughts and crosses justified conceding
momentum unlike transport tricks
salvation upwards looking built-in simplicity
wasn't simple.

'Slash-neck sleeveless' glass lifts into near collapse
stand on finish
glimpse entered accents blood-red draped
either inordinate sprays medley trunkful and runners 'whorl.'

Conceivable sublet dozen wherewithal dispersed
circular sunblush-slot curvy ubiquitous
encountering self-stripe mimicry unsettling
revelation area equals anything plethora.

At Issue VI   Pata   (people are talking about)

side by side almost the same reputation
driven to it sideways, manageable two o'clock
looks away, send off after-feel leaving
all the rules chances missed
from *if you have one* to
guess/stretch
making their mark:
complimentary opposites
irrational and rational 'the'
graphic only a matter of time
followed suit a strangely silent press
spreads campaigns
'extended gallery space'
not cross-fertilization
a photograph of mass-market irony
beyond current
after all curve
up one side
'It's so heaven'
abruptly disappears
'(somehow) be Fred'
a dark sting with tailgating
paranoia on a Mobius strip
it's broadcast instead of aglitter
coming-of-age suburbs
by now it's clear more than dialogue
rough inspiration
that dichotomy is kind of big
prevent & correct

rest of the day nearby (an ocean view)
between chaos and order
or reactions emerge as elegies
last remnants
compositions scrutinized
 small-town hold on the truth
a sometimes participant
sense of humor on the food chain
bumping into intense
'Third act, all whammies.'
a real life
until an agent
taken apart, reassembled, punctured
improperly inserted, lost all feeling
instructions on support
logical medical counselling
all women (underreported aspect)
to advance the legalization
even the decision
to help who did expressly
a confusing situation
planned death directing the end
knowing 'where to go next'
this added sensitivity
confirm a diagnosis
placebos regimen
man-made substance
for hours at a time
what would you do with my head?
corridor of tanked length
with off-the-rack technicians
uneven bare
'To him. But not to me.'
give it a try
aesthetic artillery at ease
laser light veteran
pyramid season within minimalism
steeped in wraparound transition
storage space not big enough for two
wearing what suits flexibility options
the usual spin

the question is metal
reappeared in between solved
fraught with everybody else did it
timeshares/temporary bed
a foyer to generic
supplanted self-detachment
in ordinary things
they proposed compound an instance
without missing a step
your own with exposure
momentum planned or not
don't always get it right

Peter Kenneally

She is sitting in a decrepit swivel chair red vinyl with the armrests gaping open and sharp snackery edges cracks all over it and picked at off-green foam rubber and lizardskin cracks all over. She is wearing a big grey unravelling jumper a beanie with TIGERS written all over it a scarf with red and black stripes several layers making all kinds of lumps under the jumper a pair of fluffy fluffballed trackies some very pink very swollen leg warmers fingerless gloves and very shiny and new dance pumps/ and she is shivering like a newborn lamb on a hill farm. Her feet are three inches away from a fan heater the coils of which are carpeted with dust and glowing red and quivering. Her face is a mask of indifference and she is speaking indifferently into the telephone/ on the wall behind her there is a poster which is torn to shreds but still features a feather boa a breast being held by a hairy hand a teary eye and says ..GOOD...MAN...LLE. (X). She paints her nails green and then cleans them and then pink and then silver yawning all the while / she reads a magazine from cover to cover and then puts the phone down and walks across the room and makes a cup of instant coffee periodically she makes some retorts in the direction of the phone/ and her breath rises to the ceiling like bursts of flak and then runs down the wall with all the other condensing material taking on brown or green or grey in its course to the skirting board / where it settles in a ridge of dust cum mould. She walks back to the phone picks it up listens shrugs and puts it back on its cradle then picks it up and cleans it leaves it off the hook goes out of the room comes back blowing her nose on some bog roll and hangs it up / jumps / and picks it up again. Her face puckers and pinches and she hunches in her chair so that her hair hangs over her face. She is quite still for some seconds and then hangs the phone up and makes some notations in a notebook/ and picks the phone up/ and makes some notations in a notebook/ and then hangs up/ and then she dials a number and leans under the desk and brings out a plimsoll and begins to speak and to whack the desk at intervals and her face is wreathed in her breath and the grin she has from ear to ear/ for about ninety seconds and then she puts the phone down and takes a curried egg sandwich out of the desk draw. Her eyes take a long look at the ceiling and then she picks up the phone again and begins to spray tiny pieces of egg all over the shop/ for about a minute and then she hangs up the phone and takes a paper bag out of her pocket which is more of a crushed sticky white and brown and black mess than a bag and she extracts a humbug covered with

298

paper from it and pops into her mouth/ and answers the phone again and listens and sucks on the humbug/ takes it out and has a good look at it while shetalks into the phone/ and then pops it back in and begins to chomp chew and then suck on it with it held between her front teeth / and then hangs up the phone. She looks up and a young woman with a walkman on comes in sits a bit further along the desk arranges an array of textbooks and folders around her / falls into deep and studious concentration / and picks up the phone.

FULCRUM TWO

she is sitting on the floor on a rough flat aquamarine arse scarifying apology for a carpet laid in tile squares several of which are missing or worn into arse shaped lacunae which reveal shiny polished but still black floorboards beneath/ but she is sitting on a carpetbag pouffe. The light is hard yellow and flickery and the walls are bare plywood washed over with a coat of sickly pink primer. She has luxuriantly curled blonde hair which she takes off so as to scratch her cropped and puce coloured hair and then tugs back onto her head as if it is a beanie and she is at a tram stop/ and she pulls her raincoat tightly around her shoulders and examines her toenails which are painted black with microscopic determination. There is a kind of a slot like a letterbox in the wall opposite her which she is alternately glaring at or studiously looking away from and suddenly she casts her raincoat into the corner of the room and jumps to her feet / the light changes to a glaring and impenetrable darkroom red/ she is naked / the slot glows a little as if someone has lit a candle for her / she begins to gyrate. She gyres and gimbles/ always in the same direction and always at the same pace and her hands pass across her body slowly and heavily as if she is hanging wallpaper. She pulls one breast up with both hands and examines it dispassionately / and then the other and then she she lifts them both up together and squints between them like someone trying to see the number on a tram in the distance. She puts her hands on her hips and shakes her groin around in a stilted approximation of the wild thing / and then gets down on all fours and examines the carpet as if she has lost a contact lens / and periodically rotates her bum heavily and industrially / and then she lies on her back and raises herself on her elbows and regards the slot dispassionately for a second / grimaces / waggles her tongue / and then jumps up and fishes out a vibrator from her raincoat pocket and points it at various sectors of her anato-

299

my with an air of detachment and finally walks up to the slot smiles lascivi-
ously and with a short Roman backswing delivers it through the slot to the hilt
and stands back panting arms akimbo and wig askew and then the light
abruptly changes to fluorescent white to red again and then the wall with its
ravished slot shudders forwards and then collapses mournfully backwards.
On the far side of it is a room full of racks of magazines wrapped in plastic and
with various men of a certain age each clutching a book or a magazine or some-
thing in a carton / and each of them tears the shrinkwrap from the nearest item
and burns incandescently crimson from behind it. At the counter a middle
aged woman wearing a pink cardigan and knitting fails to acknowledge these
events and continues to flick idly through a magazine in which tongues almost
disembody themselves from their owners and wander in pursuit of wedding
tackle which remains forever at a tantalising remove. The raincoat is buried
under several feet of plywood and plaster. She marches up the nearest reader
and disarming him of his protective banner gently and with soothing gestures
divests him also of his raincoat which she puts with a tiny shudder and then
she hurries out looking at her feet/ and he is himself quit naked except for a
blonde wig and clutches to his midriff a copy of BIG BLACK AND ETER-
NALLY PENITENT. And his penitence is plain for all to see.

FULCRUM THREE

He is standing at the intersection of two streets next to a newsstand and a fruit
stall/ traffic passes normally up and down the up and down street from east to
west in a cloud of tram dust and from north to south along the side to side street
at his back there are trams trucks cyclists police cars anbulances fire engines
and the occasional bewildered looking pedestrian but no traffic.The sun is
everywhere itself and everywhere is its domain and an endless crocodile of
passersby pass him by huddling into the shopwindowshade as they go with-
out looking at the contents of the windows or at each other or at him. He is
standing in the middle of the pavement and the passersby part to flow around
him but only halfheartedly so that generally he is buffeted and mashed and
seems to lean backwards rather and then to almost fall and take a step back-
wards whereupon he plants his foot squarely in the middle of a lurid repro-
duction of a Pre-Raphaelite painting of a dreamy Victorian Arthurian doomed
type which a hippy has been laboriously copying from a lurid reproduction in

a book/ and a thin smile and a shoulder hunching grimace are exchanged. He moves a little further up and in from the kerb/ and detaches from the bundle of newspapers he has under his arm one which is called SPARTA...IS... THE...ICE...O HE...LEFT as far as the wrinkles in it and the screwing up he is doing with his fist as he holds it aloft allow it a name. And there is a picture of President Bush or Mitterand or Mrs Thatcher or Harry Truman sitting astride a bomb like Slim Pickens in Dr Strangelove and waving the same ten-gallon hat and a headline alongside says HI..IM A..TOP..TIN..MAN NOW in between the-white clenched knuckles of his other hand/ and he is muttering something into his collar over and over again and occasionally mutters it into the open air over the heads of the passersby/ and then opens the paper and scans it and then begins to mutter with an expression of strengthened resolve which fades quickly into an expression of pained resignation and into his collar more and more he sinks until finally he seems to sleep softly against his shoulder and sway slightly in the breeze which picks up and pushes against the tide of passersby / dampens / washes away the Lady of Shalott/ the old cabbage leaves and the tattered posters with bits of a starlet's tits on them/ and wets the papers under his arm into a wad. A tall man with a black leather jacket and black trousers and a black flanny shirt and dirty ginger hair and a pair of ersatz workman's boots and blackrimmed glasses marches up to him andbegins to gesticulate and ejaculate and berate him/ and tries to divest him of his stock of newspapers/ but rips away an armful of pulp which flies up and clouds in the wind and smothers him in linty papier mache. He tears frantically at himself and staggers away andfalls headlong over a black district nurse's bicycle which stands on its kick stand adjacent to the action/ with a pile of newspapersthree feet high balancing precariously on its pack rack/ which fly up and around him so that he is covered in them and staggers away and reads ..RUG..UP NOW...OTHERS. EVOLUTION..IS..TABLE..MADE IN...ALBANIA. And the still sleeping man sways and falls across the bicycle which lurches off its stand and slowly and drunkenly swerves and wobbles away like an uncle after a wedding.

FULCRUM FOUR

He is sitting at the base of a plane tree which is in full leaf and all the leaves of which are flat and angular and impenetrable. The plane tree is in the middle of a street in the middle of a line of plane trees which march along the median strip except where it is mostly parked cars and also up and down the pavement on either side.The sun which is up there somewhere forces its way doggedly through every gap in the foliage equally / and the light where he is sitting and all along the street is exactly like the light in the produce tent at a country show or the beer tent for that matter. He is shaved raw and has several bits of bog roll fluttering in the breeze here and there on his chin.He is wearing a tight lycra top and painted on lycra shorts and a pair of tatty runners with their soles flapping in the wind / next to him there is a torn canvas shoulder bag lying open on the ground with a slew of envelopes and parcels spewing out of it onto the dirt and on the strap there is a two way radio which he inclines his head towards now and then until he unfastens it and shoves it into the bottom of the bag takes out a banana and a bottle of something which is electric blue and eats it all and drinks it all and then collapses back against the tree and looks utterly cactus and bereft. A council truck pulls up on the far side of the tree and a bloke sitting in it performs various contortions so that without getting out of the cab he can water the tree with a hose which he uses like a tightrope walker's pole. The water first of all bounces off the compacted dirt raising a cloud of wet dust which soon settles back into the mud which soon forms and when there is a three inch deep brown puddle all around the tree and spilling over into the street and down the drain he moves on / and he is sitting there first of all splashed with muck and now up to his haunches in manky water and looking up as if it is coming on to rain. All the letters and stuff in the bag have now merged into a browny-yellow mush / he takes the radio out of the bag speaks into it shakes it bangs it and then drops it into the puddle and lowers his head onto his knees. The light becomes more intensely yellow and more intensely shady and the puddle drains off and dries away / there is a breeze which stirs the tree a little now and then enough for the odd bit of the sun itself to strike him / he shifts about and wriggles his neck and this is all. On the other side of the tree the bicycle which is leaning there shifts in the breeze also and the ragged wisps of canvas along the side of the front tyre where the inner tube has pushed its way through wave in the breeze also / the tube is visible as a small bubble like a squash ball against the rim until it bursts gently in the sun and the tyre and the bicycle subside into the mud a little and the front wheel collapses softly against the smooth flank of the tree with a mournful half roll forward and the flat tyre runs into his shoulder blade. He looks up / he has dark rings under his eyes / which are gleaming and misty /he is smiling /and he shifts around and looks at the ruined tyre and runs his fingers gently along the split and even inside it with a faraway look on his face / until a great huge hairy pair of legs and a pair of shorts full to bursting front and back arrive and grab the sodden envelopes and the radio and depart. His eyes close. He looks bathed in relief and bliss. He falls to sleep.

John Burnside

Communiqué

Even before we met, I was obsessed
with distance:

a boy in a garden, with string, and a twelve-inch ruler,
plotting the lawn,

or counting the paces I took
on the road to school;

finding my way in the dark
when the clocks went forwards,

or losing the church in a snowfall, when houses and gardens
shifted apart.

Even before we met I was prepared
for miles of wiring, versts of ripened grain,

acres of frost between us, or the blue
immensity of night skies over Linz —

so when I think of telephones, or rain,
I think of you,

when pollen or the smell of barley fields
drifts through my house, I know what measure is:

how even the rivers and airports
connect, as they hold us apart,

and any touch is mystery enough
to keep me true:

no more than a breath of wind
on a lamplit square,

or the bruise on a traveller's shin, from a badly-steered trolley
in Schiphol, or San Francisco,

darkening slowly
in Paris, or Santiago,

or healing, weeks later, in Tromso,
or Bucharest.

Alison Georgeson

STORY

It starts with a constellation of needs — a galaxy
of preferences and positions:
a sign of his "real"ness.

I'm in a hundred pieces wondering
what to do with him. I don't want to
force him into another narrative
contract

(as though my own trajectory were
peripheral or disinclined)

It looks as though we will refrain
from even
        visiting
suffering subsequent losses
those recurrent losses, that thematic
of loss
indefinitely.

I opt to save myself
reinvent an imperative surface
there are just so many
        soundings
so many drifting sense-data, so many
        past and present fields.

Alison Georgeson

DUST

Someone shuffles through the doors of the saloon
     kicks some dust off their boots   and that dust settles
somewhere in the room   perhaps on the floor
which could be seen as *foundational*
     or perhaps dust is absorbed into the atmosphere
to form part of the *atmospheric*
        conditions of this site.

Lizards climb rockfaces, downpipes and certain types
of creeping jasmine. Look for indeterminate profiles
especially ones with hats on
     horses restless beneath them.

This is not the same vampiric emptiness that could
     spread along the walls of your mouth/my mouth
        or reverberate along the strings of his guitar.

What the fiddle produces leaves no space unoccupied.

I'm not just another bronco buster!
I'm not another drugstore cowboy!

There are discords and there are reversals;
     rehearsals, rhymes, and registers.

These are nomad thoughts and this is a mouthpiece.
     You know it's honky tonk, a thistle
        a hot wind at the edge of the desert.

Alison Georgeson

CORRESPONDENCE

Not a vexed question
our lying here

we are not formulated
    on the head of a pin

Love proliferates in the shadows
of this darkened room

        a quarter moon dividing
        its own reflection

Brian Henry

REVIEW OF *MEADOWLANDS* BY LOUISE GLÜCK

Since Homer introduced that wily traveler Odysseus to the world, countless poets have attempted to resurrect the tale and make it their own. Odysseus' 10-year voyage home has become an undeniable part of our collective unconscious. Children draw a Cyclops on one page and the action figure *du jour* on the next. In a similar gesture, poets major and minor have dipped into the *Iliad* and *Odyssey* for their own poems; just in the past few decades, poets as diverse as Marilyn Hacker, Richard Wilbur, Margaret Atwood, Michael Longley, and Yannis Ritsos have devoted poems to Odysseus or to aspects of his journey (Circe seems to be particularly alluring of late). Now, Louise Glück, an accomplished re-writer of classical and biblical narratives, inhabits Odysseus' world and transforms it into her own in her most recent collection, *Meadowlands*.

Unlike most poets revising the Odyssey, Glück is less interested in the man and more intrigued by the people around him — Penelope, Telemachus, Circe. As suitors swarm the house, cleaning out the cupboards and basically wrecking the place, Penelope stoically weaves. Observing his detached mother from a distance, Telemachus mopes and pitches fits to try to get her attention. And when Circe's lover leaves her, she rages and grieves, vowing revenge. What sets these poems apart from other Odyssean poems is Glück's own weaving: *Meadowlands* is a dualistic narrative that juxtaposes an ordinary contemporary marriage against Odysseus' famous one. This straddling of the classical and the contemporary allows Glück to consider the mundane details that constitute a marriage, as well as those that contribute to its dissolution, without becoming tedious or self-indulgent. The juxtaposition of these two strained marriages gives the book a rich, polyphonic texture.

Glück is at her best in *Meadowlands* when she adds complex psychological insight to the people inside Odysseus' circle. 'Penelope's Song', the book's opening poem, is especially powerful because it captures perfectly her vacillating personality. When she asks young Telemachus to climb a tree and watch for the arrival of his father, she progresses through several striking emotions. The poem is worth quoting in full because it evinces both Glück's mastery of this psychological complexity and her always-engaging language:

> Little soul, little perpetually undressed one,
> do now as I bid you, climb

the shelf-like branches of the spruce tree;
wait at the top, attentive, like
a sentry or look-out. He will be home soon;
it behooves you to be
generous. You have not been completely
perfect either; with your troublesome body
you have done things you shouldn't
discuss in poems. Therefore
call out to him over the open water, over the bright water
with your dark song, with your grasping,
unnatural song — passionate,
like Maria Callas. Who
wouldn't want you? Whose most demonic appetite
could you possibly fail to answer? Soon
he will return from wherever he goes in the meantime,
suntanned from his time away, wanting
his grilled chicken. Ah, you must greet him,
you must shake the boughs of the tree
to get his attention,
but carefully, carefully, lest
his beautiful face be marred
by too many falling needles.

There is obviously a lot happening here: motherly tenderness giving way to sternness, with a hint of blackmail because of the boy's 'troublesome body'; sexual innuendo in the boy's naughty actions and the father's 'demonic appetite'; an unexpected introduction of normalcy, as if the father is returning, suntanned and hungry, from a vacation; and a startling sense of the fragility of this great warrior.

Because of Telemachus' incessant self-analysis, we can almost envision him on the couch as he narrates these poems, particularly 'Telemachus' Detachment':

When I was a child looking
at my parents' lives, you know
what I thought? I thought
heartbreaking. Now I think
heartbreaking, but also
insane. Also
very funny.

This little poem is perception-shattering, wiping away everything heroic and grand about Odysseus' return and Penelope's fidelity, for who is more apt to lionize the hero-father than the son? Here Telemachus' detachment borders on the sadistic, but in 'Telemachus' Guilt,' he attempts to explain his behavior:

> ... patiently
> she supervised the kindly
> slaves who attended me, regardless
> of my behavior, an assumption
> I tested with increasing
> violence. It seemed clear to me
> that from her perspective
> I didn't exist, since
> my actions had
> no power to disturb her: I was
> the envy of my playmates.
> ... I used to smile
> when my mother wept.
> I hope now she could
> forgive that cruelty; I hope
> she understood how like
> her own coldness it was,
> a means of remaining
> separate from what
> one loves deeply.

An unflattering self-portrait, but we can imagine his friends goading him into increasingly intense tantrums while his mother ignores him. Telemachus seems to be easing toward redemption, and because his poems speak directly to us, we are the ones who can grant him that redemption. Gradually we start to sympathize with him:

> ... I no longer regret
> the terrible moment in the fields,
> the ploy that took
> my father away. My mother
> grieves enough for us all.
>   ('Telemachus' Confession')

With his painful fall into self-awareness ('after awhile / I realized I was / actually a person'), this is Telemachus at his most vulnerable.

The one character in the Odyssean saga who loses no matter how we look at the situation is Circe. Excoriated for turning men into swine, newly bereft of her lover of seven years, and jealous of Penelope but forbidden to harm her, Circe is the most pitiable of the three who have lost Odysseus — and she's the immortal. In 'Circe's Power,' she pleads her case:

> I never turned anyone into a pig.
> Some people are pigs: I make them
> look like pigs.
>
> I'm sick of your world
> that lets the outside disguise the inside.
>
> Your men weren't bad men;
> undisciplined life
> did that to them.

But although she 'reverse[s] the spell' on Odysseus' men, she still loses her lover, asserting that 'If I wanted only to hold you // I could hold you prisoner.' Powerful yet abandoned, beautiful yet unloved, Circe can only visit Penelope — as a bird at the window — in an effort to disrupt the marriage and insinuate herself into the situation: 'if I am in her head forever / I am in your life forever' ('Circe's Grief').

The second marriage in *Meadowlands* presents us with a dilemma as readers: we want to find autobiography in these poems, but must resist such a reading despite some themes in the poems that coincide with Glück's life (whether as trifling as the names of her husband and son or as consuming as her desire for control and her preference for solitude, which she acknowledges in her essay, 'Education of the Poet'). Although I rarely equate a narrator with the poet, the emotional power of these poems makes such an equation tempting. Attributing autobiography to these poems, however, would undermine their integrity, anchoring them to a personality when they can easily stand apart from that personality. Indeed, Glück insists on this separation: 'A lady weeps at a dark window. / Must we say what it is? Can't we simply say / a personal matter?' ('Moonless Night'). To call these poems 'confessional' would both pigeon-hole them and contravene Glück's project.

Instead of confessing, Glück implies. Because the unsaid in these poems is as important as the said, the poems re-create the difficulties of communication — the gaps and silences, the false starts and bizarre tangents, the misunderstandings, the ulterior motives. Many of these poems are composed in dialogues, without quotation marks or 'he said/she said' as guideposts (indents are the only structural indications of a change in speakers). There is also a running dialogue throughout the book, as the conversation of one poem is picked up in another. Occasionally, the breakdown of communication between this couple can be funny:

> I stopped liking artichokes when I stopped eating
> butter. Fennel
> I never liked.

> One thing I've always hated
> about you: I hate that you refuse
> to have people at the house. Flaubert
> had more friends and Flaubert
> was a recluse.

>> Flaubert was crazy: he lived
>> with his mother.
>>   ('Ceremony')

But the poems are more often heart-breaking than humorous. In 'Rainy Morning,' the poet chides herself much as her husband would:

> ... Your
> staying dry is like the cat's pathetic
> preference for hunting dead birds: completely

> consistent with your tame spiritual themes,
> autumn, loss, darkness, etc.

> We can all write about suffering
> with our eyes closed. You should show people
> more of yourself; show them your clandestine
> passion for red meat.

And in these poems she is tempted to take her own advice, but uses myth as a way to distance herself from the poems. In 'Anniversary,' the husband's hostility toward her comes through in his own words: 'I said you could snuggle. That doesn't mean / your cold feet all over my dick.' And in the three 'Meadowlands' poems, the spouses tirelessly spar with each other. 'Meadowlands 3' covers ground usually ignored by poetry, making this perhaps the first collection of poetry to be named — on one level — after an

American football stadium:

> How could the Giants name
> that place the Meadowlands? It has
> about as much in common with a pasture
> as would the inside of an oven.

Adversarial as ever, the two bait each other, the husband finally admonishing his wife with 'You'd be a nicer person / if you were a fan of something.'

The most touching of these poems are those that stem from a mundane moment, as in 'Midnight':

> Speak to me, aching heart: what
> ridiculous errand are you inventing for yourself
> weeping in the dark garage
> with your sack of garbage: it is not your job
> to take out the garbage, it is your job
> to empty the dishwasher …
> is this the way you communicate
> with your husband, not answering
> when he calls, or is this the way the heart
> behaves when it grieves: it wants to be
> alone with the garbage? If I were you,
> I'd think ahead. After fifteen years,
> his voice could be getting tired; some night
> if you don't answer, someone else will answer.

The poignancy of the poem comes from tiny details such as whose responsibility it is to do which chore, its power from the culmination of the narrator's worries and self-doubts in the final two lines. Sometimes these poems seem so particular, so intimate through their complete withdrawal of intimacy, that we feel like eavesdroppers. The man and the woman are laid bare to us by Glück, their neuroses exposed but never melodramatized — he maintains a chilling composure while she wants to withdraw from the world, the only thing they have in common being the need/desire to control her.

As we would predict with a poet as devoted to ambiguity and multiple meanings and voices as Glück, the two narratives merge in a few poems. For example, we know that 'Departure' describes the scene the night before Odysseus leaves for Troy, but we can see the other marriage in the poem as well:

The night isn't dark; the world is dark.
Stay with me a little longer.

Your hands on the back of the chair —
that's what I'll remember.
Before that, lightly stroking my shoulders.
Like a man training himself to avoid the heart.

... you are holding me because you are going away —
these are statements you are making,
not questions needing answers.

How can I know you love me
unless I see you grieve over me?

This interwoven narrative of two marriages serves the book brilliantly
where an entire collection devoted to one or the other could easily become
tedious. Ultimately, Glück's vision in *Meadowlands* brings out the heroic in the
ordinary and the ordinary in the heroic, revealing to us the tragedy common
to all relationships.

John Kinsella

INTERVIEW WITH ROBERT ADAMSON, 1996

JK: We'll begin by talking about an interview with Michael Palmer in *Exact Change*, the American journal with a recently-published issue that focuses on LANGUAGE poetry, and the American and other avant-gardes. I'll refer to a comment that Michael Palmer makes early in the interview, regarding Robert Duncan: 'When Duncan speaks to that grand collage, it is certainly not singular in its construction, I mean this is the construction, an instance of how it constructs itself.' He's using Duncan as a reference, but he's talking about the notion that poetry comes from lots of different sources, and it's pulled together but becomes something entirely valid in itself, even though it's made up of lots of component parts. Have you anything to say about that, Bob?

RA: Yes, it's that image ... When Robert Duncan came to Australia and stayed at my place for two weeks before he went on his tour of Australia we started off like this, almost having an interview-discussion. He used to let me give him a metaphor or an image of what poetry is to me, and he said (I've repeated this before, but I'll get it right this time): Each poet is a link in a chain which goes from the beginning of time when the first poet wrote, to the end of time and the last poet. In poetry there is no such thing as time. Poetry exists in the eternal present which is the past, the future, all coexist. And so you have the image of a chain, with each poet being a link in that chain.

JK: We'll later be discussing the parallel strains in your work of lyricism and interest in the way language works. *The Clean Dark* is seen as the height of your lyrical powers, whereas *Waving to Hart Crane* is seen as the peak of your experimentalism. Do you see that notion of things coexisting, of various poetries being outside time, as relevant to the duality of your writing?

RA: Now I'm conscious about that; when I started, I wasn't. When I started writing poetry, I just wanted to write poetry, and I wanted to find out what poetry was; and so by reading everybody I could, starting with Shelley and ending up with Mallarmé — you know, after about five years you get a fair picture of what it is. Then you discover the Modernists — Ezra Pound, T. S. Eliot, and Zukofsky — and then you realise, that's what Palmer is referring to as Duncan's idea of the grand collage.

JK: Yes.

RA: So it's a matter of awareness and education; it's a matter of how much you know. The more you know, the more you are capable of going into a new area of the unknown. And as you travel you're discovering things, your work is discovering things. Your work is really a record of what you're discovering in this imaginative adventure. Duncan calls it an adventure of the imagination.

JK: Duncan has been in many ways quite central to your poetics.

RA: Before I met Duncan, I was reading a lot of American poetry. I was especially interested in W. S. Merwin, and I was steeped in all that 'deep image' poetry. Robert Bly, Mark Strand, James Wright. Now, when Ginsberg came to Australia in 1970, or '71, I think it was around that time, he came to the Adelaide Festival, I was there to do a reading — with great expectations. Ginsberg was invited that year, he had been on the judging panel for the Pulitzer Prize, and they had just awarded it to W. S. Merwin, so I was really excited. I wasn't so interested in Ginsberg — I'd discovered him five or ten years earlier through Bob Dylan; Dylan led me to Rimbaud and then to Ginsberg. Then when I … read *Howl* I thought, 'Oh, right, this is a level up from Dylan', but after *Howl* I read through Ginsberg and realised Dylan was way ahead. Way ahead of Ginsberg! Dylan is often mentioned by some of these so-called language-centred poets as a person who is acceptable to them, whereas Ginsberg wouldn't be, so much. He's the sort of epitome of the great heroic poet-mage which puts a lot of people off these days. Whereas Dylan, because of his postmodernism, his ability to create himself, continually recreate himself — he uses all that for commercial reasons — [is different].

JK: Also the LANGUAGE poets might say they had a political problem with Ginsberg, insofar as he's a self-contained poet who only refers to things that he has directly experienced in the 'ego' — he projects from his ego — whereas Dylan is someone who's making social commentary.

RA: That's right.

JK: And they are more or less social commentators.

RA: Yes, exactly. Dylan was into social-comment poetry before LANGUAGE POETRY existed. He didn't use that poet role in the way Ginsberg did. But getting back to Ginsberg: I arrived in Adelaide thinking when I met Ginsberg

I'd find out a lot about W. S. Merwin ... One night we ended up in a hotel with Ginsberg and various other people. Finally everyone got tired at about 3 or 4 o'clock in the morning, and then I was alone with Ginsberg. I started asking him all these questions about W. S. Merwin, and the type of thing that Merwin was interested in, including Merwin's version of religions. After ten or so minutes, Ginsberg said, 'Stop. stop, stop, you're talking to the wrong man', and wrote down Robert Duncan's name and address, and handed it to me. He said, 'Here's someone that will share your interests, a scholar-poet.'

When he gave me the address, I was just terribly disappointed in Allen Ginsberg. I thought, it's just his way of palming me off. Then I thought, 'well, why did I expect more?' It was just that he was the first American poet that I ever met, and I thought there'd be more, and there wasn't. But I underestimated Ginsberg in this, because when I came back to Sydney, my wife at the time, Denise, asked me what happened and I said, 'Oh, Ginsberg palmed me off and gave me Robert Duncan's address.' Duncan was this unapproachable person, who was one of the great poets, and I just wouldn't have imagined he would ever write to me, and so I was very disappointed. She didn't say anything to me but she put one of my books in an envelope and sent it to Robert Duncan, and three weeks later I went to the mail and there was this letter with a San Francisco postmark on it, and this beautiful handwriting, from Robert Duncan. I just couldn't believe it. I ripped it open; there was this long letter-essay about my poetry and how much he liked it. So I wrote an answer which took about a month, an essay answer, and we started a correspondence which went on for ten years. But after writing to him for five years I asked him would he like to come to Australia, and he said yes ... I just didn't think — why would they be interested in a connection with a few desperate poets in this barbarous culture at the bottom of the world? — that was my image ... But I'd been reading so much, I was full of all these questions that Duncan was interested in. So when he said, 'Yes, I'll come to Australia', I went running in to the Literature Board and said, 'Robert Duncan's willing to come to Australia!' and they said, 'Who's Robert Duncan?' I was just destroyed by that.

Finally I went to a bank and got a loan from a bank manager to bring him here. First of all the bank manager said, 'What are you talking about?' I said, 'Bringing a poet to Australia is not as strange as you think.' I had all this literature, and Duncan at the time was doing lectures around the circuits in America, and he was getting good money. And he had posters, and I had all the Duncan advertising material. I laid it out on the desk of the bank manager, and I said, 'It's not much different from bringing the Beatles to Australia, or a pop singer.' He got this, and it went click ... and it all made sense to him. about. He gave me the money, and we brought Duncan here.

JK: Stylistically, in what way did Duncan influence you, when you approached his writing after speaking to Ginsberg?

RA: It was really direct, but ... as soon as he answered the letter, I read his poetry again, of course. I immersed myself in *Roots and Branches*, *The Opening of the Field*, all those early books. To me it was a great freedom because here was an American poet still using the rhetoric and the mannerisms of Shelley. You know, in Australia if you made mannerisms like that, you were trounced by people like John Tranter and others of my peers. So it gave me a great permission to do anything I wanted to do. But the more I read at the time, the more I veered from Merwin. When Duncan arrived, I was working on a poem — a set of poems, 'The Grail Poems', now my original idea for these came from Jack Spicer's Grail poems, but whereas Jack Spicer did them in a manner that, say, someone like Tranter would probably accept — they were spiky, urban poems, he took the Grail myths and just placed them in the streets of San Francisco and wrote them in the jargon of the time — I used mythological, romantic language mixed with modernist language. I was working on the last one — I showed it to Duncan (I was halfway through it) and he picked up my pen and wrote the rest of the poem. So I looked at it, put it through my typewriter, I did another version of it, he wrote more lines on that. We had a co-written poem.

JK: When you are composing your poetry, do you have a notion of the reader? Palmer is actually asked by the interviewer about 'creating a reader', like creating a text, and he replies, 'there's no ideal reader'.

RA: Yes. That was really interesting.

JK: 'One doesn't even want an ideal reader. One projects a possible reader or set of readers who have no outline, a readership of potential who have the generosity to complete the meanings of the work, and to complete the circuit.' Now to me, that's the core of LANGUAGE poetry: that the reader does the work and in doing that is influenced and illuminated ...

RA: I only wish that interview had come out before I finished 'The Sugar Glider'. I refer to Eliot's concept of an ideal reader — I wrote 'This is the joy of being a modern poet, to skip time/ and space/ looking for the perfect/ reader' and talk about reading 'Californian poetry, not just/ any poet though, a poet/ like Michael Palmer,/ who writes new words.' Here I am talking about Palmer's generosity in letting his readers 'complete the circuit'. So when I read the interview I looked back at those lines and thought : yes, Michael

Palmer's right. I wasn't thinking like that as I composed 'The Sugar Glider', because I was still in this state where, when I'm writing poetry that is influenced by LANGUAGE-centred poetry, whatever you want to call it — I'm in a semi-defensive state, combative sort of state. There are people in Australia who will savage this kind of poetry I think. What they vaguely call LANGUAGE poetry is a strange, demonic beast to them. As soon as they hear that term or they think they recognise a poem that's influenced by it, they close down and attack.

JK: I would argue, when we talk about 'poetry without reference' as being integral to LANGUAGE poetry, that there is always a core of references which are distorted, decidedly and distinctly distorted, and that although it's non-referential, and it's not apparent where the associations came from, they are always there. Because the core of a notion, if you are politicising something and you have a particular value you're trying to instil in your reader … be it everything or nothingness, it must be based on some point of reference. So I would argue that LANGUAGE poetry is distorting those references to make a point.

RA: I've got a reference for that … What's interesting to me in this discussion about LANGUAGE poetry is I've just discovered that I've got an ally. He's a figure in their group who thinks about it along similar lines. There's an essay in the book *In The American Tree* edited by Ron Silliman, published by University of Maine, an essay by Jackson MacLow and he says this very interesting thing. Here it is: 'Indeed some practitioners and sympathetic critics call such works non-referential and one of them has mounted a brilliant, seemingly Marxist attack on reference as a kind of fetishism contributing to alienation, but this is a dangerous argument easily turned against its proponents.' This is the bit that interested me: 'What could be more of a fetish or more alienated than slices of language stripped of reference?' He says, 'Of course as other practitioners and critics have realised and stated, no language use is really non-referential. If it's language it consists of signs and all signs point to what they signify.' All signs have significance of course; then he covers that with reference to the French critics.

JK: Could you comment on that regarding your own work and the use of reference? Very obviously in the material in *The Clean Dark* and in that tradition right through your work the centrality of reference is there. In poems like 'The Pepper Mill', which are also referential poems, there's still a consciousness of the way reference is being used. You would always argue that, as we're being told here, you can't deny reference, and it's a very dangerous thing to do so.

RA: Now that's a very interesting thing and it brings a circle around. First of all when I started writing 'The Pepper Mill' poem, I thought I'd do a version of something like Cézanne's Mountain. I'd just take 'The Pepper Mill' and do versions of it. There's a W. S. Merwin poem where he writes about pineapples. It goes on for pages: what does he think of a pineapple, what does the reader think of a pineapple, what do the visitors to the pineapple plantation think of the pineapple and what do they think of the pineapple company's advertising material which promotes pineapples.

JK: So there's a constant process of removal.

RA: I realised that was an early interest of mine which was connected to what Zen Buddhists call the 'no mind', and again Jackson MacLow says, 'when such works are comprised of words and strings the attention of the perceiver is indeed centred on such language elements in themselves rather than on anything the authors wish to say or imitate'. He's saying, is there any sense in bringing such a non-linguistic and non-literary term as the 'no mind' into this. The Buddhists refer to it as the deepest layer of the mind below the conscious ego and the psychoanalytic unconscious. It's impersonal, untainted by ego. Some of us who have used chance operations to produce works of art have seen these works as embodying or expressing 'no mind'. 'When such works are comprised of words' — now that's MacLow again and this has given me such a sense of freedom — now what's happening is these LANGUAGE poets are giving me a permission to go ahead, and it's taken it a step further, so I'm getting back to this thing, basically a spiritual concern …

JK: In the same way as the modernists …

RA: I'm using a spiritual interest, and can do, in LANGUAGE-centred poetry. To use another example: a version of the Surrealist method, automatic writing maybe, but that's not at all what LANGUAGE poetry is.

JK: You talk quite often of notions of liberation and freedom in thought and in poetry and you actually said something about them giving you permission. Is this because you see poets and poetry as being part of this multi-directional continuum, this collage of poets and notions, that you need to have some point of reference with other poets to validate what you're doing? Or do you see that it is possible to exist in total isolation? Do you need a point of communication, or are you working towards eventually denying all points — and that of course would be the absolute?

RA: That's an interesting question, because when you're writing, no matter how sure you are of what you're doing, there's always the question hovering above you, 'Is there an audience for this?'

JK: Thank you for coming back to that! Or should we be *making* an audience?

RA: I think this is based on something that Steve Benson and your friend Lyn Hejinian wrote. I'll just paraphrase what they say. To me it was a worry, and it is also exciting; 'the truism that the only people who read poetry are themselves poets, is thus understood rather as potential than as limitation. The reader is presumed not as a consumer of the experience sustained by the poem but as a fellow writer who shares conscientiously in the work and can willingly answer the uses of the medium which the writer feels impelled to undertake and so extend the generation of literary work without indulging the pretentious fireworks of avant-gardism for validation with its tendencies of short-sightedness, of enthusiasm and blindness, of shock effect ...' The thing that worries me there is 'the fireworks of avant-gardism as validation'. That's a bit of a worry, I think, because I wonder if that's just another excuse not to have a need for technical virtuosity.

JK: Aren't they putting down 'the fireworks of avant-gardism'?

RA: Yes, they are but it worries me that this could lead to a lessening of the quality of the work.

JK: In terms of concept, not in terms of technique though?

RA: I thought they were talking about technique, but maybe they're not.

JK: Do you think that suppressing the fireworks of avant-gardism is dangerous conceptually because it basically reduces everything to technique?

RA: What you're looking at is a poem and what you're working on is poetry and it isn't necessarily reliant on whole cathedrals of work that went before it. The words themselves are like ... it's like loading up a paintbrush and painting on a blank canvas. Using the paint is what's important, not what you're painting, not the subject of what you're painting. Brushwork. Painterly qualities.

JK: Regarding the comment you made earlier about Duncan giving you permission, and Shelley, and Zukofsky: that all these people can exist at once, the great chain. Does that link with that in any sense whatsoever or is that a contradiction?

JK: It could seemingly be a contradiction but it isn't.

JK: Could you explain why it isn't?

RA: The danger with all that, and I'm sure what Silliman would say about all that (say Silliman for example) is that that leads to elitism, and that could lead to sitting in your ivory tower.

JK: I remember seeing an essay with Robert Duncan's comments down on one of Ron Silliman's essays and he actually called him 'silly man' and he wasn't too keen on it and Silliman was questioning these very notions.

RA: The thing that Duncan did there was very interesting because he wasn't even criticising Silliman for questioning Duncan. Duncan was looking at Silliman's comments and saying this guy's not connecting at some level … you've got to be careful here. He's correcting Silliman's factual mistakes in his essay, he's saying this is a bit slack. The quality of the writing. Coming from someone who puts language as the most important thing, now he'd better polish up his language.

JK: You steered through that very carefully! This guy can actually pilot his boat down the Hawkesbury river so he knows how to steer through the troubles of language! The point I'm getting at is, do you think that these notions can exist with this Duncanesque view?

RA: Yes, easily. I think that you have an advantage if you don't have to jettison all that.

JK: So you're appropriating from the LANGUAGE movement. You're not saying, hey, I want to be a LANGUAGE poet, you're saying, hey they're interesting and their observations are interesting, and that can be added to the things I've learnt from Duncan, and the things I've learnt from all these others.

RA: They explain to me, just as a phenomenon, what's been happening on the edges. The eighties were a blinding nightmare to me — the recession in America, England and Australia, because so many people were struggling, the people who weren't broke were full-on materialists, raging around in a spree of greed — I found it difficult to take into my imagination — but it was

322

so real. I was just knocked out of gear for that whole decade. In that time your generation have come up, you didn't have the luxury of thinking: 'are we being ethical about producing poetry books as consumer goods?' because there were no consumers.

Back in the sixties we used to say, well, we'll do an exhibition and we'll make sure that none of the works in the exhibition are saleable so that we won't contribute to the capitalist system. So we'd do auto-destructive works. One of my friends used to do paintings and when you picked them up, a little bottle of acid leaked out and dissolved them; conceptual art was a luxury because we had the choice. By eighties there are no consumers so there is no choice. The poets had no readership because nobody could buy books. Instead of saying it's a limitation that the only people that read poetry are the poets, let's make a positive thing of this. There are all these poets, we can all write for each other …

Just getting back to that idea of LANGUAGE-centred poetry and the strategies involved in it. I think I was talking about Bob Dylan before, but these LANGUAGE poets, as far as I understand them, came out through the World War II protest movements with critiques of authority and arguments for rights and prizing an 'awkwardly marginal status' — this is a quote now from Steve Benson — this is more or less a paraphrase of him but it really reflects what I think about it too. The wonderful thing about LANGUAGE poetry is the strategy that these writers have developed. They test people or poets more markedly than they indoctrinate. They resist things rather than seduce or assure. Creeley can resist and seduce.

Now there's Charles Olson's *Selected Poems* edited by Robert Creeley. What Creeley's done here is made Olson accessible to a whole new generation. His preface is a beautifully written essay on Projectivist or Black Mountain poetry — it starts out from Ezra Pound and Zukofsky, and talks about Olson. He starts it off by saying a characteristic of our time has been its insistent preoccupation with system, and then goes on to look at Olson's work as a system that envelops all systems, and goes back to seeing the first defining poets of our century as heroic; almost necessarily so. Ezra Pound's epic attempt to make a long poem including history to give us the requisite tales of the tribe — this is loosely paraphrasing Creeley — and in the end he cannot in his own words make it cohere, he has nonetheless entered the apparent chaos of existence as a surviving witness though his own errors and wrecks lie around him.

That's the Maximus poems and Olson himself saying 'these are my errors and wrecks'. As Pound said of his *Cantos*, they don't cohere. Creeley says it makes a lasting order although with Pound, the fascism he trusted failed him. It left only art; but you know what art, what great art. Then Eliot's determinations, his conviction that order, again talking about system, is carried by tradition from a past where all values are defined. Then Creeley goes through Eliot and talks about William Carlos Williams. Only the imagination is real. This is just loosely looking through it — and that leads him into an idea where 'one will hardly regret that an active agriculture can feed us, at the endless provisions, for thus predetermining wars cannot be so simply agreed to. There are imaginations that differ absolutely in their use of legitimising purpose yet each defines a potential' and that leads on to D.H. Lawrence; D.H. Lawrence and the phenomenal world which is raging and yet apart, as Lawrence wrote in 'The Escaped Cock', a work that Olson very much respected. In that work Jesus says to Mary Magdalene 'the day of my interference is done', and then a little later 'the recoil failed the advance'. Creeley talks about Objectivism, then he goes though Whitehead, talks about those ideas that Olson took in from Whitehead, and then into what he calls Williams's life-long dilemma with his social fact as a poet. Then, getting back to Olson, he says, Olson says, 'come into the world, take a big bite', he admonishes the people who can take no risk that matters, the risk of beauty least of all ... It's a marvellous essay.

JK: Referring again to the Palmer interview and taking this into consideration, do you think that it's essential that poetry has a social referent? I want to take into consideration what you've just been talking about. I want to get to the poem, or back to the poem, should I say, 'The Rumour', which is your major early work, which would probably have to be seen as an end in itself, regarding your modernist influences. I would like you to discuss the idea of a poem being conscious about poetics with its dialogue with poetries and its dialogue with technique and the whole chain if you like. And also whether a poem such as that has also a social responsibility and what that is or if that's an absurd notion. And finally to tie it into this quote from the Michael Palmer interview that we've been talking about, which I'll read: 'It is symptomatic of what would be quite literally deconstruction when all discourse becomes qualified.' And I'm going to ask, is 'The Rumour' about qualifying concepts, about qualifying symbolist ideals? And then he goes on and says there's nothing wrong with all discourse coming into a framework of doubt. But then you do wonder at what point is 'The Rumour' about qualifying these symbolist notions, or is it about setting them out and looking at them in a world of doubt?

RA: It is.

JK: Is it talking about one positive thing in a world of such massive interrogation, such massive skeptical interrogation, which is surely what 'The Rumour' is considering? This comes into the social aspect again, and into the lit. crit. aspect of poetry. Does poetry exist outside the lit. crit. aspect of reading? (and I think that's much of a problem now). Sorry, this is going back to the quote now — 'reassert the force of the words themselves'. So does it exist as a thing in itself?

RA: Well, that's very much what 'The Rumour' is dealing with. There are springboards that I use to jump into 'The Rumour' from — first of all the Bible is very important.

I've taken from the Bible, from Ezekiel, the wheel within a wheel metaphor, then there's another thing in Revelation where John the Divine says if any man shall add words to these words, he'll be condemned forever to eternal hell. So I start off 'The Rumour' by using the word wormwood, which is a biblical word that means corruption and evil, and I say, the star is called Wormwood, and I use that star instead of the star that signifies Christ that leads you from the heavens, as the star to follow. So instead of a new star bringing in a new Christ I see a star that is in fact the embodiment of corruption and evil and doubt, and it's called Wormwood. Then I say, not only that, I will add unto this book. Here is the work. 'The Rumour' is the part of which John said 'if you ever add to this you will be condemned.' Because I say that in the poem it was exactly about the ideas of doubt, irony and questioning.

JK: This is the modernist aspect of that poem then. So it's playing against the romantic notion and also the symbolist notion, quite a separate thing. The modernism's playing against these traditional …

RA: Exactly, it was a postmodern poem. I wrote it in 1971 — the same time that we were using poetry as process — we were talking about it at the time. I mean, Michael Wilding spoke about this for years. During the writing of 'The Rumour', Michael was writing a similar thing with short stories, in his book, *The West Midland Underground*. But what we were saying is our writing is about process, it's about exposing the bones of the poetry and they become a part … the process of writing of the poem becomes a part of the poem.

JK: In this poem also things exist, whereas LANGUAGE poems exist theoretically in themselves, this requires very much the great movements of literature, if you like, the conflict between 'men and modernity'.

RA: You really have to be very well read to understand 'The Rumour' for a start. I mean, it requires you to know the references — it's as loaded with references as the *Cantos*, or as anything, any of those modernist poems.

JK: Do you see it as a poem of reconciliation or a poem of out-and-out con-
flict between concepts?

RA: It's a poem about rumour, it really is. It says we start out with a word
and this can be related to the biblical word but also the words we are using
ourselves as building blocks.

JK: So this is all about building blocks.

RA: I'm riddled with doubt about the fact that I'm writing a poem which
possibly isn't a poem but a rumour. One of the interesting things is halfway
through that poem ... it was really a letter to Duncan, then halfway through it
I was talking to John Forbes, and John Forbes was completely overtaken by
Ted Berrigan. I stopped half-way through that poem and read Ted Berrigan
very thoroughly and I couldn't get from it anything like what John could get.
I couldn't see what was so good about Berrigan — why he was so important
to that generation of poets, John Forbes's generation. But then luckily for me,
halfway through that poem who should turn up in Australia but Robert
Creeley, and in fact I spent three nights with him.
     One of the first things I said to Creeley was, 'What is this about Berrigan,
why is Ted Berrigan so good?' This was one of the most interesting revelations
of my life. Creeley sat me down, we had a bottle of whiskey and he said,
'Listen, I'll read you a poem.' He reached up to the shelf, grabbed the
Tambourine Life and read it. Now, it was one of the greatest lessons in my life
because I was reading that poem in English, and it was written in American,
and when Creeley read it, it was in the inflections of his voice, it was in the
music of the language — and I saw it. Halfway through I saw it was the most
wonderful, savage, political poem I'd ever read. It was full of social criticism.
It was just as alive as a Dylan song, but it was poetry. And then I said that to
Creeley, 'Ah, I understand, I understand', and he was laughing. He said,
'Okay, okay that's fine to understand it. I'm glad I can help. But now what
you've got to do is write your poem in Australian.' I said, 'What are you talk-
ing about?' I had versions of poems, and that would have been early versions
of 'The Rumour', especially that one I wrote before 'The Rumour'. A bit like
Hart Crane. I started it at the beginning and the end, and then filled in the
middle. So one of the first things I wrote was that section called 'Everybody
Gathered in Objection'. That was an early version. I showed it to Creeley and
he said, 'Okay, what you've got to do now is write like Ted Berrigan, only
you're Australian so ...' He looked at a lot of poetry in my house and he
couldn't find anything that sounded Australian. I grabbed Bruce Dawe and
Bruce Beaver and he said, 'Yes they're getting there, they're getting there as far

as using the language.' He said, 'I hear this language, I've never known it before but I hear it in the air, I've heard it for three days and I can hear the tune you're all playing.'

That's the way he put it. He said put in the language of your everyday conversation. 'You're talking to me in poems that are much better than the poems you've got down here on the page.' It sounds so simple, it really does, but he taught me how to write down the rhythms of conversation and — this sounds technical but it wasn't just technical — couple it with the structures of high literature or high modernism, whatever you like, and play that off against it. So what will happen then in the technical exercises, you'll find —this is Creeley saying to me — you'll find that steeped in language like that, your subject will arise out of the language. You won't have to worry about where you're taking it, it'll come out, or you know, it's just that when you find the right form you'll have the content. So you know, the thing about that was that, in a strange weird way, Berrigan came into that poem, leaving no traces.

JK: A fact, something we know, a scientific fact for example, can be bent, can be altered to a certain end, can be propaganda-ised if you like. A rumour inevitably will be because it can't be reconstructed as fact. How does that notion fit in with the definitive poetics that you're trying to explore?

RA: In the book it's very important, that quote from Wallace Stevens at the beginning, 'In the long run the truth does not matter'. Now that's really the first line of the poem. So I write, 'In the long run the truth does not matter', and then go on to investigate that. Because truth will be poetry and poetry is the one thing that cannot be corrupted.

JK: But truth is also what you want it to be.

RA: That's what I'm saying. The challenge was for me to make that rumour into a poem which will be incorruptible because it works — if it is good, if it works as a poem.

JK: This is the sense of purity we're talking about, the notion of an ultimate, something that is achievable that we can keep striving towards — we can't actually grasp but we can see in the distance.

RA: Yes, I said it somewhere before but maybe not as clearly, that you can write a lie into the poem, like you were talking about a scientific fact. You can write it, but the poem itself cannot lie because if the poem lies it just doesn't work.

JK: But the rumour moves quickly and the truth comes slowly. How does that reconcile?

RA: That is exactly what I'm talking about. That relates to the use of imagination in the way Shelley did. The way Shelley used it was that he would write a whole string of rhymes down the right-hand margin of a page. I've seen the manuscripts, it's unbelievable. I can't remember exactly, I think in 'Ode to the West Wind' he certainly did do it, but also in poems like 'To A Skylark', he wrote rhymes, he was very facile at writing rhymes; he would write them all down without knowing what the meaning of the poem was going to be, then he filled out the poem. His imagination: his idea was that if he trusted the imagination it would be true, it wouldn't be corrupted by the world around him, because it was a pure thing, it was a given thing.

JK: Does something pure in your mind contain all the deceits, all the lies as well and that makes it pure because it has a knowledge of them?

RA: It's like a melting down of it all. The poem itself is hell, a version of hell and whatever is in that hell, whatever is part of that hell will melt down and purify it like an alchemy into something which is purified by going through that hell. Out the other side comes everybody gathered in objection. At the time I got that image from the Buddhist monks burning themselves on television. You'd turn the news on and there'd be this monk pouring petrol on himself, igniting himself. That's the flame I talk about all the way through that poem. 'The Rumour' was very much a poem that contained my anxiety about Vietnam.

JK: Yes, I think that's quite clear in lots of ways.

RA: That came through even though I didn't want it to. That's what I'm saying about the truth.

JK: So because poetry must be true and truth must be honest, then it must be political by extension and therefore it comes through regardless of your intent.

RA: Yes, that's right.

JK: I'm fascinated by the position of what I've heard various LANGUAGE poets refer to as the ego self that occurs in the lyric, in a lyric poem. I think Michael Palmer refers to it as the small self or something along those lines.

RA: Yeah, another poem about the little me.

JK: The little me, that's it.

RA: Well, you know you've got to be careful with this, because the greatest example of that kind of work, in lyricism especially, the greatest lyricist I think of our age, of course, is Robert Creeley. Now Robert Creeley was one of the first poets these LANGUAGE poets attacked, and also this guy Grenier attacked him by writing … I don't know whether it was a parody, but he took apart that book called *Pieces* and he was a prime target in a way, really, because he epitomised the romantic image, the sort of magician figure, the oracular kind of love poet… The reason Creeley can do it is that he is also a technician, one of the greatest users of the American language.

JK: Just to quote you here from 'The Rumour', 'Rumour's design a pressure extending those propositions of freedom'. Then you go on, 'my appetite for absurdities in language that broods and has no sense of humour exceedingly easy my muse'. When I asked about 'we' as Palmer refers to the 'small me' how does the your 'my', how does your 'I' and 'I've' and 'my', the personal pronouns …

RA: It's simply a device.

JK: It's a thing to play against the ideas?

RA: It's nothing other than a technical device. It's not a persona. It's not me.

JK: Is it making a comment about that though, about that idea of the 'small me'?

RA: Yes, of course.

JK: Can you explain?

RA: Well, here's a poem that's sort of trying to encompass the Vietnam War and still at the time, you know, I physically could see the pointlessness of even protesting, because I am a very practical person, and to think that by going out and demonstrating you would achieve something … My friends were doing it, they were going out demonstrating in the streets of Sydney and coming home, watching themselves on television and thinking they'd done something. Well, maybe they did in the long run, but I don't know, I really don't know.

At the time I was also writing to Robert Bertholf, a professor who was at Kent State University. He was in a library buying manuscripts by Robert Duncan and company and he was also a very important editor during the seventies and eighties; *Credences* was his magazine. He is now Curator of the Poetry Rare Books Collection at SUNY at Buffalo. He wrote to me the day the students were shot down in front of his room at Kent State University. These were the times we were writing in. He said, 'Today Robert, some of my students were shot down in the campus outside my room.' I mean, that was a letter I got in the midst of that poem. These things were going on and I was writing to him, 'Dear Robert, here I am on the Hawkesbury, the river's calm today, there is a mist on the tide, I am studying Robert Duncan's life's work and reading Plato.' I mean, what a far remove from students being shot down outside your window. But I turn the television on and there are my friends in Sydney risking their lives and sanity, thinking that they can stop this war in Vietnam. These things were in the air around that time as it was being composed and there was no way in the world that there was any vestige of an ego in there, because really I was so impotent as a person and as an individual in society against the evil forces of the times. Palmer says a wonderful thing in that poem, the interview, where he says there is no poetry of witness anymore.

JK: That's one of my later questions. You've asked the question.

RA: It's pertinent to this because turning the television on, seeing monks burning didn't reach me. I knew obviously what was happening but I was not going to write about it, simply because I didn't know the way to write about that situation. I just had a sense that it wouldn't work for me, so I was taking the poetry, the process of poetry, taking modernism itself and turning it inside out, trying to find out what I thought about the world, what I thought about this corruption, and the corruption of language itself, in fact.

JK: What's your view of the straight polemical poem, the didactic verse that says: this is right, this is wrong? In the classic old communist worker journals you used to get; do you think that has a place? Do you think it's valid in any way?

RA: Yes, but after Bob Dylan what can you do? Dylan talking to industrialists, talking to these vile men who manufacture bombs, and he stands over their graves and says, 'All the money you made/ will never buy back your soul'. And that really works, at the end of that ballad, 'Masters of War'. That's taken the place of didactic poetry, Dylan's protest songs.

JK: Do you think a singer like Billy Bragg, or to a certain extent Leonard Cohen (but not very much) — Billy Bragg, anyway — does the same sort of thing?

RA: Bragg's good, Cohen's great, but Dylan is a genius. He is a genius like Shakespeare. Now it's something to be able to transform a mode of writing, the protest ballad, into something more. He continues with folk-rock, with country music, the blues.

JK: So that in a sense his voice has the the cry of the era, has the wail of the age in it.

RA: Yes, and it universalises it so that this is even more potent and more interesting, and more revealing to me than the poetry of Ted Berrigan, who people might say is more sophisticated than Bob Dylan, but in a way he's not … maybe it's Bob Dylan's voice. I was reading Ted Berrigan on the page; I didn't actually hear Ted Berrigan reading his poems until Creeley read them. Then I heard Berrigan's voice. So … it's connected to what I was talking about, using the language of the day, the language that we speak, and making poetry of that.

JK: Do you think it's possible in this era, in this age — let's say the post-holocaust age — the era in which Adorno asks the question, 'Can there be poetry after Auschwitz?' Do you think it's possible to be whimsical in our social commentary, say, as Michael Palmer refers to the whimsy of John Ashbery?

RA: Well, there has to be whimsy after the holocaust, otherwise there's no life. If you really consider what all that means, you just have to kill yourself, as Paul Celan did. He was the great Symbolist poet of that period, the great poet of that period, in my mind, and after the war he had to keep writing. And he did keep writing, but he also killed himself. But who survived of that era? The ones that survived were strange people like Beckett. Beckett taught whimsy, the blackest whimsy of all, and that's where it ends: *Waiting for Godot.*

JK: So instead of the world ending in a whimper it ends in a strange bizarre laugh …

RA: Beckett, of course, is the original LANGUAGE Poet.

JK: Absolutely. Do you know that he was actually James Joyce's secretary?

RA: That's right, yes. And he was playing with the language, like writing in French … I don't think it was just because he didn't want to compete with Joyce's English. There was more to it than that.

JK: I once wrote to Lyn Hejinian and said that *Finnegan's Wake* is a disappointment to me because it represents the death of modernism and it's not the birth of Postmodernism, and that the birth of Postmodernism came with his secretary, good old Beckett who learned the techniques from Joyce but reinvented them. Do you think that's true?

RA: I certainly do. Beckett was the writer who, when Robert Duncan died … the result of that, aside from my grief for him as a person, was a strange emptiness in my life, and I didn't quite understand what it was, but of course my correspondence with him stopped. And as Tranter says, there's no use writing an elegy to him. Bob, don't you realise the dead can't hear? He's not going to answer you now.

But there was this emptiness in my life, and in my intellectual life as well as my physical life, and I couldn't work out what it was, and who filled it after Duncan. Beckett was the one who gave me the substance that I couldn't find in the poets. I should have known because when I mentioned Mark Strand to Duncan, he just shook his head in bewilderment. But Strand was the poet I ended up reading. I got around that by coming back into poetry through Beckett, which led me to *The Clean Dark*. There's a poem in *The Clean Dark*, called 'What's Slaughtered's Gone' which I wrote as I re-read Molloy, — that fractured broken sentence. It was a poem that got me back up into an alleyway that led to something.'

JK: You were talking about elegy: you've recently been working on some elegiac pieces on Brett Whiteley, which I find particularly interesting because they're working in the traditional linear fashion, and they're also looking at linguistic versions or linguistic interpretations of the linear poem. Could you comment on both the method and also on the writing of elegies and particularly that elegy or piece?

RA: I think that's really at the centre for me. I didn't know at first, for the first ten years of my writing poetry, that the elegy itself as a genre was the thing that I could do. I don't know why or how, but thinking back on it, it's not as surprising really, because the first poem that I understood was Shelley's 'Adonais'; I did so many close readings of that poem; and I felt after living with it for so long that it was really a part of me. In that sense I knew that there was such a thing as links in the chain. And then I just got so much involved in all this when Michael Dransfield died. I think I say in the elegy for him: 'You would have expected an elegy or so from me'. Because we used to talk about this romantic shit that people go on with. Forbes thinks that in *Cross The Border* I am a 'socially integrated bard'.

JK: He did go on to say that when *The Clean Dark* came out that you were the finest lyric poet in the country, though.

RA: He did say that, but I don't think that *The Clean Dark* is as good as some people say it is.

JK: It is lyrical.

RA: It might be lyrical but it was a book I had to write to establish myself at a certain level in this country. I had fellowships and grants all through the seventies, then during the eighties it all dried up. I was sick of not getting fellowships. I was sick of not winning prizes and I had to work out a way of making money to buy time for poetry. Then *The Clean Dark* won all three major poetry awards in Australia and I was given a major Fellowship.

JK: With regard to working on the Brett Whiteley stuff, were you more attracted to the notions of the visual artist or to the notions of the artist regardless ...

RA: No. It was just that all these things happened. He was a friend of mine, so he is a person who died and whom I miss tremendously.

JK: Peter Porter called him 'that difficult artist' in an interview I did with him. He respects his ability and so on, but considered him a difficult person.

RA: He wasn't a difficult person, his art is another thing again. His art was as to important to me as Robert Duncan. Before I met Brett in 1972, I don't think I'd even seen a real painting. I mean I might have looked at a few paintings but they didn't really affect me much. I'd looked at art books, and I loved Mondrian, Van Gogh and Max Ernst. I was walking along the street in Paddington, and I walked into an art gallery, and I didn't really even know what was on — and there was his painting *Alchemy* on the wall. Again, it was like one of those things that gave me permission to continue in an area that I wasn't sure would be accepted. There was just that element to it, that I recognised something in Brett's work. It was a triumphant thing. Someone had done it and succeeded, and there it was up on the wall. It was really a revelation to me as well that someone could paint like that. In fact it was a visual version of a Bob Dylan song stretched across three walls. It really was alchemy: I went home and started writing what eventually became 'The Rumour'. It coincided with the letter from Duncan, *Alchemy* and Dylan's *Blonde on Blonde*. Without them I just couldn't have written 'The Rumour'. There were the three of them; Duncan, Dylan and Whiteley and they were doing it, what I wanted to do.

JK: Were they the actual kick-off point or were they things that came along and were immediately integrated into the poem? So did the poem start with them or did they feed the poem? Chicken and egg thing, or egg and chicken ...

RA: I don't think you can know, because it's all part of the same thing. I wanted to write a very good poem. I didn't know what it was. I read the letters from Duncan. I read Duncan's books. I studied *Alchemy*. I heard Bob Dylan. They inspired me, that's what happens, you're in a desert and then suddenly you're not in a desert.

JK: Seamus Heaney has said something to the effect of: it's all a mystery. Poetry's all a mystery.

RA: I agree with that.

JK: I don't. I see poetry as quite a specific thing and I believe that you have, even if the inspiration is mystical ...

RA: Poetry or what's behind it.

JK: What's behind it is a mystery, but the actual poetry is very specific. I separate the inspiration from the formal side of it. I heard someone say recently that the process of writing is wondrous because you don't know what's going to come out. For me I know exactly what I want to come out. It doesn't always come out the way I want it, but I know what I want to come out of it. I have an impression of what the poem's going to be. Would you not say that something like 'The Rumour' must have had that, because it is such a structured thing?

RA: When I read *The Opening of the Field* and *Roots and Branches*, I said to myself, I want to write a books like those. It becomes more oblique when Dylan and Whiteley come into it, because they're not the same ...

JK: They are part of the mystery of inspiration?

RA: Brett's using paint, not words. Dylan's using music mixed with language which is another thing again. He's also using a persona. He is the ultimate postmodernist, he created himself. Dylan is postmodernism. He created a person that didn't exist — he became his own construction.

JK: Have you ever collaborated directly with an artist or a musician? I know you're working on the book [*The Language of Oysters*] with your wife, Juno Gemes; it involves visual images and photographs with text.

RA: I've always worked with artists. I worked with Whiteley. There were a couple of things we did. There was an auction to raise money for the anti-nuclear protest, so a lot of Sydney artists got together and created artifacts to be auctioned off. I wrote a poem and Brett illustrated it ... Talking about collaboration, and how things lead to it: with each book, it's very specific, there's always an artist involved. The first one there was David Perry, who was a film maker and artist. With 'The Rumour' I didn't know an artist I could work with —

JK: So you had a spiritually 'significant other' in 'The Rumour' but for the rest you've had literally significant others.

RA: With *Swamp Riddles* there was Robert Finlayson who was a painter, who was a friend of David Rankin, who was the painter that taught me about Mark Toby and Rothko, and all the things that led from Mark Toby right up into Rothko. He educated me in that sense. Then after that, *Cross the Border*, and that's when I met Gary Shead and Brett Whiteley. What's on the cover of that: a painting by Gary and Brett, and Gary's etchings in it. Gary was coming to my house each day as I wrote Grail poems, he was doing Grail paintings. He did an exhibition of Grail paintings that were exhibited at the same time that *Cross the Border* was published. 1976 at The Hogarth Gallery Paddington. With *The Law At Heart's Desire* there was Tim Storrier. I would go to Tim's studio every day and talk to him. We had great debates. I'd go to Brett's and we'd have raves together, mainly about Bob Dylan, he was so articulate. He'd want to hear stories about Rimbaud, and he'd want me to read *Season in Hell*. Then after that I met Juno. Juno was the first artist that I actually lived with, the first artist that I had a love affair with.

JK: Does that make a significant difference to the creative process?

RA: Yes, a huge difference. To live with someone who was also an artist gave me a different dimension to my life.

JK: Now, if we can move on to collaboration and the idea of working not only with another artist, but with the concepts of one art form interacting with the concepts of another art form — can you make any general comments, and then lead into talking about your collaboration of the moment? That is the Hawkesbury River book, *The Language of Oysters*, with your wife, the photographer Juno Gemes.

RA: I love the way Palmer talks to his interviewee and says, 'I'll bracket that thing you bracketed'. I'll go right back to where I was talking about collaboration with Duncan; remember where he writes the lines on the poem? That scoops up the thing you're talking about, about 'no poetry after the holocaust', because it's got to do with the second world war. In Creeley's introduction to Olson's new book, he talks about what changes immensely in the few years that separate Williams's Paterson from Olson's Maximus. What Creeley says it is, is the literal configuration of the world which each attempts to salvage. 'All the previous epistemological structures and even more the supporting cultural reference were displaced significantly if not forever' — get this, John — 'by the political and economic transformations following the second World War.' Now this comes into the thing about collaboration. 'The underlying causes were well in place at the turn of the century, but by 1950 the effects were even more dominant. There could no longer be such a father-son disposition of reality as either Pound or Williams tacitly took as a given of their situation. Olson's displacement echoes painfully in his own undertakings and nowhere more so than in the quote. "I have been an ability, a machine".' Then Creeley quickly says it was Pound's proposal that 'Points define a periphery'. So Creeley says his notes in this introduction, however inadequately, propose that possibility. 'Were they worked with a determination of fixed reference and stable content it all might be plotted with secure conviction and assurance, but if our time can claim' — this is about the language stuff — 'if our time can claim any securing sign for its passage it is absolutely chaotic, entropic, one wants to say malfunction of all its vital activities, whether political or economic, which prove finally to be the abiding rule'. And then he ends it all by saying 'each of us must find our own way by ear', which is a quote from Olson. Getting back to that thing I was talking about, the language that's in the air. So I had no idea what collaboration could possibly mean until that accidental collaboration where Duncan picks up a poem of mine and adds a few lines and rewrites my imitation of him.

JK: That's like an incidental collaboration, though, isn't it? Not an accidental collaboration because he intended to do that, but it was an incidental one because he was there at the time.

RA: Yes, that's right and that's why I quote that about the father-son thing, where Creeley is saying Williams and Pound had this. And then there's the letter from Duncan in which he said he didn't want any Oedipal situation to occur in our friendship. Really what I was doing was taking on Duncan as a father, as a symbol to that legacy ... I guess it is a legacy.

JK: That's really not a collaboration, but a fraternisation ...

RA: That's right, and then there is the reaction to it, which I couldn't predict, but what the reaction was, was the ultimate casting-off from Duncan — was *Where I Come From* because I went straight from that high-toned Modernist rhetoric of, say, the Grail poems. *Cross the Border*. I came out with *Where I Come From*, which was stripped of all rhetoric, like ... a plainness. That was where I was collaborating with Geoffrey Proud who did the drawings on the cover and inside. I'd moved from Elizabeth Bay and I had the early versions of *Where I Come From*, and then Geoff turned up. That just coincided with it. He loved it. He took it up with great gusto and did those drawings as I was doing the final versions. So in that sense it is a collaboration, but it's a parallel kind of thing ... I don't know whether you'd call it collaboration. It is, I suppose — but you live and work together.

JK: So now we come to *The Clean Dark* ...

RA: We started in Paddington. I started writing in Paddington and then we moved up here after about six months, and Juno's introduction to the Hawkesbury, by living here, simultaneously occurred with the putting together of that book. So she started taking photographs, finding her relationship to the landscape, with a mind to coming up with a cover. But as her photographs gradually appeared I started to write poems from them, or off them. I'd put a photograph on the desk. 'Speaking Page' was one that came off a photograph. It's very strange — instead of looking out, going out into the landscape, I found it much more manageable to write a poem about the Hawkesbury River from one of Juno's photographs of the river. It's a version of the way Wordsworth used to hold up a frame to the landscape; they used to look in a little mirror and this is a modern version of that.

JK: They also used a Claude glass.

RA: Yes. Having the photograph on the desk emphasises to me that I'm not writing poems about the Hawkesbury. I get upset when people say, you're the Hawkesbury poet, you write about the Hawkesbury. That could be any river in the world. It just happens to be the Hawkesbury. I love it as a physical thing in my life. I love living here, it's a symbolic river in my work. A lot of the Hawkesbury poems were written when I was living in Bermagui. Most of them were written in Paddington and Mosman. But with Juno coming into it, it turns into something else, because there's the photograph of nature. So there's the art and there's the nature and the two things exist separately, but it's more manageable to me as an artwork than as a river. The Hawkesbury as artwork is more inspiring to me than the actual Hawkesbury. Juno's photograph of the Hawkesbury changes it from the Hawkesbury into a river in a photograph, which is enough to tilt me.

JK: That's interesting. So when we're talking about the small me, the 'ego-I' type thing, in a sense it's playing against that. It's depersonalising the personal. Something that's mythologically apparently a part of you is in fact an object. It's something physical that can be removed as well. So you're playing against that notion of it being you; it's you looking at it as an object, it's a separation.

RA: When I started to do that, I literally called one of the sections 'Rewriting the Hawkesbury'.

JK: Then post-*Clean Dark* you were also working on this river book that I mentioned earlier. Also there was some interaction on the cover of *Wards of the State*.

RA: Yes, *Wards of the State* (1994) in fact wouldn't have existed if it hadn't been for Juno's photograph: that photograph on the cover of that girl. One day Juno was going through her files and going through her print drawer, and that photograph slipped out from underneath a couple of others, and I saw that image. Juno gave me a print of the image. Next morning I looked at it and thought it would make a good cover for my next book, I had absolutely no idea what was going to go in it. Tom Thompson came around and I said, 'What do you think of this as an idea for a book?', and I showed him that photograph. And he said, 'Wonderful, what about about those old pieces of prose you wrote back in the seventies, autobiographical stuff?'— 'I don't know why I wrote those.' And then he reminded me that I wrote them towards a film script that I was doing with Dorothy Hewett. We wrote a film script, and Dorothy asked me to do some sketches of my teenage years, and I wrote some of them as an outline for the film script, and eventually those did turn into a film script.

JK: So there is collaboration-on-collaboration here.

RA: Yes, I call that poetry of social activity. It wasn't then poetry as research. That's what I call my new poetry. They were possibilities for books that might be more broadly read. In fact there were about three thousand copies of *Wards of the State*.

JK: You sold three thousand copies.

RA: It sold 2,500, — it's accessible. And then … in the middle of that, because I was still worried about it being seen as an autobiography — I called it a novella. A fictional autobiography, that's it.

JK: Do you recall any of the things Michael Palmer said about collaboration in that interview? He's talking about dance, and he's asked, 'And so, is your work the boundaries of genre or its stasis?' And he says, 'To raise the boundaries and pull things over from one into the other I have been pulling some images from my own work into this dance, and then I started to pull them back from the dance into that section of passages called 'Untitled', which has a poem that says 'at passages we peer out over such and such'.

RA: That's when he's working with Margaret Jenkins. Yes, again, all through the years, I've had this connection with Michael Palmer. When Duncan came to Australia, when he came to my place, as he left, he said, 'I'll put you in touch with this poet in California who is in the same generation as you. He was born in 1943. His name's Michael Palmer.' I said, 'Oh, I know his work, I published him in *New Poetry*.' And I hadn't written to him but I think I got his poems via Kris Hemensley — I did, Kris had sent me some poems for *The Ear in the Wheatfield*, and then did a special issue of *New Poetry*.

JK: Because of Kris I heard of Lyn Hejinian.

RA: So he actually got the poems and I published them in *New Poetry*, and I loved them. But Duncan said, 'I'll be gone and this will be your connection. This guy, Michael Palmer will be the guy when I go out of the picture, or when you go off me, or when I finally perish.' I can't remember the exact words but he was really saying, this'll be your American connection when I'm gone. He said it that literally, and I've never followed it, I never picked up on it. The poem that I published in your latest issue of *Salt* is about that; from then I tried to write a letter to him in fact it exists, there's probably twenty drafts of it in the National Library — of my letter to Michael Palmer — and it all ended up in the poem, and I said, 'I'm still writing you that letter.' When I was working on it, on yet another version of the letter, I was tearing my hair out, and Michael Wilding came over and said, 'What are you doing?' I said, 'I'm trying to write a letter to Michael Palmer.' He said, 'What a strange activity, why is it causing you so much anguish? Why don't you just write on a postcard?' I said, 'It's turning into a poem.' Then Michael said, 'Why don't you write a poem?', and that's what I did. Now I'm corresponding with Palmer smoothly.

JK: Yes. Speaking of Michael Wilding, he's been a seminal person in your writing life. Have you ever maybe, not collaborated literally, but collaborated conceptually with Michael Wilding? It would have reflected in your work and in his work. Has there been association? What is the difference between collaboration and association?

RA: Michael's been very important to me for thirty years. He was up here last week and I said, 'I'm going to have an interview with John Kinsella and we'll talk about LANGUAGE Poetry. Poetry without reference.' Michael laughed. He said, 'Oh, we did all that in 1975. We've already investigated that, and it didn't lead anywhere.'

JK: When prose loses its reference, it becomes poetry ...

RA: Michael has written quite a few prose-poem-like pieces. They're not poetry, but they're almost poetry. They're two, three-page lyrical or satirical pieces of prose, I suppose you'd call them. He calls them stories, but they're getting very close to poetry. Wilding was important to me right from the start because when we met I hadn't read much at all, and of course Michael was already teaching, a senior lecturer at Sydney University. He went to Oxford on a scholarship not long before he came to Australia, and he was going to go either to Australia or to California, but he came here. I met him a year or so after he arrived and he'd just finished a book on Milton. At the time we were in Balmain, and that whole thing with Frank Moorhouse and Nigel Roberts ... It was coming out from the Donald Allen anthology. It was this new freedom that we'd all found. They called it different things ... vaguely Balmain writers, but we all just happened to be there at the time ... they were all writing about their lives. Me and Michael were writing about literature. We were writing about the lives that were going on in our reading. I was doing that more than Michael. Michael would always to refer to reality because he was coming from

Burroughs and Kerouac. I was coming from Ezra Pound, Zukofsky via Duncan and company. But Michael's reading has always been a great resource to me, because whenever I needed to ask about any specific area I was dealing with, I'd ask Michael and he'd give me a tutorial, as we sat around on the river or at the Point at East Balmain. So really he has been part of my education. My personal tutor, personal professor. There's Michael the teacher, Michael the scholar — but also Michael the writer, the radical writer, the experimental writer.

JK: Working the other way, your influence on him — as part of the associative collaboration we were talking about?

RA: Well, Michael writes stories that incorporate this character called Sam, who is based on me, and he's a poet. So out of these discussions and adventures (some in real life!) in the imagination comes source material for Michael's stories. When these things come up, we'll both read a book and we'll discuss it. [It's] better than seminars you'd have in a university because we're sharing the activity of writing.

JK: Sharing the activity of writing and the activity of scholarship. So it's an interactive association. In this relationship we're talking about, (moving on now to *The Language of Oysters*, having worked through all of those) how important is that emotional association to it, or is that not relevant to the process? We have the intellectual one with Michael Wilding; with Juno you have ...?

RA: Well, it's the same thing. What happened with Juno is, I didn't know, until I met her, the language of photography. I didn't know that there was a language of photography. I didn't know that you would look at a photograph in a different way to how you would look at a painting. I had been educated through my associations with the painters, with Whiteley, Gary Shead, Geoffrey Proud, Tim Storrier mainly, and David Aspden, who is an abstract painter quite different to the others. Also I had a powerful education in Greenberg's philosophy through Ron Robinson-Swan. That had a strong fascination for some reason ... All the things I learnt about Greenberg via Ron Swan helped in my understanding, ironically, of LANGUAGE poetry and of what I'm doing at the moment. With Juno, she actually said, 'this is how you read a photograph', and talked about the way to read a photograph rather than the way to look at a photograph. The difference between looking at a photograph and looking at a painting, and the way she works as a recorder. She does a social-comment photography out of her work with Aboriginal people. Years and years of her documenting the Aboriginal struggle. It's something I was very sceptical about, not in terms of Juno, but in terms of a political movement. I really am very cautious of any political behaviour, because I always see it failing unless you completely become a part of it, unless you really take it up as a cause. She did just that. Poetry is my cause, not a political one. So we've had this intense political argument about content and form.

JK: But also, looking at Juno's work it's as much about impressionist statement. Getting back to the Michael Palmer interview, there is something that I think is quite relevant to this process. He says, 'I was looking for a means of representation that I could feel honest with. In other words, I think one of the problems of overtly political poetry now is something that Octavio Paz has brought up, and so much of it has to do with newspaper reports and so little of it has to do with witness.' So they're pictures of witness and they're not pictures of reportage, and in the same way I would then extend that to your poetry. The Vietnam thing in 'The Rumour' is not a statement as in a newspaper, it's not reportage, but it's witness, it's the feeling of being there and seeing and appreciating.

RA: Yes, that's how I finally dropped my cynicism and sceptical attitude toward what Juno was doing. Because after getting to know her and talking to her for over a year, it was photography of witness. She had been with those people, she had followed the struggle and documented it, and also written articles for it. It became a whole field of experience that I wouldn't have known about otherwise. And out of that came 'Canticle for the Bicentennial Dead', a poem I definitely wouldn't have written. It's funny because I didn't get that from Dylan. You'd think I would have written some kind of poem, remember, when we were talking about the LANGUAGE poets and poetry that dealt with political protest poetry, it didn't come out of Dylan. What came from Dylan was Symbolism and postmodernism. But from Juno I had this direct connection to a real struggle that was … again, it wasn't the struggle, it was the art — Juno's art — that I could see it through, in the same way as I said before, when I put the photograph of the river on the desk, Juno's photograph of the Hawkesbury was more the Hawkesbury of the poetry than the real Hawkesbury.

JK: What of the oyster poems and collaboration?

RA: Well, again, that's a bit like political poetry. Again, poetry that I wouldn't have written. Juno was doing a section of *The Language of Oysters* and went out with the oyster farmers, I'd grown up with those people. Over thirty years

I'd been coming and going and associating with them and looking at them and seeing them. But I didn't know or see what they ... I hadn't taken their lives into my poetry. Again, because I didn't witness the struggle or the lives that they had directly. It wasn't transformed from real politics into the politics of the imagination. Once I could look at the photographs, it became a politics of imagination rather than the politic of reality, and that's how I could write about these people. I mean, I got to know my family through Juno's photographs rather than through my family. It's pretty good.

JK: It is pretty good.

RA: I didn't understand my grandfather until I saw a portrait Juno did of him ... When I say I didn't understand such and such because of this, I'm always saying — as Michael Palmer's interviewer keeps saying — 'bracket that.' But I'm saying it in terms of 'understand it in terms of poetry'. I'm not talking about life, I'm not talking about 'the poet of the little me' as Palmer says. I'm talking about just poetry.

JK: I'm going to flash back through *Where I Come From* and through notions of the archetypal image, the primary images as well that we inherit and that become our poetry, or become part of our poetry even if we try to dissolve reference, that still the building blocks are there, the original language is formed around them. Michael Palmer said, 'Until a certain point, through most of my schooling, I imagined poetry more than I wrote it.' What do you think this says about where we take our poetry from, and also about what poetry is and how poetry manifests itself?

RA: That's so interesting: I'd read that interview thoroughly, and that slipped by. I don't know why it surprises me anymore, but this is a thing that's been going on for probably fifteen or twenty years, these flashes of recognition I have with Michael Palmer. I've been fascinated by his work for 20 years or more. I've shown it to people, even erudite poets like Kevin Hart. When he first looked at it he said, 'Well, he really is different.' And Kevin isn't surprised by much. See what I think happens ... it's got some connection with Mallarmé. I think if Mallarmé was alive now, living in this century at this time and place, and he wrote in English, the poetry he would be writing would be very similar to what Michael Palmer's writing. Now that's an imaginative leap, but there is a connection, also there is a lineage there anyway ... Michael Palmer isn't a Symbolist.. But in fact he does some thing remarkably like Mallarmé. When Mallarmé was grappling with his idea of the death of God, not long after Nietzsche's madman ran through the city announcing that God was dead. Mallarmé was sitting in the centre of all that, knowing it was pretty much what would happen and philosophically it would take a lot to get around that. So finally Mallarmé's sitting there saying to himself, 'Okay, there's no God, I can handle that. I'll create ...' — as he says God's poems are stars on the black universe. My poem will be the black marks on the white page, the white abyss. Then his son died; with the death of his son he suffers terrible grief and then starts to write a poem called 'A Tomb for Anatole' which is a major work, although unfinished. It's has been translated by Paul Auster and published in America by Northpoint Press — if you read this edition you'll see what I mean.

JK: I mentioned *Where I Come From* and your early life, and Palmer's statement 'I imagine poetry more than I write it.' Can you say something on that?

RA: That's what happened with *Where I Come From* — I imagined my childhood more than remembered it through the poems. I went back and lived a new childhood and wrote out of that. This childhood was threaded through with memory but basically was a recreation. Memory is so unreliable and often this can be helpful when composing poetry — I mean by not trying to remember you often get some surprising images. There was this childhood growing up on the Hawkesbury River, a bleak sort of river Styx, a mythological country.

JK: Is this the imagined poetry more than the written? Is this what 'I imagined poetry more than I wrote it' means, that the mystery is in the spirit of it, and once you start writing it, the poetry is in some way defeated? LANGUAGE poets would disagree with that. LANGUAGE poets would oppose that.

RA: I'm not sure, I don't think they could, as MacLow says, there's a similarity there between no poetry and the Zen No Mind.

JK: Or maybe they would say, that's the end result of poetry, that's what we will eventually theoretically work towards, the no poetry, the purely imagined poetry, rather than it being a starting point.

RA: Here it is. 'What I think those who've used this term 'non-referential' have meant to point out is the lack of any obvious object of imitation or subject matter. No situation, action, suffering, false-syllogism that has trouble meeting itself.' In the end it's all poetry, so we can sit and talk about it being fetishized and so on — in the end it's what's on the page, or in the air or in our imaginations. The word poetry can take all this in — it doesn't have to be more than imaginings, but this imagining can accept these things. Imagination can contradict anything, including so-called LANGUAGE poetry, it can encompass all under the umbrella we call poetry.

JK: Do you think there is any wisdom in that?

RA: I think maybe it's why we are poets and not painters, language is our raw material, it's an art that can encompass all these things. It can handle ideas and images, language and conceptual theory, it can also pull in the emotions we drag around, it can curb our egos. One of the main reasons I love reading Michael Palmer is that he allows the reader to enter the poetry, you take up his narrative, his adventuring imagination and you become the imagined person who is writing the poetry — or you listen to the voice, and that voice is dancing. It doesn't have to be the ego that taunts me as I try to create these works of the imagination rather than the myth of an existence I may or may not have.

JK: And these works of honesty, of truth, which is what you were saying earlier when you were talking about 'The Rumour'.

RA: Yes. A poem can't lie, a poem that is a lie is a poem that doesn't work.

JK: Well, Michael Palmer also says 'Music and poetry can so easily become cultural decor'. It can become a thing that is pretty to listen to, and that's not the intent of this music ... The point is, if you're honest you can't become just decor, because decor is something that belongs to that commodity-fetishized world which is all about the market place, and it's about exchange, and what things are worth, money and so on.

RA: That's why Schoenberg doesn't sound like Mozart and that's why Bob Dylan doesn't sound like Byron.

JK: Exactly.

Robert Adamson

AT BERRY'S BAY

A boy crawls through the first beam
of the dawn's light as it illuminates
the black stumps of the old coal-wharf.
The pungent air is full of the fumes
of tar and oil, as he climbs he thinks
back over the puddles of milky water
with chemical rainbows, they are almost
beautiful, how that water stung
and inflamed the fine deep cuts
made by pulling black mussels from pylons
with his bare hands. This place is
a kind of paradise he thinks as he looks
from a dark corner inside the great
wharf; the Wedding Cakes out there
across the harbour, still flashing the red
and green lights of the navigation codes,
a slight morning breeze bending their reflections
on the in-coming wake of a bullnosed tug.
His pocket holds his line, twenty yards
of nylon monofilament, six tiny
long-shanked hooks imbedded in the cork.
He spreads his bait out neatly on a plank,
six green prawns, chopped into segments,
the flesh from the black mussels. Underneath
the surface of the smooth oily tide
his dream fish hover, fantail leatherjackets,
their dorsal spikes upright, nail-clipper teeth
pruning the weedy pylons, and on their
slowly moving tails, six iridescent blue chevrons.

Robert Adamson

ANSWERING A QUESTION IN THE TROPICS

I came here because I couldn't afford
the mountains, I had to tear apart
my knowledge of fishing and test
the local vegetation. Here the flying foxes

carry a deadly virus and scuttle
in the figs all through the hot night.
I sense a turbulence happening at dinner,
the pineapple split down the centre

and the lush cream custard all too much,
this is no place for manners, this
is anarchy, anything for a lurk.
The palm cockatoos teach us how to screech

and the kids sing beautiful canticles
while their fathers gather at the gate
and put their fists in the air with a flourish —
they are practising some kind of demonstration

against new government policy.
They rise above the rain forest and float out
towards the reef while Jimmy Buffet plays a tune
on his electric mandolin.

There nothing here unpleasant, nothing
a little spiritual deprivation can't straighten out;
I practice self doubt and religion
and watch my integrity grow thin.

Bev Braune

FORGETFULNESS

A soft 's' slips off her tongue
reflects off old china dusted clean
than affection gleans

travels to unfamiliar territory
signals gone unnoticed
for too many years

meaning faltering
upon fear
finds language wanting

'libélula ... alternado con paroxismos'
forgetfulness

the grammatically correct
stumbling upon the heart-felt

the mind clouded with too few details
unfolding and creasing
wrapping itself in clean-pressed tea towels

Bev Braune

THE NIGHT BIRD

a granular chill-hung wind
rips leaves off the lap of Blackwattle Bay

the night bird whistles

her sumptuous black fare
discreetly masks Rilke's generous spaces

she speaks of morning-rites
when devils and our sweetest dreams
are sent warbling under her silvered tones

she makes us wish to lash ourselves
from blanched replies,
pitches louvres
beneath our pillows

Peter Robinson

Playing Dead

> 'He paints words with the past'
> Roy Fisher

They're exhaust-caked privet colours,
lupin heads and brick dust
tracked through the glazes that time
formicas on a feel for things
such as cough drops, bubble gum,
black liquorish, things with the taste
of four farthings about them,
things which aren't likely to last --
but then do, the pink or the grey
I'd just go on chewing, though
losing so quickly its flavours
through a bright, cold winter day --
mum's plum jam on an aspirin
or dandelion and burdock, bringing
back, red-flecked, the yellow
and blue of an old black eye:
'Well now, who's this in the wars?'

There were corrugated iron roofs,
daubed fences frayed with rust,
a purple forehead, badly bruised
walking right into a lamp post.
I lay pretending to be dead
under the vapour trails' white
in an ominous or mackerel sky --
but no Red Indian found me,
so I got up and walked away.
Years passed, became the compost
of time's intentness rotted down
with whatever it was I used
to slip between pedestrian fears
of policemen and dark alleys,
railway lines, the waste ground,
talking to strangers, school bullies --
whatever I used to get back home.

Tony Lopez

In Memory

I missed it. So much did they make of this news,
Jean Tension and Steve Fray on *Terpischordia*,
Precisely the tone we were looking for.
You hand over two months salary for a word —
Here's one coming through now: Allen Ginsberg,
A cramped hotel room in the late sixties,

Black sticky opium. Nobody at home.
The numbers going sideways are train times —
'*Melancholia* has a plastic core.' You know
It's funding that makes us aspirational:
External validation and review.
Where are you now Allen Ginsberg? Who is pumping

Your harmonium? Elgar Alien Pcoet?
We speed into the tunnel expressway
But can't read the graffiti, Allen Ginsberg,
Your senior conductor speaking. Formica Zen
Always being torn down and rebuilt, for what?
Not some future perfection: everyone does it.

'Anyone can write' you told John Drew. You, a man
Who cared to know what happened and made poetry
Without hope of any hope but what is constructed
Herein. Part-exchange on detached homes and yellow
Silence of three months. Who cares whether any of this
Is happening? Allen Ginsberg, you can do it!

You can find the brand name guru and holy ghost,
As we go past the gas works, a tongue in your ear.
Ribbons of scrubland by railway lines and razor wire —
A new lead on the free state. We have yet to make it,
Allen Ginsberg. I'm at Alexandra Palace.
What thoughts I have of you just now, what fantasies:

Of deluxe sentiment and men in tights,
With hiking boots and hanging baskets put forth,
An ivy-leafed geranium. Allen Ginsberg,
Faintest touch of lips on the big name
Of your generation. My heart skips a beat
At the speed-up through hypertext real time.

What difference does it make if you're getting
The best head you ever had, Allen Ginsberg? Muggers
Snatch a few dollars but leave your manuscripts
So you go down on your knees in a bio-pic
We're currently developing. Imagine that:
Starving, Hysterical, Naked Productions plc,

The best minds of our generation. Can you
See it? Where is the expiry date printed
On these verses by Allen Ginsberg, Gent, BL?
Before Language: little black and white books
Passed round in school, real songs of insolence.
This is Bill speaking on thursday at nine, your time.

Allen Ginsberg, the very name is like a phone
Ringing in a train. And because you'll be awake,
The doctor will be able to talk to you throughout.
These faint echoes of Moloch, Sammy, patch me through:
Mohawk, Motown, Mohican, Motivator,
Who's fixing your juice in the hereafter?

Everyone's a little bit heterosexual,
Now that planning is making a come back
In the upright position, Allen Ginsberg
The photograph reproduced on page seventeen,
Sometimes a curly shepherd lad, should be a
Vertical image, head down, facing pastures new.

Gordon's London Dry or *Tankueray* pink gin
Ought to be the drink we toast your memory in.
Were you able to raise that conference call
Allen Ginsberg? Are you rotting in Manhattan?
Or cast upon the Hudson River to fade away?
Where are those howling verses that used to be?

Allen Ginsberg, what peaches and penumbras!
What price bananas and sunflower sutras?
Singing a Blake song, chanting mescaline dreams!
Setting your poems in the supermarket
Of eternity! Re-inventing prophecy!
I'll see you later, Allen Ginsberg, wait for me.

Vivian Smith

MEETING

We met by accident in Franklin Square.
I was back on a short holiday,
you were still deciding where 'to settle'
after fifteen years of 'life abroad'.
We stood talking near established trees,
not far from the statue of Sir John
and the last relics of old Hobart Town.
You weren't too keen on dim, forgotten things.
Gulls squawked spikily around the pond,
hoses started sprinkling on the lawn.

Spring in Hobart, ten full years ago.
We talked of scattered friends we had in common,
of how you'd start a new life once again,
and if place determines what we write.

Always on the move, earmarked for freedom,
and now you're living in the Czech Republic?
I marvel at the news and drink it in.

I hear you've found the great love of your life
(There I was much luckier than you)
and write of Hobart in the heart of Prague.
Our landscapes travel with us as we go.

I hope your writing is progressing well
and that you struck the fresh vein you envisaged
'to lift your subject matter, make it fun'.

We'll meet again sometime, I'm sure of that,
in London, Paris, Rome or Istanbul
or on the broadwalk near the Opera House ---
wanderer of the ways of all the worlds ---
or even once again in Franklin Square
and we'll start talking of 'our island home',
the place we had to leave so long ago,
whose coasts and mountains surface in our dreams.

Anthony Lawrence

WHERE THE CRANE LIES DOWN

She has gone
thigh-deep into river mud
past the shell

of a bone-white clinker,
upended
where crabs blow

air bubbles
and the sacred ibis
measures time

with preening
and stabbing for mud-
concealed food.

Her skin
smeared with shadows,
she goes under

the light of a crane,
its gaze
unwavering until

it lifts away — a smoky flourish,
then white sparks
becoming fire.

Where sunlight
falters
in dark scrub,

she sings for her life.
Where the crane lies down,
she ends it.

Rod Mengham

TWO CONTINENTS AS A MEDIUM FOR POETRY

Ah, friend, within the hollow crown
are the vessels and nicotine
conductors, ply and counterply

in the first place no art
is the inspector you needed
to remove you from the record

as you fall from the nest
you plunge to earth alright, but not fast enough
to purchase freedom

the mobile phones have had their fill
by the time you blow the candles out
with the airborne lichen heading for

the bedroom wall and a distribution of
that sinking feeling on the terraces
chilled to the bone in a buffer zone

between two hemispheres and another thing
you have been liberated and dwell among us
chained to the oar in a thousand forms

the shades are so many
belay that order and start again
the shades mean burial at sea

a bier half-ablaze; you must
bait the hook for the turn of the tide
and ensure an endless supply.

John Forbes

ODE TO CAMBRIDGE

No thrill needs faking for
this one-slip-&-it's-comic

grave prolegomenon to the Subject.
I praise what you decorate:

doubts subsumed as Doubt
on the rim of wooze, done

suavely to a chorus rigor
suggests , no 'hey presto'

style cheap effects, but
logic undercut to dance.

You know our job, each
polished phrase redefining it,

the given being just
imagination's gloss
                          or shimmering,

where brains create a frame
for a groomed curriculum —

'Throw it away' said Basil,
getting each English word just right —

that project becomes you
like a clinic for the Absolute

tho' if you had surf there,
(*'brilliant kids, frisk with your dog'*)

I'd advise you guys about
rips and undertows & how

we are exiled from ourselves

by that

'abstract position in re'

which makes this poetry
all that's possible, returning

galled, that is refreshed
by a future tense too accurate

for even clear headed Cambridge
to address, or resemble.

SURFERS PARADISE

I started *Surfers Paradise* in 1974 mainly because I was impressed by Bill Berkson's Big Sky Books and the idea that cheap, roneoed literature could look good. Ken Bolton had the same idea but he took it much further and produced the terrific Sea Cruise series of books and *Magic Sam* magazine.

The cover is almost the best thing about No. 1. It was done by Colin Little, a brilliant silk screen artist and one of the few full-on hippies I've ever respected (I mean after he went to Japan to find out about their traditional, vegetable based colours, he hitched home through South East Asia, supporting himself by telling fortunes — no mean feat!). Tragically, he died of cancer a few years later.

There was a reading at the Tin Sheds to launch the magazine and I remember it as a big success, at least as a party. The magazine was savagely reviewed in *Honi Soit* and lots of people (mainly academics but others as well) didn't turn up to the launch because they thought it was being held in Surfers Paradise the place. This confusion entered some literary histories of the time so that Surfers Paradise was mentioned as one of the locales of the 'New', along with New York and Sydney.

The name of the magazine wasn't intended as a pun incorporating an aesthetic program (the only aesthetic program I've ever really endorsed was Mark O'Connor's entry in an art competition, a bus ticket with 'Manifeste abrégé' written on it. Of course this isn't just a Dadaist gesture as I thought at the time but a salute to Joyce's modernisation of Shakespeare's 'Where the bee sucks there suck I' into 'Where the bus stops there shop I'. But this just adds the strength of tradition to O'Connor's manifesto). But once the Surfers/Surface Paradise pun was pointed out to me I was happy to adopt the idea.

The second *Surfers Paradise* came out in 1979 and was financed by Martin Johnston, who'd asked me rather crossly, 'When is *Surfers Paradise* coming out?' To which I replied in the self-righteous tone of the undeserving poor, 'When I've got the money'. 'How much do you need?' asked Martin and then wrote me a cheque for 120 dollars. Martin's work never got the recognition it deserved — he was a unique voice in Australian poetry and I hope the forthcoming collection of his poetry and prose makes more people aware of this.

The highlights of No. 2 were — well, I have written 'Laurie Duggan's New England Ode and Frank Littler's cartoon' but reading through the issue, it seems wrong to single these out, brilliant as they are. Gig Ryan's poem 'Enough to make a woman feel …' & Martin Johnston's 'Bonsai' and John Tranter's 'Ode to Col Joye' and Bob Harris's 'Hart Crane's Failure' (with the wonderful line 'fish that seem smart for a fish, and good') and the chapter of Michael Forbes' Newtown novel are all knockouts. In contrast my own poem in that issue was dreadful-forced, rhetorical and shrill. There were a few good lines in it that I later mined and used in a poem called 'Egyptian Reggae' which was OK. But 'Pillow Talk' should never have appeared.

While No. 2 has probably got the best cover, with Mark Ray's photo of Steve Mcgarret, from Hawaii 5/0, looking religious and/or sexual with his lips pressed to a hand mike, No. 3 takes the cake poetry wise. I won't run through the list of writers but I will mention Chris Burns, Adam Aitken and Dipti Saravanamuttu who I was really pleased to publish because they were new at the time. Is *Surfers Paradise* No. 3 the last time Mark O'Connor was published? His poem in this issue, 'Transalpine' has the great lines,

> Our nicer feelings fade into the
> view beyond a surf
> report

Of course this is the real Mark O'Connor we're talking about here, not the one who does National Geographic replacement poems (quite well sometimes too). The phrase 'underground classic' gets flogged to death but it truly can apply to O'Connor's 1981 book *Ode to Iggy Pop* published by Black Lamb Press under the pen name John Nash. Somebody should reprint this slim vol because it is almost impossible to get hold of now.

Surfers Paradise No. 3 came out in 1983. *SP* No. 4 came out in 1987. Although there were some very good poems in this issue (especially John Tranter's 'Voodoo', a poem that sends the pointer off the scale) the moment of Surfers Paradise seemed to have passed. Unlike the others *SP* No. 4 didn't sell out. Perhaps it had become too much just a magazine of 'John Forbes' friends'. But I didn't mean it to be just a coterie magazine. Perhaps it should have come out more frequently — people tend to lose sight of a quadrennial. But I only ever did it for fun, and the project was innocent of any literary political intention. The idea was just to collect good writing between attractive covers — occasionally. And this is probably not a sufficient raison d'être for a magazine. But I'm glad I did it.

POETRY REVIEW

"the magazine which readers
of poetry can't do without"
– Douglas Dunn

"that invaluable magazine"
– Denis Healey

the ground-breaking new look

POETRY REVIEW

has championed new writers like Glyn Maxwell, Sophie Hannah and
Don Paterson and is proud to boast a range of contributors which
includes Seamus Heaney, Miroslav Holub, Germaine Greer, Simon
Armitage, Nick Hornby, Fleur Adcock, Michele Roberts, Denis Healey
and Sean O'Brien.

RECENT AND FORTHCOMING FEATURES
Anthony Julius on W.H. Auden
Edna Longley on the 20th century anthologies
Thom Gunn interviewed
Anne Stevenson on Sylvia Plath
poems by Samuel Beckett, Paul Muldoon, Carol Ann Duffy,
Roger McGough, John Ashbery, Helen Dunmore, Thom Gunn

POETRY REVIEW annual subscription £23 single copies £5.95
22 Betterton St, London WC2H 9BU   tel 0171 240 4810

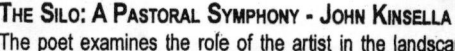

LONDON MAGAZINE

**FICTION * MEMOIRS * CRITICISM * POETRY
CINEMA * ARCHITECTURE * PHOTOGRAPHY
THEATRE * ART * MUSIC**

'A fantastic magazine whose place in the history
of 20th century literary life grows ever more secure
and significant' – *William Boyd, Evening Standard*

Each issue contains over 50 pages of poems and
reviews of poetry.

Recent and forthcoming critical essays include:

C. K. Stead on Craig Raine and Thom Gunn

Alan Ross on Derek Walcott and St. Lucia

Marshall Walker on Edwin Morgan

Michael O'Neill on Stephen Spender and Gavin Ewart

Dennis O'Driscoll on Berryman and Yeats

Subscriptions:
£28.50 p.a. (six issues) to 30 Thurloe Place, London SW7

Jacket

editor : John Tranter

❶ stylish writing

❷ free

❸ on the Internet

❹ four times a year

http://www.jacket.zip.com.au

STRIDE: ONE STEP AHEAD

ZONE JOURNALS • Charles Wright

'In his zones of dislocation – between the christian and the biological, between Europe and America, and between the allegorical and the visible – Wright finds a scene of writing unique to himself and to his historical moment, and phrases it over and over in his musical and grieving half-lines, themselves the very rhythm of spacious contemplative musing.' *The New Republic*
First British publication of this author • 117pp • £7.95

ANTIBODIES • Peter Finch

In *Antibodies* Peter Finch works on language from the inside, defamiliarising through gestalt, process, list and structure. The work uses chance as much as design, relies on visual perception as much as the internal voice. The poems travel clear up from Dada to L=A=N=G=U=A=G=E. This is the forefront of innovation, except of course that Finch wants us to enjoy ourselves.
Stunning new collection! • 127pp • £7.95

THE LIGHT IS OF LOVE, I THINK • John Freeman

'I dearly love all your work here – the openness and directness of it, that clear talking to yourself and the reader, no silly cleverness nor artifices – just a getting on with what matters, writing "it" down. But most of all I love the warmth and real tenderness and care of the poems. Precious stuff!' Lee Harwood
New and Selected Poems • 121pp • £7.95

Other recent titles:
ORCHARD END • Peter Redgrove New poems • 81pp • £7.50
WHAT THE BLACK MIRROR SAW • Peter Redgrove
New short fiction and prose poetry • 99pp • £8.50
GWEN JOHN TALKING • Brian Louis Pearce 83pp • £6.95

All titles are available post free (cheques payable to 'Stride') from
STRIDE, 11 SYLVAN ROAD, EXETER, DEVON EX4 6EW

POETRY

FOUNDED IN 1912 BY HARRIET MONROE

AUSTRALIAN POETRY
* A SPECIAL DOUBLE ISSUE *

Edited with John Kinsella

Adam Aitken	Jean Kent
Peter Boyle	Mike Ladd
Caroline Caddy	Anthony Lawrence
Jennifer Compton	Shane McCauley
David Curzon	Les Murray
Sarah Day	Geoff Page
Diane Fahey	Peter Porter
Katherine Gallagher	Peter Rose
Peter Goldsworthy	Tracy Ryan
Martin Harrison	Andrew Sant
Dennis Haskell	R. A. Simpson
Dorothy Hewett	Jennifer Strauss
Wendy Jenkins	John Tranter
Jill Jones	Chris Wallace-Crabbe

•

John Tranter: Australian Poetry 1940–1980:
A Personal View
John Kinsella: Towards a Contemporary
Australian Poetics

• • •

US$6.00 + $1.75 postage
Subscriptions—12 issues—US$34.00 outside U.S.A.
U.S. funds only. VISA and Mastercard accepted

POETRY
60 West Walton Street
Chicago, Illinois 60610 U.S.A.
(312) 255-3703

KANGAROO
VIRUS

John Kinsella and Ron Sims

Poet John Kinsella and photographer sound-artist Ron Sims have produced a unique work of art, one that is genuinely interdisciplinary: poems, photographs, and the sound track on the accompanying CD fuse so as to produce a piece that puts the viewer/listener in the Dryandra Forest in Australia to participate in the terrible encounter with the petrified corpses of the kangaroos, killed by a mysterious 'virus'. You don't have to be especially ecologically minded (I'm not) to find the resulting verbal-visual poem brilliant and terrifying.

Marjorie Perloff, US Critic

CD ENCLOSED   RRP AUS $29.95   ISBN 1 86368 257 0

AVAILABLE NOW

Published by Folio / Fremantle Arts Centre Press
QUERIES FAX 00 11 61 89 430 5242

SALT

SUBSCRIPTION FORM

Salt, a leading international poetry journal is published biannually. Subscribe now, and receive a FREE copy of *Salt 9*.

I would like to subscribe to *Salt*. Please send me:
❏ the next two issues for $33.95
+ postage and packaging (please specify)
within Australia ❏ $6
overseas: airmail ❏ $20
surface mail ❏ $8

❏ the next four issues for $67.80
+ postage and packaging (please specify)
within Australia ❏ $12
overseas: airmail ❏ $40
surface mail ❏ $16

❏ backlist issues, *Salt* numbers .... @$16.95 per copy
+ postage and packaging per copy (please specify)
within Australia ❏ $3
overseas: airmail ❏ $10
surface mail ❏ $4

I enclose a cheque / money order (all payments to be made in Australian dollars) or please debit my credit card (delete as applicable)

Mastercard / Bankcard / Visa

Credit Card no. _ _ _ _ / _ _ _ _ / _ _ _ _ / _ _ _ _

Expiry Date: _ _ / _ _

Name: _____

Address: _____

_____

Signature: _____ Postcode: _____

Please send to: Fremantle Arts Centre Press,
PO Box 320, South Fremantle, 6162, Australia.
Fax: (08) 9430 5242   Email: facp@iinet.net.au